THE ESSENTIALS OF
BIBLICAL HEBREW

THE
ESSENTIALS OF
BIBLICAL HEBREW

by

KYLE M. YATES, Ph.D.

NEW AND REVISED EDITION

HARPER & BROTHERS
NEW YORK   LONDON

*This Volume is
affectionately dedicated to*

JOHN R. SAMPEY

INCOMPARABLE MASTER AND TEACHER
OF THE HEBREW OLD TESTAMENT

TABLE OF CONTENTS

SYNTAX OF HEBREW VERBS

APPENDICES

INTRODUCTION

PRESIDENT JOHN R. SAMPEY

Doctor Kyle M. Yates has introduced many hundreds of theological students to the study of the Hebrew Scripture. Through his skill in presenting the "Essentials of Biblical Hebrew" he reduces the toil of the student to a minimum in acquiring sufficient mastery of the language to be able to read and interpret the Hebrew Old Testament.

By the time the student has completed the course of study required to master "Essentials of Biblical Hebrew" he is prepared to use to advantage a Hebrew lexicon like that of Brown, Driver and Briggs and a large grammar such as Cowley's English edition of Gesenius–Kautzsch. He can now understand the best critical commentaries on the Hebrew Old Testament.

I congratulate the hosts of young men who come to the class room of Doctor Yates to study Hebrew under his leadership, and I congratulate students of Biblical Hebrew in other institutions that they now have access to a textbook which will make attractive the study of the language in which the Hebrew historians, poets and prophets wrote. May the number of preachers who can make use of the Hebrew be greatly increased by this excellent manual.

executives have given of their time, energy, and counsel that we might have a useful book. A sincere word of thanks must go to each of them. Of these, Dr. J. Wash Watts, Dr. H. Cornell Goerner, Dr. J. Leo Green, Dr. Claude L. Howard, Dr. Virtus Krauschults, Dr. J. L. ...., and Wm. T. Bruner have rendered exceptional help.

PREFACE

Professor Ernest Sellin has given much encouragement to one who seeks to lead students to learn Hebrew. He asserts that a working knowledge of the language is obligatory unless the preacher is willing to become a helpless plaything in the hands of the unfair critics of the Old Testament. Surely we must do all that we can to stimulate a genuine interest in the study and then present the facts of grammar and syntax in a manner that men will be enabled to learn to be interpreters of the Word.

These lessons have been used in a class numbering one hundred and forty. The men have been led to learn and love the Hebrew Scriptures. The familiar words of the Bible are used over and over while the student masters the rules and laws of the language. The needs of the class of beginners have determined the method and order of presentation. The earlier grammar has been rewritten and enlarged. The exercises are completely new.

Lessons on syntax have been added so that the class may use this same book for two years. The author is aware of the fact that Hebrew syntax is best learned by reading the Old Testament in the original under the guidance of a wise teacher who directs the search for truth. It is hoped that these brief lessons will help both instructor and pupil in the task of interpretation.

It gives genuine joy to record my great debt to President John R. Sampey, D.D., LL.D., for years of guidance, counsel, instruction, encouragement and actual assistance. He taught me to love Hebrew and to seek to become an accurate scholar.

In the actual preparation of this volume several friends and associates have given of their time, energy, and counsel that we might have a useful book. A sincere word of thanks must go to each of them. Of these, Dr. J. Wash Watts, Dr. H. Cornell Goerner, Dr. J. Leo Green, Dr. Claude U. Broach, Dr. Verlin Kruschwitz, Dr. J. J. Owens, and Dr. Wm. T. Bruner have rendered exceptional help.

All the available grammars have been consulted and used freely in the preparation of this volume. The lexicon of Brown, Driver and Briggs has been used constantly. Grateful acknowledgment is hereby made for all the help received.

Kyle M. Yates

Louisville, Ky., February 22, 1938.

PREFACE TO THE SECOND EDITION

It has been a labor of love to revise this grammar in the light of the criticisms and suggestions of friends from all sections of our land. It humbles one to know that the grammar is so widely accepted. I take this occasion to salute with best wishes all toilers in the sphere of Hebrew exegesis.

Kyle M. Yates

Louisville, Ky., May 15, 1943.

THE ESSENTIALS OF
BIBLICAL HEBREW

LESSON I

THE ALPHABET

Form	Final form	Represented in transliteration by	Name	Pronounced as
א		'	'Ālĕph	(Silent)
ב (ב)		b (v)	Bêth	b in boy
ג (ג)		g (gh)	Gîmĕl	g in go
ד (ד)		d (dh)	Dālĕth	d in day
ה		h	Hê	h in hat
ו		w	Wāw	w in way
ז		z	Zăyĭn	z in zeal
ח		ḥ	Ḥêth	ch in "loch"
ט		ṭ	Ṭêth	t in toy
י		y	Yôdh	y in yet
כ (כ)	ך	k (kh)	Kăph	k in keep
ל		l	Lāmĕdh	l in let
מ	ם	m	Mêm	m in met
נ	ן	n	Nûn	n in net
ס		ṣ	Sāmĕkh	s in set
ע		'	'Ăyin	(Silent)
פ (פ)	ף	p (ph)	Pê	p in put
צ	ץ	ts	Tsādhê	ts in hits
ק		ḳ	Qôph	q in oblique (k)
ר		r	Rêsh	r in run
שׁ		{ s / sh	{ Sîn / Shîn	{ s in so / sh in shell
ת (ת)		t (th)	Tāw	t in to

3

Notes

1. Hebrew has twenty-two consonants. (The letters שׂ and שׁ are considered one).

2. These characters are always written separately and *from right to left.*

3. There are no special forms for capital letters.

4. Vowels points were invented and inserted in the text during the seventh century A. D.

5. Certain letters are similar in form. Examine the following characters, noting the differences:

בּ (Bêth)	כּ (Kăph)	פ (Pê)	
גּ (Gîmĕl)	נ (Nûn)		
ד (Dālĕth)	ר (Rêsh)	ך (Kăph final)	ף (Pê final)
ה (Hê)	ח (Ḥêth)	ת (Tāw)	
ו (Wāw)	ז (Zăyĭn)	ן (Nûn final)	
ט (Ṭêth)	מ (Mêm)	ם (Mêm final)	ס (Sāmĕkh)
ע ('Ăyĭn)	צ (Tsādhê)	ץ (Tsādhê final)	
שׂ (Sîn)	שׁ (Shîn)		

6. At the end of a word the letters כ מ נ פ צ have different forms, called final letters.

כ — ך (Kăph)

מ — ם (Mêm)

נ — ן (Nûn)

פ — ף (Pê)

צ — ץ (Tsādhê).

7. Six letters (ב ג ד כ פ ת) have two sounds. When written with the dot (called dāghĕsh-lēne) in the bosom, they have the

hard pronunciation. When the dot is absent, the sound is soft.
The dot is omitted after a vowel sound. In all other cases the
hard pronunciation is found.

ב = b		בּ = bh or v	
גּ = g		ג = gh	
דּ = d		ד = dh (as th in *this*)	
כּ = k		כ = kh	
פּ = p		פ = ph or f	
תּ = t		ת = th (as in *think*)	

[handwritten note in margin: בּגּדּכּפּתּ — Whenever they do not follow a vocal shĕwā or a vowel, insert a dāghēsh-lēne]

8. Other letters

א ('Ālĕph) has no sound. (Do not confuse with English "A").
It is a scarcely audible breathing from the lungs, the *Spiritus
lenis* of the Greek.

ע ('Ăyĭn) is a guttural consonant that should be pronounced
with a slight movement of the uvula. It is represented in trans-
literation by the rough breathing (*Spiritus asper*).

Exercises

1. Practice writing these letters until it can be done accurately
and rapidly.

2. Arrange them promiscuously and practice calling them by
name and by the English equivalent.

3. Write in English characters (begin at right).

ברא משלתם כרת לבשתן רדף לא תרצח ותנאף גדל
צדק ולא תגנב לקח יכל זכר הארץ החדש ענן׃

4. Write in Hebrew characters.

mym, rgl, bḳr, tmm, zmn, ṭrm, dvr, drk͡h, sml, s͡hmr, 'nn,
nts͡h, ksylym, t͡sdyḳ, mzbḥ, 'zḳ, 't.

LESSON II

THE VOWELS

Ancient Hebrew had no system of vowel notation. Finding only the consonants the reader supplied the proper vowel. In some cases help was given by the use of certain consonants (א and ה to denote *a*, י to denote *i* or *e*, and ו to denote *o* or *u*).

After Hebrew had ceased to be a living speech a system of vocalization was invented to preserve the proper pronunciation and meaning of the Sacred Writings.

The Palestinian system employs points and signs above, below, and in the bosom of consonantal letters. All vowels are sublinear except Ḥôlĕm and Shûrĕḳ.

TABLE OF VOWEL SIGNS

Sign	Name	English Equivalent	Sounded as	Illustration
⟋	Ḳāmĕts	ā (ä)	a in *father*	יָד yādh
⟋	Păthăḥ	ă	a in *hat*	עַם ʿăm
⟋	Tsērê	ē	e in *they*	שֵׁם shēm
⟋	Sᵉghôl	ĕ	e in *met*	אֶל־ ʾĕl
⟋	Ḥîrĕḳ Yôdh	î	i in *machine*	שִׂים sîm
⟋	Ḥîrĕḳ	ĭ	i in *pin*	הִק hĭḳ
ו, ⟋	Ḥôlĕm	ô, ō	o in *roll*	קוֹל ḳôl
				כֹּל kōl
⟋	Ḳāmĕts Ḥăṭûph	ŏ	o in *not*	כָּל־ kŏl
ו	Shûrĕḳ	û	u in *true*	קוּם ḳûm
⟋	Ḳĭbbûts	ŭ	u in *put*	הֻק hŭḳ

VOCAL AND SILENT SHᴱWA

In addition to the vowels given above, Hebrew employs still another sign ִ called Shᵉwa. When it stands under a consonant closing a syllable it is not a vowel but a Silent Shᵉwa, or a Syllable-divider. When it is under a consonant at the beginning of the syllable it is a vocal Shᵉwa and is pronounced as a very short *e*. It is, however, only a half-vowel. The first vowel sign in the Bible is this Simple Shᵉwa בְּרֵאשִׁית bᵉrē'-shîth.

This Simple Shᵉwa may be combined with the three short vowels to form Compound Shᵉwas. These are also half-vowels.

ֲ	Ḥāṭēph-Pătḥăḥ	very short *a* sound	חֲמוֹר (hᵃmôr)
ֱ	Ḥāṭēph-Sᵉghôl	very short *e* sound	אֱלֹהִים ('ᵉlôhîm)
ֳ	Ḥāṭēph-Ḳāmĕts	very short *o* sound	חֳלִי (ḥᵒlî)

NOTES

1. Each syllable must begin with a consonant. (There is one exception. It is the conjunction וּ).

2. When י (Yôdh) is preceded by an *i* or an *e* it combines with the vowel and loses its consonantal force. (יִם=yĭm, but שִׁים= sîm).

3. Ḥôlĕm and Shûrĕḳ, when written fully, use the letter waw (ו). The point is placed over it for Ḥôlĕm and in the bosom for Shûrĕḳ.

4. When the vowel sign Ḥôlĕm, ֹ, occurs in a syllable preceding the consonant שׁ, it coincides with the dot over the right hand tip of the consonant. מֹשֵׁל = mō-shēl. Similarly, when ֹ

occurs after שׁ, the dot does double service. שֹׁבַע = sō-vă‘. It is clear that the ◌ַ must be read, otherwise there would be no vowel for that particular syllable.

5. Occasionally we find יֵ ê and יֶ é in addition to the signs given above.

6. It will be noted that the sign for long "*a*" and for short "*o*" are the same. The beginner must be content to wait for the full explanation until he has learned the laws of the syllable and the tone (accent).

7. Short vowels may be heightened.

      ◌ַ ă to ◌ָ ā

      ◌ִ ĭ to ◌ֵ ē

      ◌ֻ ŭ to ◌ֹ ō

8. Certain vowels are unchangeable. They are ◌ָ â, יֶ é, יֵ ê, יִ î, וֹ ô and וּ û. (Note the circumflex marking). Apparently these vowels are characteristic of the forms in which they appear and these forms would lose their identity if the vowels were allowed to change.

EXERCISES

1. Practice writing, naming, and sounding the vowels.

2. Transliterate the following consonants and vowel signs:

דַּל כָּל שָׁת אֵם שִׁים עוֹד בֵּית אָדָם שָׁמֹר קוֹטֵל בְּרִית אֲשֶׁר

מָשָׁל בִּדְלוֹ שָׂנֵא אָמַר לְךָ כָּתַב מְשֻׁלָּם יַעֲלוּ סוּסִים קוֹלֵי

הָאִישׁ כָּתוּב.

3. Write the following in pointed Hebrew (right to left): bēn, băth, dôr, lēv, măr, rîv, ḳôl, ḳûm, bêth, nûn, 'elôhîm, lô, lû, lî, yîm, yĭm.

LESSON III

THE SYLLABLE

Each syllable begins with a consonant and includes only one full vowel. It may include two or more consonants. It may include a half-vowel before the full vowel. Thus there is a syllable for each full vowel but never for a half-vowel alone.

When marking syllables, begin with the end of the word. Thus the last syllable, the ultima, in קָטַל is טַל. The pathaḥ must be included to give a full vowel and the ט must be included in order to begin with a consonant. Accordingly the penult is קָ. In בְּרִית (bᵉrîth) there is only one full vowel, so only one syllable. (The one exception to this rule will be presented on page 19).

KINDS OF SYLLABLES

1. **Open,** ending in a vowel בּוֹ bô, לָ lā. The vowel in the open syllable must be long unless accented. It may then be short. בּוֹ bô, an open syllable with a long vowel. מַיִם mǎ-yǐm, an accented open syllable with a short vowel.

NOTE: The mark ◌ֵ is the accent.

2. **Closed,** ending in a consonant. טַל ṭǎl, קוֹל ḳôl. The vowel in the closed syllable must be short unless accented. It may then be long, נִקְטַל nǐḳ-ṭǎl. Each of these two syllables is closed, and each vowel is short. שֵׁם shēm, is a closed syllable, but the accent makes it possible for the vowel to be long. א and ה do not close a syllable (except when ה bears mappiḳ סוּסָה sû-ṣāh; see page 11).

3. **Sharpened,** a closed syllable which ends in a consonant that is doubled. קִטְטֵל kĭṭ-ṭēl.

NOTE: When a consonant would be repeated (as קִטְטֵל) instead of writing both of them, one is usually omitted and a point called *dāghĕsh-forte* is placed in the bosom of the one that remains. קִטֵּל kĭṭ-ṭēl.

The vowel of the sharpened syllable is short unless accented. הַקּוֹל hăk-ḳôl, אִמִּי 'ĭm-mî, הֵמָּה hēm-mā(h).

4. **Half-open,** an unaccented open syllable with a short vowel. עָבְדוּ 'ĭ-vᵉdhû, הַחֹשֶׁךְ hă-ḥō-shĕk. This violation of the rules for an open syllable is permitted because it is impossible to tell, when the word is pronounced normally, whether or not the letter following the vowel is repeated. The syllable sounds like a closed syllable and its vowel is allowed to stand like that of a closed syllable.

VOCABULARY

אָב	'āv	father	בֵּן	bēn	son	יוֹם	yôm	day
אָח	'āḥ	brother	בַּת	băth	daughter (f.)	קוֹל	ḳôl	voice
אֵם	'ēm	mother (f.)	טוֹב	ṭôv	good	שֵׁם	shēm	name

EXERCISES

1. Pronounce, transliterate, and divide into syllables. Indicate the kind of syllable.

לֹא אָתָם מַיִם אָדָם אֲשֶׁר בְּרִית טוֹב עִיר אֱלֹהִים הֶחָרֵב
שָׁנָה קוֹלוֹ בָּרָא בְּרֵאשִׁית קְטָלָתַם הַבֵּן הַשָּׁמַיִם הַסּוּסִים עֲבָדוּ׃

2. Write in pointed Hebrew:

way-yar' 'ᵉlô-hîm 'ĕth-kŏl-'ᵃshĕr 'ā-sā(h) wᵉhĭn-nē(h) ṭôv mᵉ'ᵒôdh wă-yᵉhî 'ĕ-rĕv wă-yᵉhî vō-ḳĕr yôm hăsh-shîsh-shî.

NOTE: The consonants in parentheses represent letters tnat have lost their consonantal value and remain as vowel letters only.

LESSON IV
SOME TECHNICAL MATTERS

Dāghĕsh-lēne

The dot placed in the six letters, ב ג ד כ פ ת, when they do not immediately follow a vowel or a vocal shᵉwa, is called *dāghĕsh-lēne*. It serves to harden the pronunciation. כָּתַבְתָּ kā-thăv-tā.

Dāghĕsh-forte

Any letter, except א, ה, ח, ע, ר, may receive in its bosom a point called *dāghĕsh-forte*, indicating that it is doubled. It is always preceded by a vowel sound. הַמַּיִם hăm-mă-yĭm. הַקּוֹל hăḳ-ḳôl.

Măppîḳ

Măppîḳ is a point placed in final ה to indicate that it is to be treated as a consonant and not as a silent vowel letter. עְמָה 'ĭm-māh. גָּבַהּ gā-văh.

Syllable-divider

The syllable-divider is a silent shᵉwa which is used to mark the end of certain syllables. It is used with closed syllables only, and with them only in the following cases: (1) when they

are not final, as in the penult of יִקְטֹל; (2) When they end in דּ,
as in לַדּ (lēkh); ③ when they have two consonantal characters
at the end, both receiving a syllable-divider and both consonants being pronounced, as in the ultima of קָטַלְתְּ. Only the first
receives it when the second is silent, as in the ultima of וַיֵּרְא.

The Gutturals

take a compound shewa & prefer a vowel

The letters א, ה, ח, ע, (and for some purposes ר) are called
gutturals. א and ה do not close a syllable. They are usually
silent at the end of a word and lose their consonantal character
completely. This is always true of א at the end of a syllable
within a word. However ה, when within a word, remains a
guttural consonant and does so at the end when the dot (măppîķ)
is placed in its bosom.

The following peculiarities are to be noted:

1. They **refuse to be doubled.** Daghesh-forte cannot be placed
in a guttural. When the dot is rejected the preceding vowel is
usually heightened, ־ִ to ־ֵ, ־ֻ to ־ֹ, ־ֻ to ־ֹ. Before ה and ח
the vowel is not heightened. (Cf. note on the half-open syllable).
יְקַטֵּל yᵉķăṭ-ṭēl but יְקָאֵל yᵉķā-'ēl, קַטֵּל ķĭṭ-ṭēl but קָהֵל ķĭ-hēl.

2. They **prefer compound shᵉwa under them** rather than simple
shᵉwa. (Usually ־ֲ, but may be ־ֱ, especially with א). אֱלֹהִים
'ᵉlôhîm. יַעֲטֹל yă-'ᵃṭōl.

3. They have a decided **preference for the "a" class vowels**
around them. (In most cases this is ־ֲ. It may be ־ֱ). יִקְטֹל
yĭķ-ṭōl but יַעֲטֹל yă-'ᵃṭōl.

The makkeph is a small horizontal line like the English hyphen used to join words which are connected in thought or utterance. The words become one and the accent is on the last word. From two to four words may be united in this way. אֶת־כָּל־אֲשֶׁר־לוֹ 'ĕth-kŏl-'ăshĕr-lô.

The Accents

In the Hebrew text one finds a large number of marks in addition to the regular vowel points. These marks of accentuation are placed above, below, and between the consonants. They are designed: (a) to mark the tone syllable of the word; (b) as punctuation marks; (c) as musical notations. There are about thirty of these signs in the Hebrew text. Since it will be impossible to treat them adequately here, we may give ourselves to a consideration of the more essential matters.

The main accent or tone falls generally upon the ultima, מָשַׁל mā-shăl. In certain nouns (מֶלֶךְ) and some verbal forms (מָשַׁלְתִּי mā-shăl-tî) it falls on the penult. The syllable that bears the main accent is known as the tone syllable. In this grammar words which are accented on the last syllable are not marked (קָטַל kā-tăl); those accented on the penult have ־ָ under the vowel of the accented syllable to call special attention to the accentuation, קָטַלְתִּי kā-tăl-tî.

Metheg

Metheg is a secondary accent used in the same word with the regular accent. The natural position for this secondary accent is on the second and fourth syllables before the tone,

הַכּוֹכָבִים hăk-kô-khā-vîm. The sign used is a small perpendicular stroke under the syllable to the left of the vowel to be accented, הָאָדָם hā-'ā-dhām. *when there is a deviation from the short vowel chart*

The sign is used:

1. Usually on the second syllable before the tone if the vowel is long. In case that vowel is short it goes back to the third syllable, הָאִשָּׁה hā-'ĭsh-shā(h), הָאַרְבָּעִים hā-'ăr-bā-'îm.

2. With all vowels before compound shᵉwa, וַאֲנִי wǎ-'ᵃnî.

3. With all long vowels before vocal shᵉwa pretonic, מָשְׁלוּ mā-shᵉlû.

4. With a long vowel in a closed syllable before maḳḳeph, שֵׁם־הַנָּהָר shēm-hăn-nā-hār.

Pause

In a Hebrew verse there are two natural pauses. The accents *silluḳ* (ـ) and *'Athnah* (ـ) mark these pause syllables. *Silluḳ* occurs on the last tone syllable and *'Athnah* on the principal syllable near the middle of the verse. A syllable bearing either of these marks is said to be *in pause*. The vowel so marked usually becomes long. מַיִם mǎ-yĭm, in pause, becomes מָיִם mā-yĭm.

VOCABULARY

אִישׁ 'îsh	*man*	יָד yādh	*hand* (f.)	עֵץ 'ēts	*tree*
אָדָם 'ā-dhām	*man*	סוּס sûṣ	*horse*	עַם 'ăm	*people*
לֵב lēv	*heart*	עִיר 'îr	*city* (f.)	עַל 'ăl	*upon*

LESSON V

THE ARTICLE

Hebrew has no indefinite article. Indefiniteness is generally indicated by the absence of the article, קוֹל ḳôl, *a voice*, שֵׁם shēm, *a name*.

The definite article is always a prefix. It is joined to the word so closely as to make one word in writing and pronunciation. It suffers no change for gender or number.

TABLE FOR WRITING THE ARTICLE

- הַ before non-gutturals   הַקּוֹל hăḳ-ḳôl *the voice*.
- הָ before א, ר (ע generally)   הָאָב hā-ʼāv *the father*. *Compensation*
- הַ before ה and ח   הַחֹשֶׁךְ hă-ḥō-shĕk *the darkness*.
- הֶ before חָ and unaccented עָ, הָ הֶחָג hĕ-ḥāg *the festival*.

NOTES

1. The usual way of writing the article is to prefix הַ to the substantive and put daghesh-forte in the first consonant, הַשֵּׁם, הַגָּדוֹל, הַטּוֹב, הַבַּת.

2. Gutturals (א, ה, ח, ע) and ר refuse the daghesh-forte and hence the vowel changes noted above. The short vowel of the article is left in an open syllable, unaccented. The normal thing is to heighten the ־ַ to ־ָ.

3. When the substantive begins with א or ר (ע usually) the normal change of vowel takes place, הָעֵץ hā'ēts, *the tree*.

4. In the case of ה and ח the doubling is refused, but the

vowel is allowed to remain short. They are said to be doubled by implication, הֶחָרֵב. (See note on half-open syllable, p. 10).

5. אֶרֶץ 'ĕ-rĕts, *earth*, with the article becomes הָאָרֶץ hā-'ā-rĕts, *the earth*. עַם 'ăm, *people*, becomes הָעָם hā-'ām, *the people*. הַר hăr, *mountain*, becomes הָהָר hā-hār, *the mountain*. (These syllables are accented and the vowel is at liberty to change its length for the sake of euphony).

6. The interrogative particle הֲ is usually prefixed to the first word of an interrogative sentence. It may be written הֲ, הָ or הַ; הֲיִקְטֹל *will he kill?*; הַאֶקְטֹל *shall I kill?*; הֶאָמַר *did he say?*

VOCABULARY

דָּבָר	dā-vār	*word, thing*	מָקוֹם	mā-ḳôm	*place*
שָׁלוֹם	shā-lôm	*peace*	שָׁנָה	shā-nā(h)	*year* (f.)
נָבִיא	nā-vî'	*prophet*	בֹּקֶר	bō-ḳĕr	*morning*
רֹאשׁ	rô'sh	*head*	בְּרִית	bᵉrîth	*covenant* (f.)

EXERCISES

1. Prefix the article with the proper pointing:

סוּס, רֹאשׁ, שָׁלוֹם, אֵל, חֹשֶׁךְ, אֵם, יֶלֶד, אוֹר, זָהָב, יָם, הַר, מֶלֶךְ, עַד, רֶגֶל, אֶחָד, עֵת, פֶּה, חוּץ, נַעַר, יַיִן, חֶסֶד, לָשׁוֹן, פְּרִי, עָנָן.

2. Write in Hebrew:

The man, the father, the day, the voice, the head, the city, the peace, the place, the morning, the covenant, the darkness, the prophet, the heart, the horse.

LESSON VI

PREPOSITIONS

The Inseparable Prepositions

בְּ *in, by, with*

כְּ *as, like, according to* ~~about~~

לְ *to, for, at*

} *always prefixes*

They are pointed as follows:

ְ usually

בְּ	בְּשֵׁם	*in a name*
כְּ	כִּדְבַר	*according to a word*
לְ	לְקוֹל	*to a voice*

ִ (ĭ) before another sheʷa

בִּ	בִּדְבַר	*by word of*
כִּ	כִּבְרִית	*according to a covenant*
לִ	לִפְרִי	*to fruit*

ֲ (ă)	before compound sheʷa	בַּ, בֶּ, בָּ		
ֱ (ĕ)	corresponding short vowel:	כַּ, כֶּ, כָּ	כַּאֲשֶׁר	
ֳ (ŏ)	ֲ ֲ , ֱ ֱ , ֳ ֳ	לַ, לֶ, לָ	*according as*	

ַ (ă)	before the article,	בַּ	בַּיּוֹם *in the day*
ָ (ā)	with the vowel	בָּ	כָּרֹאשׁ *like the head*
ֶ (é)	of the article	בֶּ	לֶחָג *to the festival*

NOTES

1. Sometimes the preposition may receive ָ (ā) before the tone syllable. This is usually true before an "a" sound in a monosyllabic word, לָעַד *to eternity.*

2. When the preposition precedes the article the הַ of the article is lost, and the preposition takes the vowel of the article.

Instead of בְּהַיּוֹם we find בַּיּוֹם. Instead of לְהַקּוֹל we find לַקּוֹל. Instead of בְּהַחֹשֶׁךְ we find בַּחֹשֶׁךְ. Instead of לְהָעִיר we find לָעִיר.

The Preposition מִן *from*

It may stand alone or be prefixed to the substantive.

It is pointed as follows:

מִן־	before the article (usually)	מִן־הַקּוֹל	*from the voice*
מִ	before non-gutturals, with the nun assimilated	מִקּוֹל	*from a voice*
מֵ	before א, ע, and ר (usually)	מֵאִישׁ	*from a man*
מְ	before ה and ח (usually)	מְחוּץ	*from abroad (outside)*

Vocabulary

אוֹר	'ôr	*light*		יָם	yām	*sea*
חֹשֶׁךְ	ḥō-shĕkh	*darkness*		זָהָב	zā-hāv	*gold*
סֵפֶר	sē-phĕr	*book*		מֶלֶךְ	mĕ-lĕkh	*king*
מְאֹד	mᵉʾôdh	*exceedingly*		רֶגֶל	rĕ-ghĕl	*foot* (f.)

Exercises

1. Pronounce aloud, translate and transliterate.

מִבָּקָר, כַּדָּבָר, כְּדָבָר, מֵאִישׁ, בַּמָּקוֹם, לַבֵּן, בָּעִיר, מֵרֹאשׁ, לְיָד, לַבְּרִית, מִן־הַמֶּלֶךְ, מֵחֹשֶׁךְ, מֵאוֹר, מִן־הָרֶגֶל.

2. Write in Hebrew.

To the day, in a name, for the man, from the father to the mother.

according to the word, in the city, from day to day, for a man, for a woman, from father to son, in the morning, in the light.

LESSON VII

The Conjunction and the Adjective

The Conjunction

The inseparable prefix וְ *and*, is written as follows:

וְ usually, וְשֵׁם wᵉshēm, *and a name.*

וּ before בּ, מ, פּ, and consonants with simple shᵉwa וּבֵן û-vēn, *and son*, וּמָקוֹם û-mā-ḳôm, *and place*, וּדְמוּת û-dhᵉmûth, *and likeness.*

וִ before the form יְ, וִיהִי wî-hî (instead of וְיְהִי), *and let it be.*

וַ, וֶ, וָ before compound shᵉwa (the corresponding short vowel), וַאֲנִי wǎ-ᵃnî, *and I.*

Note: It may be written וָ before a heavily accented syllable, וָרַע wā-rā', *and evil.*

The Adjective

In Hebrew the adjective may be used attributively or predicatively.

1. When it qualifies (modifies) a substantive it stands after the substantive and agrees with it in gender, number and definiteness, שֵׁם טוֹב shēm ṭôv, *a good name*, הַשֵּׁם הַטּוֹב hǎsh-shēm hǎṭ-ṭôv, *the good name* (the name, the good), הַקּוֹל הַטּוֹב וְהַגָּדוֹל hǎḳ-ḳôl hǎṭ-ṭôv wᵉhǎg-gā-dhôl, *the voice, the good, and the great = the good and the great voice.*

2. The predicative adjective agrees with the substantive in gender and number, but it never takes the article. It usually

stands before the substantive, but may follow it, טוֹב הַקּוֹל ṭôv hăk-ḳôl or הַקּוֹל טוֹב hăk-ḳôl ṭôv, *the voice (is) good,* טוֹב וְגָדוֹל הַשֵּׁם ṭôv wᵉghā-dhôl hăsh-shēm, *the name (is) good and great.*

VOCABULARY

תָּמִים	tā-mîm	*perfect*	קָדוֹשׁ	ḳā-dhôsh	*holy*
גִּבּוֹר	gĭb-bôr	*hero*	יֶלֶד	yĕ-lĕdh	*child*
אָדוֹן	'ā-dhôn	*lord*	עֵד	'ēdh	*witness*
חֶרֶב	ḥĕ-rĕv	*sword* (f.)	כּוֹכָב	kô-khāv	*star*

EXERCISES

1. Pronounce aloud, translate, and transliterate.

הַבֵּן הַטּוֹב וְהַבַּת, טוֹב הַיֶּלֶד, הַיֶּלֶד הַטּוֹב, תָּמִים הַבְּקָר,
הָעֵץ נָדוֹל, קָדוֹשׁ הָאָדוֹן, הַיֶּלֶד וְהָאֵם בָּעִיר, הַגִּבּוֹר עֵד,
נָדוֹל הַכּוֹכָב, הַחֹשֶׁךְ הַגָּדוֹל, הַמֶּלֶךְ קָדוֹשׁ:

2. Write in Hebrew.

A great day, the good brother, in the great day, the great man (is) good, mother and son, father and daughter, light and darkness (are) in the day and in the book. The morning (is) perfect. The hand and the heart (are) for the son.

LESSON VIII

THE VERB

Hebrew has no "tenses." Tense indicates time. The time of a Hebrew verb is indicated by its context.

The inflections of a Hebrew verb indicate state instead of

time. They present the condition as complete, incomplete, continuous or imperative. The completed states will be called perfects, the incomplete ones imperfects, the continuous ones participles and the imperative ones imperatives. Infinitives are not verbs but nouns or adverbs used to name the action of a verb or to modify a verb.

EXAMPLES

Perfect	קָטַל	ḳā-ṭăl	*he killed, he has killed, he will have killed.*
Imperfect	יְקְטֹל	yĭḳ-ṭōl	*he began to kill, he kills, he will kill.*
Participle	{ קוֹטֵל קָטֵל }	ḳô-ṭēl	*(he) was killing, (he) is killing, (he) will be killing.*
Imperative	קְטֹל	ḳᵉṭōl	*kill thou.*
Infinitive	{ קָטוֹל קְטֹל }	ḳā-ṭôl ḳᵉṭōl	*killing.*

The Perfect

The fundamental part of any verb is the root. The simplest verb form is the third person masculine singular of the perfect. The consonants of this form, as a rule, constitute the root. The letters of the strong verb like קָטַל appear in all forms of the verb without change. The vowels of the 3rd masculine singular perfect continue in all other forms unchanged except as the laws of syllable and tone require a change when afformatives are added. Afformatives are remnants of personal pronouns, which are added to indicate variations in person, number and gender.

The afformatives for the perfect are:

Singular			Plural		
3 m.	——	*he*	3 c.	וּ——	*they*
3 f.	הָ——	*she*	2 m.	תֶּם——	*you*
2 m.	תָּ——	*thou*	2 f.	תֶּן——	*you*
2 f.	תְּ——	*thou*	1 c.	נוּ——	*we*
1 c.	תִּי——	*I*			

When we start with the root קטל and add these afformatives we find the following forms:

Singular

3 m.	קָטַל	ḳā-ṭăl	*he killed*
3 f.	קָטְלָה	ḳā-ṭᵉlā(h)	*she killed*
2 m.	קָטַלְתָּ	ḳā-ṭăl-tā	*thou didst kill*
2 f.	קָטַלְתְּ	ḳā-ṭălt	*thou didst kill*
1 c.	קָטַלְתִּי	ḳā-ṭăl-tî	*I killed*

Plural

3 c.	קָטְלוּ	ḳā-ṭᵉlû	*they killed*
2 m.	קְטַלְתֶּם	ḳᵉṭăl-tĕm	*you killed*
2 f.	קְטַלְתֶּן	ḳᵉṭăl-tĕn	*you killed*
1 c.	קָטַלְנוּ	ḳā-ṭăl-nû	*we killed*

Explanation of Vowel Changes

1. With vowel afformatives

Two of these afformatives, הָ and וּ, begin with a vowel and are called vowel afformatives. Since they begin with a vowel, they cannot form separate syllables and so attach themselves to the final consonant of the root. They draw the accent to themselves. Then the vowel of the original ultima, being left in an unaccented open syllable, must be either heightened or volatilized. It is usually volatilized. Thus the ultima of קָטַל becomes טָלָה or טָלוּ. The sheʷa of this syllable, being a volatilized vowel, is vocal. It is also <u>pretonic</u>. Therefore the vowel preceding it receives a metheg. Thus the penult of קָטַל becomes (קָטְלוּ, קָטְלָה קָ).

2. With consonant afformatives

The other afformatives begin with a consonant and are called consonant afformatives. When they include a full vowel, they form separate syllables which are not accented except in the case of the heavy suffixes, תֶּם and תֶּן. When these heavy afformatives draw the accent from the penult, the vowel of the antepenult, standing in an open syllable two places before the tone, must receive a metheg or volatilize. Usually it volatilizes (קְטַלְתֶּם).

In the case of the 2nd feminine singular the ת cannot form a separate syllable and so attaches itself to the ultima. Both the final consonants then receive a syllable divider (קָטַלְתְּ).

Vowel afformatives and תֶּם and תֶּן take the accent. The nearest vowel in an open syllable is shortened to sheʷa.

VOCABULARY

מָשַׁל	mā-shăl	*he ruled*	גָּדַל	gā-dhăl	*he was great*
נָתַן	nā-thăn	*he gave*	דָּבַר	dā-văr	*he spoke*
שָׁמַר	shā-măr	*he kept*	כָּרַת	kā-răth	*he cut*
לָבַשׁ	lā-văsh	*he put on*	פָּקַד	pā-ḳădh	*he visited*

EXERCISES

1. Write the perfect using מָשַׁל *to rule* and פָּקַד *to visit*.
2. Translate, pronounce aloud, and transliterate.

מָשַׁלְתִּי, לָבַשְׁתָּ, כָּרְתוּ, נָתְנָה, גְּדַלְתֶּם, שְׁמַרְתָּן, פְּקַדְנוּ,
מָשְׁלָה, נָתַן אֶת הַסֵּפֶר לָאִישׁ הַטּוֹב, כָּרְתָה אֶת הַסֵּפֶר:

NOTE: The direct object (if definite) is usually marked by the placing of אֵת immediately before it. The אֵת is not to be translated. It may be written as a separate word (אֶת הַקּוֹל) or joined by maķķeph to the following word (אֶת־הַקּוֹל). When joined to the word the vowel is shortened.

The verb stands first in the sentence unless special emphasis is desired, שָׁמַר הָאִישׁ אֶת הָעֵץ *the man kept the tree.*

LESSON IX

THE IMPERFECT

The imperfect, expressing unfinished action, is formed from an abstract substantive, (*nomen actionis*) preceded by the fragments of the personal pronouns (נ, א, ת, י) which are called preformatives, תִּקְטֹל tĭk-ţōl, *thou wilt kill* (lit. *thou (to) kill*).

In the perfect (complete action) we are more particularly interested in the fact, and the part denoting the person comes last קָטַלְתָּ. In the imperfect (action still incomplete) we are more interested in the person of the agent, and the pronoun stands before the root of the verb תִּקְטֹל. In some forms of the imperfect we have preformatives and afformatives.

Singular			Plural		
3 m.	--- י	*he*	3 m.	י --- וּ	*they*
3 f.	--- ת	*she*	3 f.	תּ --- נָה	*they*
2 m.	--- ת	*thou*	2 m.	תּ --- וּ	*you*

2 f.   תָּ – – – ֖י   *thou*   2 f.   תָּ – – – נָה   *you*

1 c.   א – – –   *I*   1 c.   נ – – –   *we*

Beginning with the root קטל and adding the afformatives and preformatives we have:

Singular

3 m.	יִקְטֹל	yĭḳ-ṭōl	*he will kill*
3 f.	תִּקְטֹל	tĭḳ-ṭōl	*she will kill*
2 m.	תִּקְטֹל	tĭḳ-ṭōl	*thou wilt kill*
2 f.	תִּקְטְלִי	tĭḳ-ṭᵉlî	*thou wilt kill*
1 c.	אֶקְטֹל	'ĕḳ-ṭōl	*I shall kill*

Plural

3 m.	יִקְטְלוּ	yĭḳ-ṭᵉlû	*they will kill*
3 f.	תִּקְטֹלְנָה	tĭḳ-ṭōl-nā(h)	*they will kill*
2 m.	תִּקְטְלוּ	tĭḳ-ṭᵉlû	*you will kill*
2 f.	תִּקְטֹלְנָה	tĭḳ-ṭōl-nā(h)	*you will kill*
1 c.	נִקְטֹל	nĭḳ-ṭōl	*we shall kill*

NOTES

1. The vowel of the preformative is ־ִ (ĭ) (thinned from an original ă), except under א which prefers ־ֶ (ĕ). (See rules for gutturals for this preference for the "*a*" class vowel).

2. The second vowel in most strong verbs is ־ֹ (ō). It is a tone long *o* heightened from an original ־ֻ (ŭ). This stem vowel

is volatilized before the vowel afformatives וֹ and יִ_. (Instead of יִקְטְלוּ we find יְקַטְלוּ).

3. The preformative syllable יִק is closed. Thus we know the sheʷa under the first radical ק is a syllable-divider. Watch for daghesh-lene following this closed syllable, יִקְדַּשׁ, יִשְׁבֹּר, יִכְתֹּב.

VOCABULARY

מָלַךְ	mā-lăkh	*he reigned*	סָפַר	şā-phăr	*he numbered*
כָּתַב	kā-thăv	*he wrote*	קָדַשׁ	ķā-dhăsh	*he was holy*
זָכַר	zā-khăr	*he remembered*	כָּשַׁל	kā-shăl	*he stumbled*
לָמַד	lā-mădh	*he learned*	רָדַף	rā-dhăph	*he pursued*

EXERCISES

1. Write the imperfect using מָשַׁל *to rule* and שָׁמַר *to keep*.

2. Translate and locate* fully:

יִמְלֹךְ, אֶלְמֹד, יִפְקֹד, תִּכְתֹּב, תִּזְכְּרִי, אֶכְשַׁל, יִסְפְּרוּ,
תִּקְדַּשְׁנָה, תִּכְשְׁלוּ, נִרְדֹּף, תִּזְכַּרְנָה, תִּמְשְׁלִי, יִלְבְּשׁוּ, אֶשְׁמֹר,
תִּגְדַּלְנָה, נִכְרֹת:

3. Translate.

I shall write, you (m.) will keep, we shall speak, they will remember the word. Thou wilt reign in the city. She will learn, we shall remember. You will visit the son and the daughter.

*NOTE: To locate the verb form מָשַׁלְתָּ let the student say: "Perfect, 2nd, masculine, singular from מָשַׁל, to rule. Thou didst rule." For the word שׁוֹמֵר let him say: "Active participle from שָׁמַר, to keep. Keeping or a keeper."

LESSON X

IMPERATIVES, INFINITIVES AND PARTICIPLES

The Imperative, used only for affirmative commands, is identical with the imperfect except that it drops the preformative, תִּקְטֹל *thou wilt kill*, but קְטֹל *kill thou*.

	Singular		Plural	
2 m.	קְטֹל ķᵉṭōl *kill thou*		קִטְלוּ ķĭ-ṭᵉlû *kill ye*	
2 f.	קִטְלִי ķĭ-ṭᵉlî *kill thou*		קְטֹלְנָה ķᵉṭōl-nā(h) *kill ye*	

The Imperative is never used with a negative. Prohibitions are expressed either by לֹא (*not*) with the imperfect or by אַל with the jussive. (The jussive is usually an abbreviated form of the imperfect. It is employed in the second and third persons to express commands, wishes and prohibitions.)

The Infinitives appear in two forms.

The Absolute קָטוֹל is rare.

The Construct קְטֹל is more common.

The usual infinitive is the short form קְטֹל, being used frequently with prepositions prefixed, לִמְשֹׁל *to rule*. It is identical in form with the 2nd masculine singular imperative (except in Hiphʻil).

The Absolute infinitive קָטוֹל does not admit of any prefix or suffix. It has the effect of throwing forward prominently the bare idea of the verb without defining it in any way. It merely paints an action, without regard to agent, time or circumstance. It usually accompanies a finite verb for added emphasis or to

denote continuance of the action, שָׁמוֹר שָׁמַרְתִּי *keeping, I have
kept,* מָלוֹךְ תִּמְלֹךְ *ruling, thou shalt rule (thou shalt verily be
king).* (Do not confuse with the participle).

The Participle represents action as continuous. It is unbroken.
The simple stem of the verb has two forms, an active participle
(קֹטֵל) קוֹטֵל *killing* or *one who kills,* and a passive participle
קָטוּל *killed* (dead).

By way of summary we have the simple verb as follows:

PERFECT

	Singular			Plural	
3 m.	מָשַׁל	*he ruled*	3 c.	מָשְׁלוּ	*they ruled*
3 f.	מָשְׁלָה	*she ruled*	2 m.	מְשַׁלְתֶּם	*you ruled*
2 m.	מָשַׁלְתָּ	*thou didst rule*	2 f.	מְשַׁלְתֶּן	*you ruled*
2 f.	מָשַׁלְתְּ	*thou didst rule*	1 c.	מָשַׁלְנוּ	*we ruled*
1 c.	מָשַׁלְתִּי	*I ruled*			

IMPERFECT

	Singular			Plural	
3 m.	יִמְשֹׁל	*he will rule*	3 m.	יִמְשְׁלוּ	*they will rule*
3 f.	תִּמְשֹׁל	*she will rule*	3 f.	תִּמְשֹׁלְנָה	*they will rule*
2 m.	תִּמְשֹׁל	*thou wilt rule*	2 m.	תִּמְשְׁלוּ	*you will rule*
2 f.	תִּמְשְׁלִי	*thou wilt rule*	2 f.	תִּמְשֹׁלְנָה	*you will rule*
1 c.	אֶמְשֹׁל	*I shall rule*	1 c.	נִמְשֹׁל	*we shall rule*

IMPERATIVE

	Singular			Plural	
2 m.	מְשֹׁל	*rule thou*	2 m.	מִשְׁלוּ	*rule ye*
2 f.	מִשְׁלִי	*rule thou*	2 f.	מְשֹׁלְנָה	*rule ye*

INFINITIVES

מָשׁוֹל *ruling*

מְשֹׁל *to rule*

PARTICIPLES

מוֹשֵׁל (מֹשֵׁל) *ruling, or one who rules (a ruler)*

מָשׁוּל *ruled (under complete subjection)*

VOCABULARY

דָּבַק	*cleave, cling*	קָבַר	*bury*
לָכַד	*capture*	צָדַק	*be righteous*
שָׁכַן	*dwell*	שָׂכַל	*be wise, prudent*

EXERCISES

1. Translate and locate the verb forms.

שָׁמְרוּ, אֶשְׁמֹר, מָשַׁל, קָבַר, צָדַק, כָּתוּב, לָמוּד, נָתַן,

סְפָרְנָה, זִכְרוּ אֶת הַדָּבָר, זָכוֹר תִּזְכֹּר לִשְׁמֹר אֶת הַבְּרִית,

מָשׁוּל, קָדָשְׁנוּ, נִשְׂכֹּל, מָשְׁלִי, דְּבַק:

2. Write in pointed Hebrew.

Learn ye, rule thou in the city, we will learn to keep the head and the heart, thou wilt be great, I shall visit, they will stumble, number ye, remember thou, keeping thou shalt keep the covenant, we shall be righteous, they wrote in the morning.

LESSON XI

PERSONAL PRONOUNS

In order to use the personal pronoun correctly one must know the separate forms and the abbreviated forms. The former are

distinct words and are used to express the nominative case.
They are unchangeable and indeclinable.

The abbreviated forms, called pronominal suffixes, are used
to represent the oblique cases. Attached as suffixes to the verb
or to the particle אֵת they stand as the direct object of the verb
(Accusative). When attached to a noun they denote possession
(Possessive). When they are joined to the inseparable prepositions they may stand as the object of the preposition.

אֲנִי אִישׁ   *I* (am) *a man* (separate form)

מְשָׁלַנִי $\}$ *he ruled me* $\left\{\begin{array}{l} \text{suffix attached to verb} \\ \text{suffix attached to אֵת} \end{array}\right\}$
מָשַׁל אֹתִי

סוּסִי   *my horse* (suffix attached to a noun)

לִי   *to me* (suffix attached to a preposition)

Separate Forms

Singular			Plural		
אֲנִי	'ᵃnî	$\}$ *I*	נַחֲנוּ	năḥ-nû	$\}$ *we*
אָנֹכִי	'ā-nō-khî		אֲנַחְנוּ	'ᵃnăḥ-nû	
אַתָּה	'ăt-tā(h)	*thou* (m.)	אַתֶּם	'ăt-tĕm	*you* (m.)
אַתְּ	'ătt	*thou* (f.)	אַתֵּנָה	'ăt-tē-nā(h)	*you* (f.)
הוּא	hû'	*he*	הֵם, הֵמָּה	hēm	*they* (m.)
הִיא	hî'	*she*	הֵנָּה, הֵן	hēn-nā(h)	*they* (f.)

These separate forms are rarely used to express the subject
of the verb, except with the participle. The verb form contains
the pronominal subject (מָשַׁל *he ruled*). Only when the writer

wished to place special emphasis on the subject would he use
הוּא מָשַׁל *he ruled.*

THE PRONOMINAL SUFFIXES WITH A PREPOSITION

Singular		Plural	
לִי	*to me*	לָנוּ	*to us*
לְךָ	*to thee* (m.)	לָכֶם	*to you* (m.)
לָךְ (לֵכִי)	*to thee* (f.)	לָכֶן	*to you* (f.)
לוֹ	*to him*	לָהֶם	*to them* (m.)
לָהּ	*to her*	לָהֶן	*to them* (f.)

THE PRONOMINAL SUFFIXES WITH אֵת (DIRECT OBJECT)

↳ the note of the accusative

Singular		Plural	
אֹתִי	*me*	אֹתָנוּ	*us*
אֹתְךָ	*thee* (m.)	אֶתְכֶם	*you* (m.)
אֹתָךְ	*thee* (f.)	(אֶתְכֶן)	*you* (f.)
אֹתוֹ	*him*	אֹתָם	*them* (m.)
אֹתָהּ	*her*	אֹתָן	*them* (f.)

THE PRONOMINAL SUFFIXES WITH A NOUN

Singular		Plural	
סוּסִי	*my horse*	סוּסֵנוּ	*our horse*
סוּסְךָ	*thy* (m.) *horse*	סוּסְכֶם	*your* (m.) *horse*
סוּסֵךְ	*thy* (f.) *horse*	סוּסְכֶן	*your* (f.) *horse*
סוּסוֹ	*his horse*	סוּסָם	*their* (m.) *horse*
סוּסָהּ	*her horse*	סוּסָן	*their* (f.) *horse*

EXERCISES

1. Pronounce and translate.

אָנֹכִי אָב, אַתָּה הָאִישׁ, הוּא הַיֶּלֶד, מָשַׁל הַבֵּן אֶת סוּסוֹ,
קוֹלָהּ טוֹב, גָּדַל יוֹמָם, נָתַן אֶת הַסֵּפֶר לִי, הוּא הַנָּבִיא הַטּוֹב,
נָתְנוּ אֶת סוּסָם לַמֶּלֶךְ:

2. Translate into Hebrew.

*The father gave the covenant to him. Her horse (is) in the city.
The king ruled the people. The mother kept him. Thou (art) the
woman.*

LESSON XII

OTHER PRONOUNS

The Demonstratives

	Singular			Plural	
this	m. זֶה	zě(h)	*these* c.	אֵלֶּה	'ēl-lě(h)
	f. זֹאת	zô'th			
that	m. הוּא	hû'	*those*	m. (הֵם) הֵמָּה	hēm-mā(h)
	f. הִיא	hî'		f. (הֵן) הֵנָּה	hēn-nā(h)

These pronouns conform to the same rules as the **adjective**
with regard to the article; i. e., they take the article when **quali-**
fying, but not when predicative.

זֶה אִישׁ טוֹב	*this (is) a good man.*
זֶה הָאִישׁ הַטּוֹב	*this (is) the good man.*
הָאִישׁ הַזֶּה	*this man.*
הָאִשָּׁה הַזֹּאת	*this woman.*
הָאִישׁ הַטּוֹב הַזֶּה	*this good man.*

The Relative

אֲשֶׁר *who, which, what,* is the one relative pronoun. It is invariable for all genders, numbers, and cases. (In later Hebrew שַׁ or שֶׁ followed by daghesh-forte is occasionally found for אֲשֶׁר).

The Interrogatives

מִי (mî) *who,* refers to persons,   מִי אַתָּה *who (art) thou?*

מָה (mā(h)) *what,* refers to things, מַהדִהִיא *what (is) that?*

The pointing of מָה varies according to the consonant which follows it. (cf. the pointing of the article).

מַה plus daghesh-forte, (usually)	מַהדּלָךְ	*what to thee?*
מַה before ה and ח	מַהדִהִיא	*what (is) that?*
מָה before א, ע and ר	מָהדאֵלֶּה	*what (are) these?*
מֶה before gutturals with "a"	מֶהדעָשִׂיתִי	*what have I done?*

NOTE: אֵי (*where*) plus the demonstrative (אֵידזֶה) may be used as an interrogative, אֵידזֶה הַדֶּרֶךְ *which way?*

NOTE: The pronoun מִי stands alone while מָה is always joined to the following word by makkeph.

VOCABULARY

מָכַר	mā-khăr	*sell*	שָׁבַת	shā-văth	*rest*
שָׁלֵם	shā-lēm	*be whole*	שָׁבַר	shā-văr	*break*
קָרַב	ḳā-răv	*draw near*	שָׁפַט	shā-phăṭ	*judge*

EXERCISES

1. Translate.

זֶה הַדָּבָר, הַדָּבָר הַזֶּה, הָאִישׁ אֲשֶׁר הָאָב, הַסּוּס הַהוּא,

הוּא הַסּוּס הַטּוֹב, מָהֹאֵלֶּה, מִי הַנָּבִיא, הַשֵּׁם הַקָּדוֹשׁ הַזֶּה, הָאֵם הַזֹּאת:

2. Write into Hebrew.

Who gave the good book to the prophet? What (is) in the hand? This woman sold the horse. They rested in the light. Ye will draw near. We shall judge the child.

LESSON XIII

THE SUBSTANTIVE

Cases

Strictly speaking there are no cases in Hebrew. There is no clear set of case endings as we find in other languages. The old accusative ending ה‍ָ is found occasionally at the end of nouns to denote *direction* or motion toward, הָהָרָה *toward the mountain*. Usually, however, there is no ending to indicate the accusative. It is the case of the direct object and, if the word is definite, it is preceded by אֵת, *he kept the man* שָׁמַר אֵת הָאִישׁ (The pronominal suffix attached to the end of a verb expresses the accusative, מְשָׁלָם *he ruled them*).

The Genitive is clearly indicated by a combination of words which is called the **construct** relation. It is the use that corresponds to the expression "*of*" in English, סוּס הָאִישׁ *the horse of the man* (*the man's horse*). The substantive סוּס is said to be in the **construct** state, and the substantive אִישׁ is in the **absolute** state. The governing substantive always stands first, never takes the article, and must be followed immediately by the substantive in the absolute state. They form a compound word,

since the accent has been lost from the word in the construct.
When the accent is lost, the long vowels (unless unchangeable)
are volatilized (shortened).

דָּבָר	*word*	but	דְּבַר אִישׁ	*a word of a man.*
יָד	*hand*	but	יַד הַבֵּן	*the hand of the son.*
כֹּל	*all*	but	כָּל־הָאָרֶץ	*all (of) the earth.*
תּוֹרָה	*law*	but	תּוֹרַת יָהוֶה	*law of Yahweh.*

Gender and Number

Hebrew has two genders, masculine and feminine, and three
numbers, singular, plural, and dual. The dual is confined to
substantives. It is used in the names of objects that go in pairs
(ears, eyes, feet, etc.). The following table gives the various
endings for gender and number:

		Singular		Plural	
Masc.	Abs.	סוּס	*horse*	סוּסִים	*horses*
	Const.	סוּס	*horse of*	סוּסֵי	*horses of*
Fem.	Abs.	סוּסָה	*mare*	סוּסוֹת	*mares*
	Const.	סוּסַת	*mare of*	סוּסוֹת	*mares of*

Dual

Masc.			Fem.	
Abs.	סוּסַיִם	*horses* (a pair)	סוּסָתַיִם	*mares* (a pair)
Const.	סוּסֵי	*horses of* (a pair)	סוּסָתֵי	*mares of* (a pair)

NOTES:

1. The masculine singular has no separate ending.

סוּס *horse*, טוֹב *good*, קוֹל *voice*.

2. The masculine plural ending ◌ִים is usually added to the masculine singular form.

סוּסִים *horses*, טוֹבִים *good (ones)*.

3. The feminine ending is ◌ָה, formed from the original ending ◌ָת. (Watch for the return of this old ending ◌ַת before suffixes.)

שָׂרָה *princess*, טוֹבָה *good*, סוּסָה *mare*.

4. The feminine plural ends in וֹת.

דּוֹר *generation*, דּוֹרוֹת *generations*, שָׂרוֹת *princesses*, פָּרוֹת *cows*, טוֹבוֹת *good (ones)*.

5. The dual ending is the same for masculine and feminine ◌ַיִם.

יָדַיִם *hands (a pair)*, אָזְנַיִם *ears (a pair)*

6. Irregular plurals

    (a) Some masculine nouns use the feminine plural ending.

שֵׁמוֹת, קוֹלוֹת, מְקוֹמוֹת, אוֹתוֹת, אָבוֹת.

    (b) Some feminine nouns use the masculine plural ending.

יוֹנִים (from יוֹנָה *dove*), מִלִּים (from מִלָּה *word*).

    (c) Some substantives have two plurals, one in ◌ִים and one in וֹת.

דּוֹר *generation*, שִׁיר *song*, שָׁנָה *year*.

    (d) Some substantives are found only in the plural.

שָׁמַיִם *heavens*, מַיִם *waters*, פָּנִים *faces*.

VOCABULARY

אֵשׁ	*fire (f.)*	גֵּר	*sojourner*	לַיְלָה	*night*
גַּם	*also*	חַג	*feast*	כֹּל (כָּל-)	*all, every*
גַּן	*garden*	חֹק	*statute*	צוּר	*rock*

Exercises

1. Translate.

הַסּוּסִים הַטּוֹבִים, הָאוֹר הַגָּדוֹל, אִישׁ שָׁלוֹם, קוֹל הָאָב,
הַקּוֹלוֹת הַטּוֹבוֹת, הַסּוּסוֹת וְהַפָּרוֹת, חֶרֶב הַמֶּלֶךְ, מֶלֶךְ הָאָרֶץ
הַגָּדוֹל, קוֹלוֹת הָעָם, הַשָּׁמַיִם וְהָאָרֶץ, הָאָזְנַיִם וְהַיָּדַיִם:

2. Write in Hebrew.

He has kept the law of the covenant. They pursued the man toward the mountain. The word of God (is) perfect. They will write the book for the king.

LESSON XIV

Pronominal Suffixes with Substantives

The possessive pronouns, *my, thy, his, her, our, your,* and *their,* are not found as separate words in Hebrew. As stated on page 29 they are represented by fragments of personal pronouns attached to the substantive. This is really another example of the *construct* state. The substantive is in the construct before a fragment of the pronoun. Instead of saying *my horse,* we are forced to say *the horse of me* סוּסִי. *Your word* = דְּבַרְכֶם, *the word of you.*

Masculine Substantives with Pronominal Suffixes

	Singular	Plural
	סוּס *horse*	סוּסִים *horses*
	סוּס *horse of* (Const.)	סוּסֵי *horses of* (Const.)
1 c. sg.	סוּסִי *my horse*	סוּסַי *my horses*

2 m. sg.	סוּסְךָ	*thy horse*	סוּסֶיךָ	*thy horses*
2 f. sg.	סוּסֵךְ	*thy horse*	סוּסַיִךְ	*thy horses*
3 m. sg.	סוּסוֹ	*his horse*	סוּסָיו	*his horses*
3 f. sg.	סוּסָהּ	*her horse*	סוּסֶיהָ	*her horses*
1 c. pl.	סוּסֵנוּ	*our horse*	סוּסֵינוּ	*our horses*
2 m. pl.	סוּסְכֶם	*your horse*	סוּסֵיכֶם	*your horses*
2 f. pl.	סוּסְכֶן	*your horse*	סוּסֵיכֶן	*your horses*
3 m. pl.	סוּסָם	*their horse*	סוּסֵיהֶם	*their horses*
3 f. pl.	סוּסָן	*their horse*	סוּסֵיהֶן	*their horses*

This paradigm gives all the suffixes attached to substantives. Many words will present variations in vowels, due to the influence of the tone, but these endings remain the same after all substantives. We may recognize the ending ִי as "*my*," the the ending ךָ as "*thy*," the ending נוּ as "*our*," the ending כֶּם as "*your*." We see that instead of many "declensions," we really have none in Hebrew. We merely have substantives in the construct plus these suffixes. Let nothing hinder a complete mastery of these endings.

FEMININE SUBSTANTIVES WITH PRONOMINAL SUFFIXES

The same endings are used with feminine substantives. When the substantive does not have the ending ָה the suffixes are attached directly. When the ending is ָה the suffixes are added to the original form of the substantive ַת (the construct). סוּסָה becomes סוּסַת when suffixes are to be added.

	Singular		Plural	
	סוּסָה	*mare*	סוּסוֹת	*mares*
	סוּסַת	*mare of* (Const.)	סוּסוֹת	*mares of* (Const.)
1 c. sg.	סוּסָתִי	*my mare*	סוּסוֹתַי	*my mares*
2 m. sg.	סוּסָתְךָ	*thy mare*	סוּסוֹתֶיךָ	*thy mares*
2 f. sg.	סוּסָתֵךְ	*thy mare*	סוּסוֹתַיִךְ	*thy mares*
3 m. sg.	סוּסָתוֹ	*his mare*	סוּסוֹתָיו	*his mares*
3 f. sg.	סוּסָתָה	*her mare*	סוּסוֹתֶיהָ	*her mares*
1 c. pl.	סוּסָתֵנוּ	*our mare*	סוּסוֹתֵינוּ	*our mares*
2 m. pl.	סוּסַתְכֶם	*your mare*	סוּסוֹתֵיכֶם	*your mares*
2 f. pl.	סוּסַתְכֶן	*your mare*	סוּסוֹתֵיכֶן	*your mares*
3 m. pl.	סוּסָתָם	*their mare*	סוּסוֹתֵיהֶם	*their mares*
3 f. pl.	סוּסָתָן	*their mare*	סוּסוֹתֵיהֶן	*their mares*

NOTES

1. In the singular the old feminine form is used, and the endings are joined directly to it. There is no vowel change before the heavily accented syllables כֶם and כֶן, but before all the light suffixes the ־ is heightened to ־. We have סוּסָתוֹ instead of סוּסַתוֹ (The vowel must be long in an open syllable unless accented.) סוּסַתְכֶם can stand because the ־ is in a half-open syllable.

2. In the plural there is a double plural ending. The feminine plural וֹת is retained and the regular plural suffixes are added, סוּסוֹתֵינוּ.

EXERCISES

1. Write the pronominal suffixes to the following:

יוֹם *day*, יוֹנָה *dove*, דּוֹרוֹת *generations*, טוֹבִים *good*.

2. Translate.

אוֹרִי, אוֹרִים, אוֹר הַבֹּקֶר, אוֹר פָּנִים, קוֹלוֹ, אָבִי, קוֹלְךָ,
קוֹלְכֶם, קוֹלָהּ, גְּבוּרֵנוּ, דּוֹרוֹתֵיהֶם, יֹנָתָם, טוֹבוֹתֶיךָ, יֹנָתָהּ,
יוֹמָהּ, דּוֹרוֹתַי, טוֹבִים, סוּסֶתְךָ, סוּסוֹתֵינוּ, קוֹלוֹתֵיהֶם, תּוֹרָתְךָ,
תּוֹרוֹת, סוּסַיִם, צוּרִים, צוּרֵינוּ, גְּבוֹרִים, גְּבוֹרֶיךָ, גְּבוֹרָם,
בְּרִיתִי, בְּרִיתוֹ, בְּרִיתְכֶם:

LESSON XV
OTHER SUBSTANTIVES WITH SUFFIXES

In our last lesson the student was introduced to the pronominal suffixes as attached to a word that had unchangeable
vowels in it. In other words, we were concerned with the terminations. We now turn to the consideration of a word that is
subject to internal vowel changes when suffixes are added. In
this study let the student remember that the vowel of an open
syllable must be long unless accented. The vowel of the ante-
penultimate syllable is usually volatilized, מְלָכִים, דְּבָרִים.

	Singular			Plural	
	דָּבָר	word		דְּבָרִים	words
	דְּבַר	word of (Const.)		דִּבְרֵי	words of (Const.)
1 c. sg.	דְּבָרִי	my word		דְּבָרַי	my words
2 m. sg.	דְּבָרְךָ	thy word		דְּבָרֶיךָ	thy words
2 f. sg.	דְּבָרֵךְ	thy word		דְּבָרַיִךְ	thy words
3 m. sg.	דְּבָרוֹ	his word		דְּבָרָיו	his words
3 f. sg.	דְּבָרָהּ	her word		דְּבָרֶיהָ	her words

1 c. pl.	דְּבָרֵנוּ *our word*	דְּבָרֵינוּ *our words*	
2 m. pl.	דְּבַרְכֶם *your word*	דִּבְרֵיכֶם *your words*	
2 f. pl.	דְּבַרְכֶן *your word*	דִּבְרֵיכֶן *your words*	
3 m. pl.	דְּבָרָם *their word*	דִּבְרֵיהֶם *their words*	
3 f. pl.	דְּבָרָן *their word*	דִּבְרֵיהֶן *their words*	

There are many classes of substantives. In each class the vowels show a different behavior. We present two of these examples and then append a list of some other nouns with the construct form of each.

Eternity		*King*	
עוֹלָמִים	עוֹלָם	מְלָכִים	מֶלֶךְ
עוֹלָמֵי	עוֹלָם	מַלְכֵי	מֶלֶךְ
עוֹלָמַי	עוֹלָמִי	מְלָכַי	מַלְכִּי
עוֹלָמֶיךָ	עוֹלָמְךָ	מְלָכֶיךָ	מַלְכְּךָ
עוֹלָמַיִךְ	עוֹלָמֶךְ	מְלָכַיִךְ	מַלְכֵּךְ
עוֹלָמָיו	עוֹלָמוֹ	מְלָכָיו	מַלְכּוֹ
עוֹלָמֶיהָ	עוֹלָמָהּ	מְלָכֶיהָ	מַלְכָּהּ
עוֹלָמֵינוּ	עוֹלָמֵנוּ	מְלָכֵינוּ	מַלְכֵּנוּ
עוֹלְמֵיכֶם	עוֹלַמְכֶם	מַלְכֵיכֶם	מַלְכְּכֶם
עוֹלְמֵיכֶן	עוֹלַמְכֶן	מַלְכֵיכֶן	מַלְכְּכֶן
עוֹלְמֵיהֶם	עוֹלָמָם	מַלְכֵיהֶם	מַלְכָּם
עוֹלְמֵיהֶן	עוֹלָמָן	מַלְכֵיהֶן	מַלְכָּן

	Absolute	Construct		Absolute	Construct
overseer	פָּקִיד	פְּקִיד	*death*	מָוֶת	מוֹת
wise	חָכָם	חֲכַם	*fruit*	פְּרִי	פְּרִי
old man	זָקֵן	זְקַן	*sea*	יָם	יָם (יָם)
book	סֵפֶר	סְפֶר	*queen*	מַלְכָּה	מַלְכַּת
youth	נַעַר	נַעַר	*righteousness*	צְדָקָה	צִדְקַת
work	פֹּעַל	פֹּעַל			

SOME IRREGULAR NOUNS

	Singular		Plural	
	Absolute	Construct	Absolute	Construct
father	אָב	אֲבִי	אָבוֹת	אֲבוֹת
brother	אָח	אֲחִי	אַחִים	אֲחֵי
one	אֶחָד	אַחַד	אֲחָדִים	אַחֲדֵי
sister	אָחוֹת	אֲחוֹת	אֲחָיוֹת	אַחְיוֹתַי
man	אִישׁ	אִישׁ	אֲנָשִׁים	אַנְשֵׁי
house	בַּיִת	בֵּית	בָּתִּים	בָּתֵּי
wife	אִשָּׁה	אֵשֶׁת	נָשִׁים	נְשֵׁי
son	בֵּן	בֶּן (בִּן)	בָּנִים	בְּנֵי
name	שֵׁם	שֵׁם	שֵׁמוֹת	שְׁמוֹת
daughter	בַּת	בַּת	בָּנוֹת	בְּנוֹת
water	——	——	מַיִם	מֵי (מֵימֵי)
day	יוֹם	יוֹם	יָמִים	יְמֵי
city	עִיר	עִיר	עָרִים	עָרֵי

	Absolute	Construct	Absolute	Construct
mouth	פֶּה	פִּי	פִּיוֹת	פִּיוֹת
head	רֹאשׁ	רֹאשׁ	רָאשִׁים	רָאשֵׁי
heavens	———	———	שָׁמַיִם	שְׁמֵי
implement	כְּלִי	כְּלִי	כֵּלִים	כְּלֵי

Exercises

Translate.

זְקֵנִים, זִקְנֵי, חַכְמֵי, יָמִים, מְלָכוֹת, זִקְנֵי, מוֹתִי, נְעָרִים,
סִפְרֵי, פְּרִיהֶם, זִקְנֵיכֶם, מוֹתִי, נַעֲרָה, סְפָרִים, פָּעֳלוֹ, פְּעָלִים,
פְּקִידִים, פְּקִידוֹ, צִדְקָתִי, צְדָקוֹת, צִדְקוֹת, דְּבָרַי, קוֹלָם,
יוֹמָן, קוֹלְךָ, פִּיךָ, בְּרִיתָם, אֱלֹהֵינוּ:

LESSON XVI

Some Principles of Syntax

1. The verb usually stands first in the sentence. However
when either the negative or the interrogative pronoun occurs
in the sentence it precedes the verb.

מָכַר הָאִישׁ סוּס   *the man sold a horse.*

לֹא שָׁמַר אֶת הַתּוֹרָה   *he did not keep the law.*

מִי כָתַב אֶת־הַסֵּפֶר   *who wrote the book?*

2. When particular emphasis is wanted, any word may be
given first place.

לִי הַכֹּהֵן נָתַן סֵפֶר   *the priest gave me a book.*

3. The subject usually follows the verb.

אָמַר אֱלֹהִים *God said.*

4. The subject is followed by its modifiers. The adjective agrees with the substantive in gender, number, and definiteness.

הַסּוּס הַטּוֹב *the good horse.*

הַסּוּסִים הַטּוֹבִים *the good horses.*

הַסּוּסוֹת הַטּוֹבוֹת *the good mares.*

5. The demonstrative behaves like the adjective. When attributive, it follows the substantive and both take the article.

הַקּוֹל הַזֶּה *this voice.*

If another adjective is used, the demonstrative follows it, and each word is made definite by the article.

הַקּוֹל הַטּוֹב הַזֶּה *this good voice.*

6. The direct object of the verb is the next in order. If definite, it is preceded by the particle אֵת.

מָכַר הָאִישׁ אֶת הָעֵץ *the man sold the tree.*

7. By way of summary, we may note the regular word order. Verb, subject (and its modifiers), direct object (and its modifiers), indirect object. When any other order is used, it is for special emphasis.

כָּתַב הַמֶּלֶךְ הַגָּדוֹל הַזֶּה אֶת הַדָּבָר הַטּוֹב לַשַּׂר *This great king wrote the good word to the prince.*

8. The comparative degree is expressed by means of the preposition מִן.

הָאִישׁ גָּדוֹל מִדַּרְבֵּן *the man is larger than the son.*

9 The use of *He directive* to express the idea of the accusative

[handwritten marginal notes:]

Definite object
1. אֵת
2. Proper name
3. If it has a pronominal suffix
4. Construct is def. when absolute is def.

of verbal sentence

Heb. has no adverbs to modify nurs except, now,

Superlative
a. Use construct state & follow it w/ plural.
1. King of kings
2. Song of songs
b. Or just put the article in front of the adj.

as the limit of motion is common. The suffix הָ is attached
to the substantive.

אַרְצָה *toward the land.*

10. The <u>Cohortative ending</u> הָ is attached to the first person
of the imperfect or to the imperative to give added strength.
In the case of the imperative the request is made more hearty
and impressive.

אֶמְשְׁלָה *let me rule* or *I will rule.*

נִכְרְתָה *we will cut* (a covenant)

שְׁמָעֶרְנָא *hear, I pray*

זָכְרָה *think!*

11. A prohibition cannot be expressed by an imperative. The
usual means is to use אַל with the jussive.

וְדָם נָקִי אַל־תִּשְׁפְּכוּ *and shed not innocent blood.*

VOCABULARY

בֵּין	*between*	דּוֹר	*generation*	עוֹד	*again*
בַּיִת	*house*	דָּם	*blood*	עֵת	*time* (f.)
גָּדוֹל	*great*	הַר	*mountain*	פֶּה	*mouth*

EXERCISES

Translate.

הַשָּׁנִים הָאֵלֶּה, הָאָרֶץ הַזֹּאת, נָתַן אֱלֹהִים אֶת־הַדָּבָר בַּיּוֹם
הַהוּא: שָׁמַר הָאָדָם אֶת־הַשַּׁבָּת: לָמַד הַיֶּלֶד מִן־הַסֵּפֶר: לֹא
מְשַׁלְתֶּם אֶת־הַיֶּלֶד: הָאִישׁ הַגָּדוֹל הַזֶּה בָּהָר: זָכְרוּ אֵת הַצּוּרִים
בֵּן בֵּין הַבַּיִת וּבֵין הָעֵץ: כָּתְבָה הַבַּת אֶת הַסֵּפֶר לַיֶּלֶד:

LESSON XVII

The Stems of the Verb

In addition to the verb forms already studied we have six other stems, each representing a different aspect of the primary meaning of the verb. To find a suitable name for these sets of forms is difficult. They can hardly be called conjugations, or moods, or voices. Perhaps it will be best to speak of them as stems. These derived stems are formed from the simple (*Qal*) stem (or the root) by means of prefixes, vowel changes, and the doubling of certain letters.

The root idea or meaning of the verb is presented in three conditions or degrees: (1) the **simple,** *to love*, (2) the **intensive,** *to love passionately*, (3) the **causative,** extending the action over a second agent, *to make to love*, *to cause to love*. Each of these has an active and a passive form. The intensive has a reflexive form also. The names for these stems, except Qal which means "light," are derived from the Hebrew word פָּעַל. (Niph'al, Pi'el, Pu'al, Hithpa'el, Hiph'il, Hoph'al).

SIMPLE	INTENSIVE	CAUSATIVE
Active	Active	Active
(Qal) קַל	(Pi'el) פִּעֵל	(Hiph'il) הִפְעִיל
Passive	Passive	Passive
(Niph'al) נִפְעַל	(Pu'al) פֻּעַל	(Hoph'al) הָפְעַל
	Reflexive	
	(Hithpa'el) הִתְפַּעֵל	

All double middle radical

Using קָטַל as the paradigm word the stems are as follows:

1. The Simple Active   קָטַל   *he killed*
   (Qal)

2. The Simple Passive   נִקְטַל   *he was killed*
   (Niph'al)   נִפְעַל

3. The Intensive Active   קִטֵּל   *he killed (brutally)*
   (Pi'el)   פִּעֵל

4. The Intensive Passive   קֻטַל   *he was killed (brutally)*
   (Pu'al)

5. The Intensive Reflexive   הִתְקַטֵּל   *he killed himself*
   (Hithpa'el)

6. The Causative Active   הִקְטִיל   *he caused to kill*
   (Hiph'il)

7. The Causative Passive   הָקְטַל   *he was caused to kill*
   (Hoph'al)

Characteristics of these Stems

1. Qal קָטַל, the simple verb stem as found in the lexicon.

2. Niph'al (נִפְעַל) נִקְטַל, the passive of the Qal, has a prefixed נ (shortened from הַן). It may be reflexive in force.

3. Pi'el (פִּעֵל) קִטֵּל, always active, middle radical always
doubled by means of daghesh-forte (in strong verbs). It may
be iterative or emphatic.

4. Pu'al (פֻּעַל) קֻטַל always passive, middle radical always
doubled (in strong verbs).

5. Hithpa'el (הִתְפַּעֵל) הִתְקַטֵּל, reflexive (middle voice),
middle radical doubled and a prefixed הַת always present.

6. Hiph'il (הִפְעִיל) הִקְטִיל active, always has a prefixed ה.

7. Hoph'al (הָפְעַל) הָקְטַל passive, always has a prefixed ה.

Notes

1. We use קְטַל as a paradigm word because the old word פָּעַל contains a guttural, the presence of which causes some irregularities.

2. The complete paradigm of the seven stems is given, although only six verbs out of fourteen hundred make use of all these stems.

3. The names of the stems indicate the vowels to be used in the perfects. Learn to pronounce each word correctly, getting the proper vowel sound.

נִקְטַל	nĭk-ṭăl	נִמְשַׁל	nĭm-shăl	*Niph'al*
קִטֵּל	kĭṭ-ṭēl	מִשֵּׁל	mĭsh-shēl	*Pi'el*
קֻטַּל	kŭṭ-ṭăl	מֻשַּׁל	mŭsh-shăl	*Pu'al*
הִתְקַטֵּל	hĭth-kăṭ-ṭēl	הִתְמַשֵּׁל	hĭth-măsh-shēl	*Hithpa'el*
הִקְטִיל	hĭk-ṭîl	הִמְשִׁיל	hĭm-shîl	*Hiph'il*
הָקְטַל	hŏk-ṭăl	הָמְשַׁל	hŏm-shăl	*Hoph'al*

4. Remember the doubling of the second radical of the three intensive stems.

5. The causative stems are increased from without. Remember the prefixed ה, הָקְטַל, הִקְטִיל.

6. The first syllable of Niph'al, Hiph'il and Hoph'al stems is closed and the second radical of the verb takes daghesh-lene if it is ב, ג, ד, כ, פ, ת; נִשְׁבַּר, הִזְכִּיר, הָרְדַּף.

Vocabulary

גָּבַר be strong, *prevail*　　סָגַר close, *shut*

דָּרַשׁ *tread, seek*　　שָׂרַף *burn*

כָּבַס *wash*   שָׁכַב *lie down*

כִּפֵּר *cover* (Pi.)   שָׁכַם *rise early* (Hi.)

EXERCISES

1. Write the 3rd masculine, singular of each of the stems treated above, using קָטַל, מָשַׁל, כָּשַׁל, גָּנַב, מָלַךְ.

2. Translate and locate fully:*

גָּבַר, נִדְרַשׁ, כָּבַס, כִּפֵּר, נִסְגַּר, הִשְׁכִּיב, הִגְבִּיר, כְּבַס,

הִתְכַּפֵּר, סָגַר, הִשְׁכִּים, שָׁכֵן, הִתְגַּבֵּר, כָּפַר, סָגֵר, נִשְׁבַּר,

הִשְׁבִּית, נִשְׁפַּט, הִסְגִּיר, נִשְׂרַף, הִשְׁכִּין, שָׁבַר, הָשְׁבַּר, שָׁלַם,

הִשְׁבִּיר, נָשְׁבַּת, הִשְׁלִים, נִקְרַב, הִקְרִיב, הִשְׂכִּיל, נִקְבַּר, קָבַר,

נִצְדַּק, הִצְדִּיק, נִמְכַּר, הִתְמַכֵּר, הִזְכִּיר, פָּקַד:

*To locate דִּבַּרְתָּ let the student use the following order: "Pi'el, perfect, 2nd, masculine, singular from דִּבֵּר *to speak*. Thou didst speak."

LESSON XVIII
THE REMAINING PERFECTS

We turn now to a consideration of each of these stems.

The Niph'al (נִקְטַל).

The simple passive stem has a prefixed נ (from the ground form נִקְטַל). Note how closely the inflection resembles the simple active (Qal) stem.

Singular	Plural
נִקְטַל *he was killed (he killed himself)*	נִקְטְלוּ *they were killed*
נִקְטְלָה *she was killed*	

נִקְטַלְתָּ thou (m.) wast killed   נִקְטַלְתֶּם you (m.) were killed

נִקְטַלְתְּ thou (f.) wast killed   נִקְטַלְתֶּן you (f.) were killed

נִקְטַלְתִּי I was killed   נִקְטַלְנוּ we were killed

The Pi'el (קַטֵּל) (קִטֵּל ground form).

The intensive active stem doubles the middle radical.

Singular

קִטֵּל he killed (brutally)

קִטְּלָה she killed (brutally)

קִטַּלְתָּ thou (m.) didst kill (brutally)

קִטַּלְתְּ thou (f.) didst kill (brutally)

קִטַּלְתִּי I killed (brutally)

Plural

קִטְּלוּ they killed (brutally)

קִטַּלְתֶּם you (m.) killed (brutally)

קִטַּלְתֶּן you (f.) killed (brutally)

קִטַּלְנוּ we killed (brutally)

The Pu'al (קֻטַּל) (קֻטַּל or קֹטַל)

The intensive passive stem doubles the middle radical.

Singular

קֻטַּל he was killed (brutally)

קֻטְּלָה she was killed

קֻטַּלְתָּ thou (m.) wast killed

קֻטַּלְתְּ   *thou* (f.) *wast killed*

קֻטַּלְתִּי   *I was killed*

Plural

קֻטְּלוּ   *they were killed* (*brutally*)

קֻטַּלְתֶּם   *you* (m.) *were killed*

קֻטַּלְתֶּן   *you* (f.) *were killed*

קֻטַּלְנוּ   *we were killed*

The Hithpaʻel (הִתְקַטֵּל) (הִתְקַטֵּל)

The intensive reflexive stem doubles the middle radical and prefixes הִת.

Singular

הִתְקַטֵּל   *he killed himself*

הִתְקַטְּלָה   *she killed herself*

הִתְקַטַּלְתָּ   *thou* (m.) *didst kill thyself*

הִתְקַטַּלְתְּ   *thou* (f.) *didst kill thyself*

הִתְקַטַּלְתִּי   *I killed myself*

Plural

הִתְקַטְּלוּ   *they killed themselves*

הִתְקַטַּלְתֶּם   *you* (m.) *killed yourselves*

הִתְקַטַּלְתֶּן   *you* (f.) *killed yourselves*

הִתְקַטַּלְנוּ   *we killed ourselves*

NOTE: When the prefix (הִת) precedes the sibilants ס, שׂ, שׁ, the ת of the prefix changes places with the sibilant, הִשְׁתַּמֵּר *he kept himself,* הִסְתַּתֵּר *he concealed himself.* The תּ of the prefix may be assimilated before ד, ת, ט. It may be changed to ט and transposed before צ, הִטַּהֵר for הִתְטַהֵר *he purified himself,* הִצְטַדֵּק for הִתְצַדֵּק *he sanctified himself.* (See Isa. 1:16 הִזַּכּוּ for the assimilation of ת before ז).

The Hiph'il (הַקְטֵל) (הִקְטִיל)

The causative stem has a prefixed הַ. The ground form is הַקְטֵל which becomes הִקְטִיל in 3rd masculine singular. Before vowel additions (הַ֗ and וּ) the ◌ִי is retained and accented (הִקְטִילוּ). Before consonant additions the original ◌ַ is restored (הִקְטַלְתָּ).

Singular

הִקְטִיל	*he caused to kill*
הִקְטִילָה	*she caused to kill*
הִקְטַלְתָּ	*thou (m.) didst cause to kill*
הִקְטַלְתְּ	*thou (f.) didst cause to kill*
הִקְטַלְתִּי	*I caused to kill*

Plural

הִקְטִילוּ	*they caused to kill*
הִקְטַלְתֶּם	*you (m.) caused to kill*
הִקְטַלְתֶּן	*you (f.) caused to kill*
הִקְטַלְנוּ	*we caused to kill*

The Hoph'al (הָקְטַל) (הֻקְטַל or הָקְטַל)

The causative passive has the prefixed הֻ with the vowel ◌ֻ (ŏ). Sometimes the original ◌ָ takes its place.

Singular

הָקְטַל   *he was caused to kill*

הָקְטְלָה   *she was caused to kill*

הָקְטַלְתָּ   *thou (m.) wast caused to kill*

הָקְטַלְתְּ   *thou (f.) wast caused to kill*

הָקְטַלְתִּי   *I was caused to kill*

Plural

הָקְטְלוּ   *they were caused to kill*

הָקְטַלְתֶּם   *you (m.) were caused to kill*

הָקְטַלְתֶּן   *you (f.) were caused to kill*

הָקְטַלְנוּ   *we were caused to kill*

EXERCISES

Translate and locate fully.

הִמְשִׁילוּ, נֶתְנָה, שְׁמַרְתָּ, גֻּדְּלָה, דִּבַּרְנוּ, לִמַּדְתִּי, לִמַּדְתֶּם,
רֻדַּף, הָפְקַדְתִּי, כֻּתְּבוּ, קֻבַּרְתֶּן, נִשְׁבַּתְנוּ, מֻשְׁלַּתֶּם, הִסְתַּתֵּר,
הִמְשִׁילָה, מָשַׁלְתִּי, הִתְקַדְּשָׁה, הִצְדַּקְנוּ, קֻדַּשְׁתֶּן, סֻפַּרְתָּ, כָּשֵׁל,
הֻכְשַׁלְתָּ, שֻׁבְּרוּ, הֻזְכַּרְתִּי, נִזְכַּרְנוּ, זְכַרְתֶּם, נִשְׁמְרָה, הִמְלַכְתִּי,
לָכַדְנוּ, הֻשְׁבַּרְתִּי:

LESSON XIX

THE REMAINING IMPERFECTS

The Niph'al (יִקָּטֵל)

The prefix in the imperfect is יִן (yǐn). Since the נ is always
assimilated when followed by a syllable-divider we have יִקָּטֵל

instead of יִנְקָטֵל *he will be killed.* (The original form was probably יְהִנְקָטֵל).

Singular

יִקָטֵל	*he will be killed*
תִּקָטֵל	*she will be killed*
תִּקָטֵל	*thou* (m.) *wilt be killed*
תִּקָטְלִי	*thou* (f.) *wilt be killed*
אֶקָטֵל	*I shall be killed*

Plural

יִקָטְלוּ	*they* (m.) *will be killed*
תִּקָטַלְנָה	*they* (f.) *will be killed*
תִּקָטְלוּ	*you* (m.) *will be killed*
תִּקָטַלְנָה	*you* (f.) *will be killed*
נִקָטֵל	*we shall be killed*

The Pi'el (יְקַטֵל) (יַקְטֵל)

The intensive active requires that the middle radical be doubled. The meaning is properly intensive; יִשְׁבֹּר (Qal) *he will break.* יְשַׁבֵּר (Pi'el) *he will break* (into bits). It may have a causative force, יִלְמַד *he will learn,* יְלַמֵּד *he will teach* (cause to learn). The preformative has ־ֲ except under א. The vowel before נָה is usually ־ֵ, תְּקַטֵּלְנָה.

Singular

יְקַטֵּל	*he will kill* (*brutally*)
תְּקַטֵּל	*she will kill*

תִּקְטֵל   *thou* (m.) *wilt kill*

תִּקְטְלִי   *thou* (f.) *wilt kill*

אֲקַטֵּל   *I shall kill*

Plural

יְקַטְּלוּ   *they* (m.) *will kill* (**brutally**)

תְּקַטֵּלְנָה   *they* (f.) *will kill*

תְּקַטְּלוּ   *you* (m.) *will kill*

תְּקַטֵּלְנָה   *you* (f.) *will kill*

נְקַטֵּל   *we shall kill*

The Pu'al (יְקֻטַּל) (יְקַטַּל)

The intensive passive requires the doubling of the middle radical. It has the dull vowel ֻ under the first radical. The ְ is under the preformative. Before נָה we usually find ֵ. It is the regular intensive passive, יְבֻקַּשׁ *he will be sought diligently*.

Singular

יְקֻטַּל   *he will be killed* (**brutally**)

תְּקֻטַּל   *she will be killed*

תְּקֻטַּל   *thou* (m.) *wilt be killed*

תְּקֻטְּלִי   *thou* (f.) *wilt be killed*

אֲקֻטַּל   *I shall be killed*

Plural

יְקֻטְּלוּ   *they* (m.) *will be killed* (**brutally**)

תְּקֻטַּלְנָה   *they* (f.) *will be killed*

תִּקָּטְלוּ‎ you (m.) *will be killed*

תִּקָּטַלְנָה‎ you (f.) *will be killed*

נִקָּטֵל‎ we shall be killed

The Hithpa'el (יִתְקַטֵּל) (יִתְקַטֵּל)

The intensive reflexive has the prefix יִת‎ and is inflected regularly. The middle radical (of the stem) is doubled. The vowel before נָה‎ is usually ‐ֵ. (See page 51 for note on change before sibilants.)

Singular

יִתְקַטֵּל‎ *he will kill himself*

תִּתְקַטֵּל‎ *she will kill herself*

תִּתְקַטֵּל‎ *thou* (m.) *wilt kill thyself*

תִּתְקַטְּלִי‎ *thou* (f.) *wilt kill thyself*

אֶתְקַטֵּל‎ *I shall kill myself*

Plural

יִתְקַטְּלוּ‎ *they* (m.) *will kill themselves*

תִּתְקַטֵּלְנָה‎ *they* (f.) *will kill themselves*

תִּתְקַטְּלוּ‎ *you* (m.) *will kill yourselves*

תִּתְקַטֵּלְנָה‎ *you* (f.) *will kill yourselves*

נִתְקַטֵּל‎ *we shall kill ourselves*

The Hiph'il (יַקְטִיל) (יְהִקְטִיל)

The causative active stem holds the original ◌ַ under the pre-formative (יַקְטִיל). The ◌ִי is retained and accented before vowel additions (◌ִי and וּ). The vowel ◌ֵ occurs before נָה.

Singular

יַקְטִיל	*he will cause to kill*
תַּקְטִיל	*she will cause to kill*
תַּקְטִיל	*thou (m.) wilt cause to kill*
תַּקְטִילִי	*thou (f.) wilt cause to kill*
אַקְטִיל	*I shall cause to kill*

Plural

יַקְטִילוּ	*they (m.) will cause to kill*
תַּקְטֵלְנָה	*they (f.) will cause to kill*
תַּקְטִילוּ	*you (m.) will cause to kill*
תַּקְטֵלְנָה	*you (f.) will cause to kill*
נַקְטִיל	*we shall cause to kill*

The Hoph'al (יָקְטַל) (יְהָקְטַל)

The causative passive is perfectly regular in its inflection. A secondary form of Hoph'al, with ◌ֻ under the preformative, occurs in a few strong verbs and certain classes of weak verbs.

Singular

יָקְטַל	*he will be caused to kill*
תָּקְטַל	*she will be caused to kill*

תָּקְטַל   *thou* (m.) *wilt be caused to kill*

תָּקְטְלִי   *thou* (f.) *wilt be caused to kill*

אָקְטַל   *I shall be caused to kill*

Plural

יָקְטְלוּ   *they* (m.) *will be caused to kill*

תָּקְטַלְנָה   *they* (f.) *will be caused to kill*

תָּקְטְלוּ   *you* (m.) *will be caused to kill*

תָּקְטַלְנָה   *you* (f.) *will be caused to kill*

נָקְטַל   *we shall be caused to kill*

EXERCISES

Translate and locate fully.

יִשָּׁבֵר, יְקַדְּשׁוּ, תְּדַבֵּר, תְּכֻפַּר, תְּקֻדְּשׁוּ, יִסָּגְרוּ, תִּתְקַדְּשׁוּ,
יַזְכִּירוּ, יָפְקְדוּ, אַקְרִיב, תִּזָּכַרְנָה, נְלֻמַּד, יִמָּכֵר, יִלָּבֵשׁ, יְקֻדְּשׁוּ,
תָּקְרַבְי, תַּשְׂכִּילוּ, נַזְכִּיר, יְשֻׁבְּרוּ, תִּשָּׁמַרְנָה, יָנְתַן, נַגְדִּיל, נִכְרַתְּ,
אֶשָּׁבֵר, אֶתְדַּבֵּר, יְסֻפְּרוּ, אֶכָּשֵׁל, אֶתְגַּדַּל, תַּזְכִּיר, נִלָּבֵשׁ,
יִמָּלֵט:

LESSON XX

THE IMPERATIVES, INFINITIVES AND PARTICIPLES

THE IMPERATIVES

The stem of the imperative is the same as the imperfect. The passive stems, Puʻal and Hophʻal, have no imperatives. The imperative is found only in the second person (singular and plural).

Niph'al

2 m. sg.	הִקָּטֵל	*be killed* (*kill thyself*)
2 f. sg.	הִקָּטְלִי	*be killed* (*kill thyself*)
2 m. pl.	הִקָּטְלוּ	*be killed* (*kill yourselves*)
2 f. pl.	הִקָּטֵלְנָה	*be killed* (*kill yourselves*)

Pi'el

2 m. sg.	קַטֵּל	*kill* (*thou*) (*brutally*)
2 f. sg.	קַטְּלִי	*kill* (*thou*) (*brutally*)
2 m. pl.	קַטְּלוּ	*kill* (*ye*) (*brutally*)
2 f. pl.	קַטֵּלְנָה	*kill* (*ye*) (*brutally*)

Hithpa'el

2 m. sg.	הִתְקַטֵּל	*kill thyself*
2 f. sg.	הִתְקַטְּלִי	*kill thyself*
2 m. pl.	הִתְקַטְּלוּ	*kill yourselves*
2 f. pl.	הִתְקַטֵּלְנָה	*kill yourselves*

Hiph'il

2 m. sg.	הַקְטֵל	*cause* (*one*) *to kill*
2 f. sg.	הַקְטִילִי	*cause* (*one*) *to kill*
2 m. pl.	הַקְטִילוּ	*cause* (*one*) *to kill*
2 f. pl.	הַקְטֵלְנָה	*cause* (*one*) *to kill*

The Infinitives

There are two infinitives for each stem. The Hithpaʻel infinitive absolute and the Puʻal infinitive construct are not found in the Bible. The Niphʻal infinitive absolute has two forms. Either form may be used. Prepositions may precede and suffixes may be added to the construct infinitives but never to the absolute.

Absolute

Niphʻal	הִקָּטֹל (נִקְטֹל)	*being killed*
Piʻel	קַטֹּל (קַטֵּל)	*killing (brutally)*
Puʻal	קֻטֹּל	*being (brutally) killed*
Hithpaʻel	(הִתְקַטֹּל)	*killing one's self*
Hiphʻil	הַקְטֵל	*causing to kill*
Hophʻal	הָקְטֵל	*being caused to kill*

Construct

Niphʻal	הִקָּטֵל	*to be killed*
Piʻel	קַטֵּל	*to kill (brutally)*
Hithpaʻel	הִתְקַטֵּל	*to kill one's self*
Hiphʻil	הַקְטִיל	*to cause to kill*
Hophʻal	הָקְטֵל	*to be caused to kill*

The Participles

Each stem has a participle. The Qal has both an active and a passive form. The Niphʻal participle has the same form as

the perfect except for the long vowel in the ultima (נִקְטָל).
The other participles are formed by prefixing מ to the stem in
the place of the preformative of the imperfect (מְקַטֵּל, יְקַטֵּל).

Qal	(active)	קֹטֵל	killing, one killing
	(passive)	קָטוּל	killed, one killed (dead)
Niph'al	passive or reflexive	נִקְטָל	killed, one killed or killing one's self
Pi'el	(active)	מְקַטֵּל	killing (brutally), one killing (brutally)
Pu'al	(passive)	מְקֻטָּל	being (brutally) killed, one killed
Hithpa'el	(reflexive)	מִתְקַטֵּל	killing one's self, one who kills himself
Hiph'il	(active)	מַקְטִיל	causing to kill, one who causes to kill
Hoph'al	(passive)	מָקְטָל	caused to kill, one caused to kill

VOCABULARY

בָּגַד	deal treacherously	בדל	(Hi.) divide, separate
בקשׁ	seek (Pi.)	שׁלך	cast (Hi.)
מלט	escape (Ni., Hi., Hith.)	תָּפַשׂ	catch, seize

EXERCISES

Translate and locate fully.

לִשְׁכֹּן, לָמוּד, לְדַבֵּר, מַשְׁכִּים, נִמְלָט, כָּתוּב, נִשְׁבָּר, מְדַבֵּר,
מְקֻדָּשׁ, מַזְכִּיר, דַּבֵּר, שָׁבוּר, נִפְקַד, מְבַקֵּשׁ, מַקְרִיב, מָפְקָד,
מִתְקַדֵּשׁ, הִנָּתֹן, הַשְׁכֵּם, בַּקְשִׁי, הִכָּרֵת, הִמָּלֵט, הִסְתַּתַּרְנָה,
הִשָּׁמֵר, לְהִתְקַדֵּשׁ, לִכְרֹת, מַלֵּט, זָכוֹר:

LESSON XXI

A Synopsis of the Strong Verb

	Simple		Intensive			Causative	
	Qal	Niph'al	Pi'el	Pu'al	Hithpa'el	Hiph'il	Hoph'al
Perf.	קָטַל	נִקְטַל	קִטֵּל	קֻטַּל	הִתְקַטֵּל	הִקְטִיל	הָקְטַל
Impf.	יִקְטֹל	יִקָּטֵל	יְקַטֵּל	יְקֻטַּל	יִתְקַטֵּל	יַקְטִיל	יָקְטַל
Imv.	קְטֹל	הִקָּטֵל	קַטֵּל	—	הִתְקַטֵּל	הַקְטֵל	—
Inf. A.	קָטוֹל	הִקָּטֹל נִקְטֹל	קַטֵּל	קֻטֹּל		הַקְטֵל	הָקְטֵל
Inf. C.	קְטֹל	הִקָּטֵל	קַטֵּל	קֻטַּל	הִתְקַטֵּל	הַקְטִיל	הָקְטַל
Ptc. A.	קֹטֵל	—	מְקַטֵּל	—	מִתְקַטֵּל	מַקְטִיל	—
Ptc. P.	קָטוּל	נִקְטָל	—	מְקֻטָּל	—	—	מָקְטָל

Notes

1. Too much emphasis cannot be given to the importance of this synopsis. Nothing short of an absolute mastery of every form can be considered.

2. Learn to pronounce the names of the stems perfectly. If the word, "Niph'al," is pronounced correctly it should be easy to write the Hebrew form, using the short *i* and the short *a*. (נִמְשַׁל ,נִקְטַל).

3. In writing the imperfects let the student make sure of the following order of the vowel of the preformative:

Qal Niph'al Pi'el Pu'al Hithpa'el Hiph'il Hoph'al

׆ ׆ ׆ ׆ יְתָ׃ ׆ ׆

Pronounce them over and over until they are mastered.

4. The imperfects have as the vowel of the first radical:

Qal Niph'al Pi'el Pu'al Hithpa'el Hiph'il Hoph'al

ק קָ קִ קִ קִ ק ק

5. The second radical with its vowel is as follows:

Qal Niph'al Pi'el Pu'al Hithpa'el Hiph'il Hoph'al

ט טֵ טֵ טַ טֵ טִי טַ

6. The Niph'al has נ in every form. It is assimilated except in the perfect and the participle.

7. The intensive stems have the second radical doubled *every-where*. The active and passive stems are distinguished by the vowels and the reflexive by the prefixes מְת, נְת, תְּת, יְת, הְת.

8. The Hiph'il has ־ under the preformative in all forms except in the perfect.

9. The Hoph'al has ־ (ŏ) under the preformative in all forms.

10. The passive stems have no imperatives (except Niphal).

11. The preformative letter for all participles (except in Qal and Niph'al) is מ.

12. Before נָה in active stems the vowel is ־. In the passive stems the vowel is ־.

13. The passive participles all have ־ in the antepenult in the derived stems.

Vocabulary

גָּנַב steal   סָפַד mourn

מָטַר rain   שָׁטַף overflow

סָמַךְ sustain   קָבַץ collect

Exercises

Translate and locate fully.

תַּמְטֵר, הִמְטִיר, אַמְטִיר, מַמְטִיר, יָמָלֵט, הַזְכִּיר, לִמְלֹךְ,

מְקַדֵּשׁ, גָּנְבוּ, גֻּנַּב, יִסָּמֵךְ, נָגוֹב יִגָּנֵב, מְדַבֵּר, לָבוּשׁ, סָמֵךְ,

סָפְדוּ, קָבַץ, יִגָּנֵב, סָמְכָה, סְפָדִים, קָבַץ, הִתְקַבְּצוּ, שָׁטַף,

יִתְגַּנֵּב, סָמוּךְ, סָפְדוּ, תִּקָּבֵץ, יִשָּׁטֵף, יָכָרֵת, יִסְפְּדוּ, לִסְפֹּר,

הַקָּבֵץ, שָׁטַף, יָסְגַּר, יִנָּתֵן, מְבַקֵּשׁ, הַשְׁכִּים, יְלַמֵּד, הַמְשִׁיל,

יַכְתֵּב:

LESSON XXII

Waw Consecutive (Conversive)

Hebrew makes a peculiar use of the conjunction. It is called
waw consecutive. The simple conjunction may connect verbs
or nouns. Waw consecutive is used to connect finite verbs
only and indicates that the state of the verb to which it is joined
is a consequence of a preceding verb. It must be joined to its
verb. Any conjunction not attached directly_to its verb is
not waw consecutive.

In continued narration after a perfect the verbs that follow
may be put in the imperfect with waw consecutive.

The man kept (שָׁמַר) *the law, and he rested* (וַיִּשְׁבֹּת) *on the Sabbath and he did not sell* (וְלֹא מָכַר) *anything.*

After a simple imperfect the verbs that follow may be in the perfect with waw consecutive.

The man will keep (יִשְׁמֹר) *the law and he will rest* (וְשָׁבַת) *on the Sabbath and he will not sell* (וְלֹא יִמְכֹּר) *anything.*

It seems from these illustrations that the waw has the power of converting the perfect into an imperfect and *vice versa*. In fact, older grammars named it "waw conversive." It is best to drop this name and use the term that more accurately describes the actual function. The verbs, connected by ן, form in the mind of the author one chain or series, in which the verbs with waw consecutive are judged from the point of view of the first verb and, from that point of view, are considered as expressing a completed or incomplete action.

מָשַׁל *he ruled*   יִמְשֹׁל *he will rule*

וּמָשַׁל *and he will rule*   וַיִּמְשֹׁל *and he ruled*

THE FORM OF THE CONJUNCTION

1. With the perfect, it is the same as the waw conjunctive with its various pointings, וְחָי ,וּמָשַׁל ,וְקָרָא.

2. With the imperfect, it is ן followed by daghesh-forte, and pointed just as the article, וַיִּקְטֹל ,וָאֶקְטֹל ,וַיִּקְרָא.

(NOTE: The daghesh-forte may be omitted when supported only by simple sh^ewa).

The Verbal Form Used

1. The usual verbal form is used in the perfect. The accent is frequently shifted from the penult to the ultima, וְאָמַרְתָּ instead of וְאָמָרְתָּ.

2. The imperfect prefers a shortened form. The accent is usually shifted from the ultima to the penult when the penultimate syllable is open, וַיֵּשֶׁב ,וַיֹּאמֶר ,וַיַּרְא ,וַיְהִי.

Vocabulary

אָסַר	bind, imprison	גָּרַשׁ	drive out
בָּלַע	swallow	נבא	prophesy
בָּרַח	flee	נָטָה	spread out

Exercises

Translate and locate verb forms:

אָסְרָה, אָסוּר, אָסְרוּ, בָּלְעוּ, מִבְלָע, בָּרְחוּ, הַבְרִיחוּ, גָּרֵשׁ, נִגְרַשׁ, יִנָּבֵא, יִתְנַבֵּא, מִתְנַבֵּא, זָכַר אֱלֹהִים אֶת־בְּרִיתוֹ וַיִּפְקֹד אֶת־הָעָם: יִפְקֹד אֱלֹהִים אֶת־עַמּוֹ וְשָׁמַר אֹתָם: דִּבַּרְתִּי אֶת־הַדָּבָר וְלֹא כְשָׁלוּ: יַשְׁכִּים וְנִמְלַט וּבִקֵּשׁ אֶת הָעִיר: יִזְכֹּר אֹתָם וְהָלַךְ וְדִבֶּר לָהֶם: הִשְׁכִּים וַיְדַבֵּר וְלֹא בָרַח מִן־הַבָּיִת:

LESSON XXIII

Pronominal Suffixes with Verbs

The direct object of the verb, when a pronoun, may be written as a suffix to אֵת (אֹתוֹ *him*) or as a suffix to the verb. These

fragmentary pronouns are joined to active verbs and point out
the person or thing acted upon.

הִקְטִילוֹ *he caused him to kill*, or *he caused (one) to kill him*.

The suffixes for perfect and imperfect, when the verbal form
ends in a vowel, are as follows:

Singular		Plural	
נִי	*me*	נוּ	*us*
ךָ	*thee* (m.)	כֶם	*you* (m.)
ךְ	*thee* (f.)	(כֶן)	*you* (f.)
הוּ	*him*	ם	*them* (m.)
הָ	*her*	ן	*them* (f.)

When the verbal form ends in a consonant, a connecting
vowel is required. In the perfects this vowel is ◌ָ or ◌ַ. In the
imperfects and imperatives it is ◌ֵ.

After verbal forms ending in a consonant

Perfect		Impf. and Impv.	
◌ַנִי	*me*	◌ֵנִי	*me*
◌ְךָ	*thee* (m.)	◌ְךָ	*thee* (m.)
◌ָךְ (◌ֵךְ)	*thee* (f.)	◌ֵךְ	*thee* (f.)
וֹ = (◌ָהֶוּ)	*him*	◌ֵהוּ	*him*
◌ָהּ	*her*	◌ֶהָ	*her*
◌ָנוּ	*us*	◌ֵנוּ	*us*
◌ְכֶם	*you* (m.)	◌ְכֶם	*you* (m.)

כֶן־	*you* (f.)	כֶן־	*you* (f.)
ם־	*them* (m.)	ם־	*them* (m.)
ן־	*them* (f.)	——	*them* (f.)

NOTES

1. These suffixes resemble very closely the noun suffixes. Note carefully the differences. (See paradigm M, page 216, for suffixes added to קָטַל).

2. The imperative takes the same suffixes and the same connecting vowel as the imperfect.

3. The infinitive construct takes noun suffixes.

4. The suffixes to the participle are practically always those of the noun.

5. Singular suffixes to the imperfect and imperative are some‐ times strengthened by the addition of *Nun* which is usually assimilated to the following consonant.

6. It is our purpose in this lesson to learn to recognize and translate the suffix to the verb. We shall use the Hiph'il form of the verb because it presents no internal vowel changes. The student will find many mystifying changes in ordinary verb forms. Let him be content, for the time being, with the location of the form and the proper translation of the verb and the pro‐ nominal suffix.

Suffixes to the Hiph'il

Perfect

הִקְטִיל   *he caused to kill*

הִקְטִילַנִי   *he caused to kill me*

הִקְטִילְךָ   *he caused to kill thee* (m.)

הִקְטִילֵךְ   *he caused to kill thee* (f.)

הִקְטִילוֹ   *he caused to kill him*

הִקְטִילָהּ   *he caused to kill her*

הִקְטִילָנוּ   *he caused to kill us*

הִקְטִילְכֶם   *he caused to kill you* (m.)

הִקְטִילְכֶן   *he caused to kill you* (f.)

הִקְטִילָם   *he caused to kill them* (m.)

הִקְטִילָן   *he caused to kill them* (f.)

Imperfect

יַקְטִיל   *he will cause to kill*

יַקְטִילַנִי   *he will cause to kill me*

יַקְטִילְךָ   *he will cause to kill thee* (m.)

יַקְטִילֵךְ   *he will cause to kill thee* (f.)

יַקְטִילֵהוּ   *he will cause to kill him*

יַקְטִילָהָ   *he will cause to kill her*

יַקְטִילֵנוּ   *he will cause to kill us*

יַקְטִילְכֶם   *he will cause to kill you* (m.)

יַקְטִילְכֶן   *he will cause to kill you* (f.)

יַקְטִילֵם   *he will cause to kill them* (m.)

(יַקְטִילֵן)   *he will cause to kill them* (f.)

VOCABULARY

אָבַד *perish*
(Hi.) *destroy*

אָהֵב *love*

אָמַר *say*

בָּרָא *create*

בָּרַךְ *bless*

עָמַד *stand*

EXERCISES

Translate and locate fully

הִלְבִּישַׁנִי, הִמְלִיכוּ, יַלְבִּישֵׁם, תְּלַמְּדֵם, לְהַבְדִּילְךָ,
הִזְכִּירֵנִי, יַמְשִׁילְכֶם, הִמְטִיר, הִמְלִיכַנִי, הִמְשִׁילָהּ, אַלְבִּישֵׁם,
הִצְדַּיְקַנִי, הִשְׂכִּילָךְ, יַזְכִּירְךָ, נַשְׁכִּימֵם, יַשְׁבִּירֵנִי, נַמְשִׁילוֹ,
יַפְקִידֵנוּ, הִשְׁלִיכוּ, יַגְבִּירְכֶם, הִגְדִּילְךָ, יַגְדִּלְכֶם:

LESSON XXIV

A STORY CONCERNING THE COVENANT WITH ISRAEL

לִמֵּד יהוה אֶת־יִשְׂרָאֵל בַּמִּדְבָּר: וַיְדַבֵּר לוֹ כַּדְּבָרִים
הָאֵלֶּה כַּאֲשֶׁר דִּבַּרְתִּי לְאַבְרָהָם אָבִיךָ כֵּן אֲנִי מְדַבֵּר לָךְ:
אֲנִי כֹרֵת בְּרִית עִמְּךָ: זְכֹר אֶת־מִצְוֹת יהוה אֱלֹהֶיךָ לִשְׁמֹר
אֹתָן וְאָנֹכִי אֲגַדֵּל אֹתְךָ: הִתְקַדֵּשׁ וְכַבֵּד אֶת־אֱלֹהֶיךָ: תְּלַמֵּד

אֶת־הַדְּבָרִים הָאֵלֶּה וּקְשַׁרְתָּם לְאוֹת עַל יָדֶיךָ וּכְתַבְתָּם עַל־
מְזוּזוֹת בֵּיתֶךָ וּבִשְׁעָרֶיךָ: גַּם לַמֵּד תְּלַמֵּד אֹתָם לִבְנֶיךָ: כָּכָה
הַשְׂכֵּל תַּשְׂכִּיל אֶת־בָּנֶיךָ: לָכֵן אָמְרוּ בְּנֵי יִשְׂרָאֵל טוֹב לָנוּ
לִלְמַד עַל יָדֵי יהוה: מִשְׁפְּטֵי יהוה אֱמֶת גַּם עַבְדְּךָ נִזְהָר בָּהֶם
בְּשָׁמְרָם עֵקֶב רָב: יהוה יִמְלֹךְ לְעוֹלָם וָעֶד:

NOTES

1. For words not yet studied see vocabulary, page 158. A translation of this reading lesson may be found on page 191. It is to be used by the student in preparation.

2. לָמַד in the Pi'el (לִמֵּד) means "make to learn, teach."

3. לוֹ "to him." The antecedent noun being a collective noun (יִשְׂרָאֵל), all the pronouns referring to it may be rendered as plurals.

4. כַּאֲשֶׁר preposition כְּ and the indeclinable relative pronoun אֲשֶׁר. Literal rendering "according to the thing which;" hence, "just as."

5. מְדַבֵּר a participle may be used as a finite verb. It denotes continuous action. The subject usually precedes (as in this case) the participle. Cf. כֹּרֵת in sentence following.

6. עִמָּךְ a pausal form. Preposition עִם + 2nd m. sg. suffix.

7. אֹתָן sign of the accusative אֵת + 3rd f. plu. suffix. So אֹתָךְ and אֹתָם later.

8. תְּלַמֵּד impf. with the force of an imperative. וּקְשַׁרְתָּם perfect with וֹ consecutive + 3rd m. pl. suffix. Again, the force of an imperative.

9. וּבִשְׁעָרֶיךָ mas. plu. of שַׁעַר "gate" + וֹ conjunctive, the preposition בְּ + 2nd m. sg. suffix.

10. לַמֵּד when the infinitive absolute precedes the verb, it adds intensity to the action. Literal rendering: "teaching, thou shalt teach;" thus, "thou shalt *indeed* teach." Cf. הַשְׂכֵּל in next sentence.

11. לְבָנֶיךָ mas. plu. of בֵּן + the preposition לְ and 2nd m. sg. suffix. The mas. const. plu. of בֵּן is בְּנֵי.

12. Literal rendering of עַל יְדֵי יהוה : "upon the hands of Yahweh." Const. plu. of יָד.

13. עֶבֶד, עַבְדְּךָ + 2nd m. sg. suffix.

14. בְּשָׁמְרָם infinitive construct (שָׁמֹר) + preposition בְּ and 3rd m. pl. suffix.

15. Literal rendering of לְעוֹלָם וָעֶד : "To the ages (collective noun) and on."

LESSON XXV
IRREGULAR VERBS

Statives

Less than one fifth of the verbs in Hebrew are inflected like the strong verb קָטַל. There are certain verbs known as "statives," usually intransitive, which express a state or condition, *he is full, thirsty, in fear, in love, heavy, strong,* etc. They are regular except in the Qal. In the ultimate syllable of the Qal they may take ־ֵ, ־ַ, or ־ֹ; שָׁכַב *to lie down,* כָּבֵד *to be heavy,* קָטֹן *to be small.* The ־ֵ is changed to ־ַ before all consonantal afformatives, יָשַׁבְתָּ but the ־ֹ is retained before the consonantal afformatives (except תֶם and תֶן) קָטָנְתָּ, but קְטָנְתֶּם.

Some of the more common statives are:

כָּבֵד	be heavy	גָּדַל	be great
זָקֵן	be old	שָׂכַל	be wise
יָכֹל	be able	שָׁכֹל	be bereaved
קָטֹן	be small	חָזַק	be strong
יָרֵא	be afraid	צָדֵק	be righteous
שָׁכַב	lie down	קָדַשׁ	be holy
שָׁלֵם	be whole	קָרַב	be near
רָחַק	be far off	שָׂמַח	be glad

Guttural Verbs

It must be remembered that gutturals have certain peculiarities, that affect the vowels under and before them. The verb that has a guttural in it differs from קָטַל only in vocalization. The consonants do not change. א and ה are not classed as gutturals at the end of a word. נָחַם, לָקַח, שָׁבַע, גָּאַל, עָמַד.

Weak Verbs

In addition to the gutturals א, ה, ח, ע and the letter ר there are other consonants that give trouble. These letters נ, י, and ו may be assimilated and disappear with or without trace. Verbs whose second and third consonants are identical show certain peculiarities that we shall consider.

The Paradigm Word, פָּעַל

It is convenient to have a system for designating the radicals, and for this purpose the old Jewish paradigm word, פָּעַל, is adopted. The letters *Pe*, *Ayin*, and *Lamedh*, are used in speaking of the radicals. פ (*Pe*) stands for the first radical. ע (*Ayin*) for the second, and ל (*Lamedh*) for the third. Thus a *Pe Nun* verb is one which has a *Nun* as its first radical, נָפַל. A *Pe Yodh* verb is one that has a *Yodh* as its first radical, יָטַב. An *Ayin Waw* verb is one whose middle radical is a *Waw*, קוּם. A verb like סָבַב whose second and third radicals are the same is called a *Double Ayin* verb. A *Lamedh Aleph* verb has an *Aleph* for its third radical, קָרָא.

Weak Verbs} Using פָּעַל and watching for א, ה, ח, ע, ר, נ, י, and ו we get:

Pe Guttural	עָמַד, חָזַק, עָבַד
Ayin Guttural	בָּחַר, צָעַק, שָׁאַל
Lamedh Guttural	תָּקַע, שָׁמַע, שָׁלַח
Pe Nun	נָבַט, נָצַל, נָפַל
Lamedh Aleph	חָטָא, קָרָא, מָצָא

Lamedh He	בָּנָה ,פָּדָה, גָּלָה
Double Ayin	מָדַד, גָּלַל ,סָבַב
Ayin Waw	שׁוּב ,רוּץ ,קוּם
Ayin Yodh	שִׁיר ,בִּין, שִׂים
Pe Yodh	יָתַר, יָלַד, יָשַׁב

hollow verb — Ayin Waw   *cl. 35, p 94*

In studying the guttural verbs it will be well to remember
that the radicals remain the same throughout just as in the
strong verb. For example the Pi'el which doubles the middle
radical (קִטֵּל) will necessarily assume a special form when the
middle radical is a guttural, as gutturals cannot be doubled. The
form is determined by the laws governing gutturals. It is not
some arbitrary thing to be committed to memory. We find בֵּרֵךְ
instead of בֵּרֵּךְ however, because the middle radical refuses the
doubling and the short vowel in the open pretone must be
heightened. So it is with the other types of "irregular" verbs,
which are thoroughly regular to one who clearly understands
the fundamental principles of the language.

VOCABULARY

אָשֵׁם	*transgress, offend*	שָׁאַל	*ask*
רָכַב	*ride*	רָגֵז	*be excited*
תָּקַע	*strike*	רָאָה	*see*
שָׁבַע	*swear*	עָרַךְ	*arrange*

EXERCISES

Designate the classes of the following verbs:

נתן, ברך, צוה, אבל, שמע, סבב, לקח, ילד, קרא, בנה,

פקד, קלל, רעע, עמד, בער, נפל, אהב, יצר, שוב, בוא,

חדל, עבר, זבח, לעט, גלה, הבא, שרת, נחם, הלל, בוש,

בין, שכח, הלך, אשם, תקע, ערך:

LESSON XXVI

THE PE GUTTURAL VERB

(First Radical a Guttural)

See Paradigm B (page 198)

Types: חָמַד *desire*, הָרַג *kill*, עָמַד *stand*.

Some peculiarities:

Review carefully the rules for the gutturals in lesson **IV**.

1. The guttural *prefers a compound sh⁰wa under it* instead of a simple sh⁰wa as in the strong verb.

קְטַלְתֶּם but עֲטַלְתֶּם.

יַקְטִיל but יַעֲטִיל.

(Wherever the strong verb has a vocal sh⁰wa under it, the Pe Guttural verb has a compound sh⁰wa. This frequently occurs where the strong verb is pointed with a syllable-divider.)

The usual form is ⁼⁻ but א prefers ⁼⁻, אָמַר, עֲטַל.

2. The guttural *refuses to be doubled* (cf. Niph'al) קָטֵל. יְעַטֵל (The ע will not take the daghesh-forte and, to compensate for it, the vowel in the open preformative syllable is heightened ־ to ־).

The student will remember that the Niph'al forms are the only ones that have the doubling in the first radical. It will be an easy matter to apply this second rule in the Niph'al only.

3. The guttural *prefers an "a" class vowel before it.*

יִקְטֵל but יֶעֱטֵל   הִקְטִיל but הֶעֱטִיל

נִקְטַל but נֶעֱטַל

In the Qal imperfect (with *o*) the original ă of the performative is restored giving us יְעֲטֹל.

In the Niph'al perfect and participle and the Hiph'il perfect the preformative vowel is deflected to ־ before the guttural. (This is true with certain verbs in the Qal imperfect.)

NOTES

1. The combination of vowel and sheʷa is as follows: ־ֲ־, ־ֳ־ and ־ֱ־.

2. The vowel immediately before a compound sheʷa must have a secondary accent הֶעֱטִיל, יְעֲטִיל.

3. Two vocal sheʷas never occur together. When compound sheʷa precedes simple sheʷa the compound sheʷa gives way to the corresponding short vowel. (This happens before vowel additions) יִקְטְלוּ but יֶעֱטְלוּ and this becomes יֶעַטְלוּ.

4. Five verbs beginning with **א** have certain peculiarities in the Qal;

אָבַד *perish,* אָכַל *eat,* אָמַר *say,* אָבָה *be willing,* אָפָה *bake.*

In the Qal imperfect the preformative vowel is ô and the second vowel is ă. (In pause the short ă may become long ē, יֹאכֵל)

לֵאמֹר becomes לֵאמֹר, יֹאכַל, יֹאמַר.

5. The verb אָהַב is irregular. The imperative is אֱהַב, plural אֱהֲבוּ.

VOCABULARY

אָסַף	gather	חָפֵץ	desire, delight *in*	עָבַר	pass over
הָפַךְ	overturn	חָשַׁב	think, devise	עָזַב	abandon
הָרַג	kill	עָבַד	serve	עָזַר	assist

EXERCISES

Translate and locate fully:

עֶזְבוּ, עֲמַדְתֶּם, יַעֲבֹר, תַּעֲבִיר, יַעֲזֹר, אֹהֵב, נֶאֶסְפָה, יַהֲפְכוּ, עָבַר, נַעֲמֹד, מֶעֱמָד, יֹאכַל, עֲבַרְתֶּם, עֲזוֹב, אֱמֹר, וַיֹּאמְרוּ, נֹאמַר, לֵאמֹר, אָכוֹל תֹּאכֵל, תֹּאמְרוּ, הֶעֱמִידָה, תַּעֲזְבִי, עֲמֹד, הָפַכְתִּי, עֹמֵד, מַעֲמִיד, יַעֲמֹד:

LESSON XXVII

THE AYIN GUTTURAL VERB

(The Middle Radical a Guttural)

See Paradigm C (page 200)

Types: שָׁאַל *ask,* שָׁחַט *slay,* בָּעַר *consume.*

Verbs whose second radical is a guttural exhibit the following peculiarities:

1. The guttural *refuses the doubling* (Cf. Pi., Pu., Hithpa.).

   (1) Before א and ר (and sometimes ע) the preceding vowel is heightened ־ to ־ָ, ־ to ־ֵ, ־ִ to ־ֵ.

      בֵּרֵךְ becomes בֵּרֶךְ

      יְבָרֵךְ becomes יְבָרֶךְ

      יְמָאֵן becomes יְמָאֵן.

   (2) Before ה, ח (and sometimes ע) the preceding vowel usually remains short (doubled by implication).

      יְנַחֵם, מִהַר, נִחַם, יְנַעֵם.

2. The guttural *prefers compound sh^ewa* **under** it. Wherever the strong verb has vocal sh^ewa, the four gutturals (ע, ח, ה, א) take ־ֲ while ר usually takes simple sh^ewa.

      שָׁחֲטָה instead of שָׁחְטָה

      בֶּחֱרוּ instead of בֶּחְרוּ

      תִּשְׂחֲקוּ instead of תִּשְׂחְקוּ.

3. The guttural *prefers an "a" class vowel*. ־ַ usually replaces ־ֹ in the Qal imperfect and imperative, יִשְׂחַט instead of יִשְׂחֹט.

In the Pi'el perfect the ־ֵ sometimes gives way to ־ַ, נָחַם instead of נָחֵם.

VOCABULARY

פָּרַד *separate*	מִהַר (Pi.) *hasten*	שָׁחַט *slaughter*
מָאֵן (Pi.) *refuse*	כָּעַס *provoke, be vexed*	בָּעַר *consume, burn*
שָׂחַק *laugh*	צָעַק *cry out*	גָּאַל *deliver, redeem*

1. Write in full:

   a. The Pi'el of גָּרֵשׁ.

   b. The Pu'al of בֹּעַר.

   c. The Qal of שָׁחֹט.

2. Translate and locate fully:

הִכְעִיס, אַכְעִיס, בֹּעַר, לְבָעֵר, גֹּאֵל, נִמְהָר, מְשַׂחֵק, שָׁחוּט,
בָּעֵר, הִבְעַרְתִּי, נִגְאַל, מִהַר, מַשְׂחִיקִים, יִשְׁחַט, בָּעַרְתָּ,
תַּבְעִיר, מֵאֵן, תִּגָּאֵל, יְמַהֵר, יְבָעֵר, מַהֵר, יִשְׁחַט, מַבְעִיר,
מֵאַנְתָּ, מְמַהֵר, שָׁחַטוּ, לִשְׁחֹט, שֶׂחֲקוּ, יִשְׂחַק, יְמָאֵן, גָּאַל, מָאֵן,
יִגְאַל, מְבַעֲרִים, יְבָעֵר, בְּעֵרָה, הַכְעִיס, גְּאוּלִים:

LESSON XXVIII
THE LAMEDH GUTTURAL VERB
(The Final Radical a Guttural)
See Paradigm D (page 202)

Types: שָׁמַע *hear*, בָּטַח *trust*, גָּבַהּ *be high*.

This class includes verbs ending in הָ, עַ, חַ. Verbs with ר as
the final guttural behave as strong verbs. Final א and ה are
not gutturals. They form distinct classes of weak verbs.

The peculiarities of the Lamedh Guttural are:

1. Every final guttural must have an "*a*" sound before it,

קָטַח, יִקְטַח, קְטַח, יָקְטַח.

2. Unchangeably long vowels naturally are retained, taking pathaḥ furtive between the vowel and the guttural.

שָׁלוּחַ becomes שָׁלוּחַ (shā-lûᵃḥ)

יַשְׁלִיחַ becomes יַשְׁלִיחַ (yăsh-lîᵃḥ).

3. When afformatives are added the form stands just as the strong verb, הִשְׁמַעְתָּם, קָטְחוּ, שָׁלְחָה, יִשְׁלְחוּ.

4. In the perfects the 2nd feminine singular forms have a helping vowel (־) under the guttural שָׁלַחַתְּ. (Note the daghesh-lene in the תּ and the syllable-divider under it. This ־ is very probably a pathaḥ furtive).

VOCABULARY

זָבַח	sacrifice	בָּקַע	cleave, split	בָּטַח	trust
לָקַח	take	פָּשַׁע	transgress	גָּבַהּ	be high, (Hi.) exalt
מָשַׁח	anoint	שָׁמַע	hear	שָׁלַח	send

EXERCISES

1. Write the 3rd singular masculine perfect and imperfect of שלח in all stems.

2. Write the participles of שמע in all formations.

3. Write the Hiphʻil perfect and the Qal imperfect of בטח.

4. Translate and locate fully:

יִבְטַח, מַבְטִיחַ, מַגְבִּיהַ, לִזְבֹּחַ, בָּקַע, הִתְבַּקְּעוּ, אֶלְקַח,

נִשְׁמַע, מְשֻׁלָּח, בְּטַח, גָּבַהְתָּ, זָבַחְתִּי, זֶבַח, יִבְקַע, לָקַח,

מַשְׁמִיעַ, בָּטוּחַ, גָּבְהוּ, מַשְׁלִיחַ, זֶבַח, לְהִבָּקַע, לְקַחְתָּ, זָבְחוּ,
לָקַח, נִמְשַׁח, שָׁלַח, יִפְשַׁע, בָּטוּחַ, יִנָּבֶה, וַיִּזְבַּח, לִזְבֹּחַ,
מִבְקָעִים, לְקַח, מָשׁוּחַ, הַמָּשַׁח, שָׁלוּחַ, נִשְׁלַח, פָּשְׁעוּ, הִבְטַחְתָּ,
יַגְבִּיהַּ, אֶזְבַּח, מִזְבֵּחַ, בָּקַעְתָּ, לְהַבְקִיעַ, נִלְקַח, יִשְׁמַע, שָׁמַע,
שָׁלַח, נִפְשַׁע, שַׁלַּח׃

LESSON XXIX

A STORY CONCERNING THE CROSSING OF THE JORDAN

אָמַר יְהוֹשֻׁעַ אֶל־בְּנֵי יִשְׂרָאֵל הַיּוֹם הַזֶּה נַעֲבֹר אֶת־הַיַּרְדֵּן׃
יַעַבְרוּ הַכֹּהֲנִים לִפְנֵי הָעָם וְעָמְדוּ בְתוֹךְ הַיַּרְדֵּן עַד־אֲשֶׁר
עָבְרוּ כָל הָעָם׃ יהוה שָׁלַח אֹתָנוּ בַּדֶּרֶךְ הַזֹּאת וְשָׁמוֹעַ נִשְׁמַע
בְּקוֹלוֹ׃ אֲנִי בָטוּחַ כִּי כֻלָּנוּ בֹטְחִים בּוֹ׃ הוּא מַבְטִיחַ אֹתָנוּ׃
נֹאמַר יהוה עִמָּנוּ וְלֹא נֹאבֵד׃

וַיְדַבֵּר יְהוֹשֻׁעַ עוֹד לֵאמֹר הַעֲבִירוּ עִמָּכֶם שְׁתֵּים־עֶשְׂרֵה
אֲבָנִים וְהַעֲמִידוּ אֹתָם בִּמְלוֹנְכֶם׃ יִשְׁאֲלוּ בְנֵיכֶם מָחָר לֵאמֹר
מָה לָכֶם הָאֲבָנִים הָאֵלֶּה וַאֲמַרְתֶּם לָהֶם נִכְרְתוּ מֵי הַיַּרְדֵּן
מִפְּנֵי אֲרוֹן בְּרִית יהוה׃ לֹא מֵאֲנוּ בְנֵי־יִשְׂרָאֵל לַעֲבֹר כִּדְבַר
יהוה וְלֹא נִמְאֲסוּ כַּאֲשֶׁר נִמְאֲסוּ אֲבוֹתֵיהֶם בַּמִּדְבָּר עַל־כֵּן
הָאֲבָנִים הָאֵלֶּה לְזִכָּרוֹן לִפְנֵי יִשְׂרָאֵל עַד עוֹלָם׃

NOTES

1. For new words consult the vocabulary on page 158.

2. בְּנֵי cf. בֵּן, mas. const. plu. of בְּנֵיכֶם.

3. הַיּוֹם emphatic by virtue of its position.

4. לִפְנֵי const. plu. of פָּנֶה + preposition לְ, "in the presence of."

5. עַד־אֲשֶׁר with finite verb, "until."

6. כָּל הָעָם a collective subject; hence, a plural verb עָבְדוּ.

7. שֹׁלֵחַ a ptc. used as a finite verb. The subject precedes when ptc. is employed.

8. וְשָׁמוֹעַ נִשְׁמַע בְּקוֹלוֹ literal rendering: "and hearkening we shall hearken to his voice." Note use of inf. absolute. שָׁמַע – – – בְּ means "to hearken to."

9. בָּטוּחַ literally: "am made trustful," ptc. used as finite verb.

10. כֻּלָּנוּ "all of us," כָּל + the pronom. suffix.

11. הַעֲבִירוּ "cause ye to pass over." Hiph. imperative.

12. שְׁתֵּים־עֶשְׂרֵה "twelve."

13. וְהַעֲמִידוּ Hiph. imperative of עָמַד.

14. מָחָר "tomorrow."

15. מֵי construct of מַיִם.

16. עַל־כֵּן "upon so"="therefore."

17. עַד עוֹלָם collective noun "unto ages."

LESSON XXX

THE PE NUN VERB

(The First Radical a Nun)

See Paradigm E (page 204)

Types: נָפַל *fall*, נָגַשׁ *approach*.

When the letter נ is supported by a syllable-divider it is as- *unaccented closed syllable.* similated into the following letter, יִנְפֹּל becomes יִפֹּל, יַנְגִּיד becomes יַגִּיד, נָתַנְתָּ becomes נָתַתָּ.

1. This assimilation comes in Qal imperfect, Niph'al perfect and participle, and throughout the Hiph'il and Hoph'al. When the נ is dropped a daghesh-forte is always placed in the second radical. This assimilation does not take place in verbs that are also Ayin Guttural.

2. The Qal imperative is usually regular (נְפֹל) although in certain cases (the Qal in *a*) the נ is lost, leaving the form טַל, גַּשׁ.

3. The Qal infinitive construct is usually regular (נְטֹל) al- though in the verbs that have *a* in the imperfect the נ is dropped. As a sort of compensation ת is added, making a segholate form. (נָגַשׁ becomes גַּשׁ then גַּשְׁתְּ then גֶּשֶׁת). *2 seghals*

4. The preposition before such a segholate form is always written לְ (לָגֶשֶׁת).

5. The verb לָקַח follows the analogy of the Pe Nun verb in the Qal and Hoph'al. יִלְקַח becomes יִקַּח, נִלְקַח (Qal im-

perfect) becomes נֻקַּח but נִלְקַח (Niph'al perfect) remains un-assimilated.

NOTE: On account of the sharpened syllable in the Hoph'al, the original preformative ־ֻ appears, יֻגַּד, הֻגַּד.

VOCABULARY

נָגַע	touch	נָטַע	plant
נָגַשׁ	approach (Hi.) bring near	נגד	announce, declare
נָפַל	fall	נבט	(Hi.) look, gaze, behold
נצל	(Hi.) snatch, deliver (Ni.) (passive) (Pi.) plunder	נָסַע	depart

EXERCISES

1. Write synopses of Qal, Niph'al, and Hiph'il stems, using נָגַשׁ, נָפַל.

2. Translate and locate fully:

יִפֹּל, נֹסַע, יִגַּע, לָגֶשֶׁת, נְטַעְתִּי, מַפִּיל, יַנְצֵל, תַּסִּיעַ, יַפִּיל,
הַבִּיט, גַּע, נִגַּשׁ, יִטַּע, מַפִּילִים, הִצִּיל, מַסִּיעַ, קַח, הִגִּיד, מַבִּיט,
נֻגַּע, יְנַגַּע, נַגִּישׁ, נֹטֵעַ, הִתְנַפֵּל, הֻצַּל, מַצִּיל, נָסְעוּ, הֻגַּדְתָּ, יַגִּיד,
הַגִּיעַ, מַגִּישׁ, נָטוּעַ, מִתְנַפֵּל, יִתְנַצְּלוּ, גֵּשׁ, מַגִּיד, הַגִּיעַ, מְגַשׁ,
אֶפֹּל, נֹפֵל, יִנָּצֵל, יִסַּע, יֻקַּח, הֻגַּד, יֻגַּד, מַגִּיעַ, הִתְנַגֵּשׁוּ, הִפִּיל,
נִצַּלְתֶּם:

weak verbs

LESSON XXXI
The Lamedh Aleph Verb
(Last Radical an Aleph)
See Paradigm F (page 206)

Types: מָצָא *find*, מָלֵא *be full*, קָרָא *call*.

At the beginning of a syllable א is always a guttural; at the
end of a syllable it is always quiescent (silent). When quiescent
the preceding vowel is always long, מָצָא *he found*, יִמְצָא *he
will find*, נִקְרָא *he was called.*   *I quit prefer a*
vowels, hence T

1. To write the **synopsis** of the Lamedh Aleph verb it is only
necessary to write the synopsis of the strong verb, substitute
an א for the ל of קָטַל and heighten the short vowels. (The
Qal imperfect and imperative prefer the *a* instead of the *o*
(יִקְטָא and קְטָא).

2. To write the various **inflections** note: *as 1.*

  (a) Before the consonant afformatives the same rule ap-
      plies קְטָאתָ, הִקְטַאתִי, מָצָאתָ.

  (b) Before the vowel additions (הָ_, יָ_, וּ) the א is a
      consonant (guttural) and is treated like a strong con-
      sonant רָפְאוּ, מָצְאָה.

Notes

1. In the inflection of the perfects the vowel before א is ָ
in the Qal, and ֵ in all the other perfects, נִקְטֵאתָ, מָצָאתָ,
קְטֵאתָ.

2. In the imperfects and imperatives before א with the termination נָה the vowel is ֵ (é) (heightened from ֶ) קְטֶאנָה.

3. The infinitive construct may be formed by adding ת (מְלֹאת) although the regular form is קְרֹא *to call.*

4. The quiescent א frequently falls out in the writing, מָצְתִי for מָצָאתִי.

VOCABULARY

חבא	(Ni.) *hide, withdraw*	נָשָׂא	*lift up*	שָׂנֵא	*hate*
חָטָא	*sin*	קָרָא	*call, meet,*	מָלֵא	*be full*
מָצָא	*find*	רָפָא	*heal, care*	צָמֵא	*be thirsty*

EXERCISES

1. Write a complete synopsis using מָצָא.

2. Translate and locate fully:

חָטְאָה, חָטָא, מַחֲטִיא, תַּחֲבִיא, מָלֵא, מָצָאתָ, מַמְצִיא,

מְנַשְּׂאִים, תֵּרָפֵא, יִקְרָא, שָׂנֵא, יִתְחַטְּאוּ, יִתְחַבֵּא, מָלֵא, נִמְצָא,

נָשְׂאוּ, יְרָפֵא, לְהִתְרַפֵּא, קְרָא, שָׂנוּא, הֶחֱטִיא, חֹטֵא, נֶחְבָּא,

מִתְחַבֵּא, מְמַלֵּא, מֹצֵא, רִפָּא, צָמְאוּ, יָקְרָא, מְשַׂנֵּא, נִקְרָא,

יְצָמָא, לִרְפֹּא, יָנְשֵׂא, נַמְצִיא, יְמַלֵּא, מָלְאוּ, תֵּחָבֵא, תַּחֲטִיא,

חָבְאוּ, מָלְאוּ, נִמְצָא, נְשָׂא, נֹשֵׂא, רֹפֵא, קָרָאת, יִשְׂנָא:

LESSON XXXII

THE LAMEDH HE (LAMEDH YODH) VERB

(Last Radical ה)

See Paradigm G (page 208)

Types: גָּלָה *reveal,* כָּסָה *conceal.*

These verbs originally ended in י (or ו). This final consonant has been lost. As a protection for the vowel and to preserve the appearance of the triliteral root the final ה is now written as the third consonant. The ה is not a genuine part of the root. It is a vowel sign with the ָ of the root. (When the ה is truly consonantal, it takes mappiḳ. The verb then belongs to the Lamedh Guttural class, גָּבַה *to be high,* תָּמַהּ *to wonder*).

1. In the **synopsis** of this verb (in all forms without afformatives) the letter ה appears as the final letter (except in infinitives construct and the Qal passive participle).

Note the endings for the various stems:

ה ָ in all perfects קָטָה, נִקְטָה, קָטָה, הִקְטָה.

ה ָ in all imperfects יָקְטָה, יָקַטָה, יְקַטָה, יַקְטָה.

ה ָ in all imperatives הִקְטָה, קַטָה, הַקְטָה, קְטָה.

Regular vowel in all infinitives absolute הַקְטֵה, קָטֹה, קָטַה.

וֹת in all infinitives construct הַקְטוֹת, הָקְטוֹת, קְטוֹת.

ה ָ in all participles (except Qal passive) מְקַטֶּה, נִקְטָה, קְטֶה, מַקְטֶה, מָקְטֶה.

Write the synopsis of the strong verb, change the ל to an ה, substitute the vowel given above and the new synopsis is complete.

2. In the **inflection,** when afformatives are added, the following rules apply:

(a) Before consonant afformatives the י is preserved as the third radical. The י unites with the preceding vowel, forming a diphthong.

In active perfects it is **יְ** (The Pi'el and Hiph'il may have **יַ**).

In passive perfects it is **יֻ**.

In imperfects and imperatives before **נָה** it is **יֶ**,

קְטִינָה‎, תִּקְטֶינָה‎, הִקְטִיתְ‎, קְטַיְתְּ‎, קָטִיתְּ‎.

(b) Before vowel afformatives (and before suffixes) the **י** with its vowel is lost.

קְטוּ instead of קְטִיוּ

קַטּוּ instead of קַטִּיוּ

יַקְטוּ instead of יַקְטִיוּ

יֵרְדוּ instead of יֵרְדִיוּ

NOTES

1. The feminine singular of all perfects has the old feminine ending **ת** to which the regular ending **הָ** is added, (קְטָתָה and קְטָתָה).

2. The jussive of all voices is formed by dropping the **הָ** of the imperfect. יְקַט instead of יְקְטָה. This process is called "apocopation" and the resultant forms "apocopated forms." The addition of **ו** consecutive also causes this apocopation, וַיִּגֶל for וַיִּגְלָה.

VOCABULARY

בָּכָה	weep	כָּלָה	be complete (Pi.) complete	רָעָה	feed
גָּלָה	disclose (Pi.) reveal (Hi.) carry away	צוה	(Pi.) command	פָּדָה	ransom
		כָּסָה	cover, conceal	קָנָה	get, obtain
אָבָה	be willing	בָּנָה	build	פָּנָה	turn

EXERCISES

1. Write a synopsis of the verb using נָּלָה.

2. Translate and locate fully:

parse

בָּכִיתִי, אָבוּ, יִגְלֶה, תִּבְכֶּה, אָבָה, הִגְלוּ, יִגְלֶה, נִבְכֶּה,
נִגְלֶה, בָּכוּ, גָּלֶה, גָּלִית, בֹּכֶה, נַּשׁ, גָּלוּי, הִגְלָה, מְבַכָּה, נִגְלָה,
הָגְלוּ, הִתְגַּלּוֹת, מְגֻלֶּה, בָּנִיתָ, יִבְנֶה, בֹּנֶה, בְּנֵה, בָּנוֹת, נִבְנָה,
נִבְנָה, לְהִבָּנוֹת, כֹּסֶה, הַכָּסוֹת, כִּסָּה, כְּסִיתִי, יְכַסֶּה, כַּסּוֹת,
מְכַסֶּה, יִתְכַּסּוּ, מִתְכַּסֶּה, כָּלוּ, כָּלוֹת, כָּלָה, אֲכַלֶּה,
כַּלֵּה, יִפְדֶּה, פְּדֵה, פֹּדֶה, יָפְדֶה, פָּנִיתָ, פָּנֶיךָ, יִפְנֶה, לִפְנוֹת, פֹּנֶה,
מַפְנֶה, מְפַנֶּה, יִרְעֶה, רָעֶה, לִרְעוֹת, רֹעֶה, קָנִיתָ, קָנְתָה, קָנֶה, קֹנֶה,
יִקְנוּ, צֻוָּה, יְצַוֶּה, וַיְצַו, מְצֻוֶּה, צֻוֵּיתָ:

LESSON XXXIII

A STORY CONCERNING THE CROSSING OF THE JORDAN (Continued)

אָמַר יהוה אֶל־יְהוֹשֻׁעַ הַיּוֹם הַזֶּה אָחֵל גַּדֶּלְךָ בְּעֵינֵי כָל־
יִשְׂרָאֵל כִּי יֵדְעוּ כִּי כַּאֲשֶׁר הָיִיתִי עִם־מֹשֶׁה אֶהְיֶה עִמָּךְ: אֱמֹר
לָהֶם בְּזֹאת תֵּדְעוּ כִּי אֵל חַי בְּקִרְבְּכֶם וְהוֹרֵשׁ יוֹרִישׁ בַּעֲבוּרֵיכֶם
אֶת הַגּוֹיִים אֲשֶׁר יֹשְׁבִים בָּאָרֶץ: כְּנוֹחַ כַּפּוֹת רַגְלֵי הַכֹּהֲנִים
בְּמֵי הַיַּרְדֵּן יִכָּרְתוּ הַמַּיִם הַיֹּרְדִים מִלְמַעְלָה וְיַעַמְדוּ נֵד־אֶחָד
וְהַמַּיִם הַיֹּרְדִים עַל יָם־הַמֶּלַח יָתַמּוּ עַד אֲשֶׁר תַּמּוּ כָל־הָעָם
לַעֲבֹר: אֶת־זֹאת יַעֲשֶׂה יהוה לְמַעַן דַּעַת כָּל־עַמֵּי הָאָרֶץ אֶת־
יַד יהוה כִּי חֲזָקָה הִיא וּלְמַעַן שׁוֹם יִרְאַת יהוה בִּלְבַבְכֶם:

וּבַיּוֹם הַהוּא הָחֵל יהוה לְגַדֵּל אֶת־יְהוֹשֻׁעַ׃ הָיוּ הַכֹּהֲנִים
עֹמְדִים בְּתוֹךְ הַיַּרְדֵּן עַד תֹּם כָּל־הַדָּבָר אֲשֶׁר צִוָּה יהוה אֶת־
יְהוֹשֻׁעַ׃ וַיְהִי כַּאֲשֶׁר תַּמּוּ הַכֹּהֲנִים לַעֲבֹר הֶחֱלוּ הַמַּיִם לָשׁוּב
לִמְקוֹמָם׃ וַיֹּאמְרוּ בְּנֵי יִשְׂרָאֵל בִּלְבָבָם חֶסֶד יְסוֹבֵב אֶת־כָּל־
הַבֹּטְחִים בִּיהוה כְּמוֹ מְסוֹבֵב הוּא אֶת־יְהוֹשֻׁעַ הַיּוֹם הַלְלוּיָהּ
הַלְלוּ אֶת־שֵׁם יהוה׃

NOTES

1. גַּדְּלָךְ Pi'el inf. const. + pronom. suffix. ־ַ is changed to
־ָ before heavy suffix ךְ.

2. בְּעֵינֵי construct plural of עַיִן + preposition.

3. בְּזֹאת is emphatic by position.

4. הַיֹּרְדִים When the article is used with the ptc., it is practically equivalent to a relative clause.

5. כְּנוֹחַ "At the resting of the souls of the feet." Inf. const.
from נוּחַ.

6. עַד אֲשֶׁר תַּמּוּ "until that all the people will have finished
with reference to passing over."

7. לֵב, בִּלְבַבְכֶם (reduplicated form) + prep. בְּ + 2nd plu.
suffix.

8. וַיְהִי apocopated (shortened) form of Qal impf. יִהְיֶה.

9. יְסוֹבֵב Po'el impf. from סָבַב.

10. מְסוֹבֵב Po'el ptc. from סָבַב.

11. הַיּוֹם "the day"="this day," "today." (Recurrence of
original demonstrative force of the article.)

LESSON XXXIV

The Double Ayin Verb
(Second and Third Radical the Same)
See Paradigm H (page 210)

Types: סָבַב *surround*, קָלַל *be light*.

The weakness of these verbs lies in the fact that the second and third radicals, being identical, are in many cases written as one letter, סָבַב becomes סַב, קָלַל becomes קַל. Where this occurs, the second radical must bear daghesh-forte before af-formatives, קַלּוּ instead of קָלֲלוּ.

1. To find the **synopsis** we write קָטַט as in the strong verb. The next step is to cancel the second radical and the vowel of the first. קָטַט becomes קַט, יְקַטַט becomes יָקַט. In the intensive stems and in the Qal infinitive absolute and participles the form remains uncontracted קָטַט, קָטוֹט, קֹטֵט.

2. The stem vowel, which, after contraction, stands with the first radical instead of the second, is the same as that of the corresponding form of the strong verb except in

Niph‘al imperfect and imperative הִקַּט, יִקַּט,

Hiph‘il perfect, imperfect, infinitive construct and participle מֵקַט, הָקַט, יָקֵט, הָקֵט.

The ground form is retained in the Niph‘al while the vowel of the ground form is heightened in the Hiph‘il.

3. The vowel of the preformative, now in an open syllable before the tone, is heightened, ֲ to ָ in Qal and Niph‘al, ֲ

to ־ in Hiph'il perfect and participle; נָקְטַט becomes נִקַט,
הָקְטַט becomes הָקַט.

4. The regular intensive stems are found frequently uncontracted, הִלֵּל praise. Certain special forms are also found,
קוֹטֵט (here called Po'el), קוֹטַט (Po'al), and הִתְקוֹטֵט (Hith-
po'el). In rare instances a Pilpel form is found גִּלְגֵּל from גָּלַל
to roll.

5. Before consonantal afformatives a long helping vowel is
inserted to insure pronunciation of the full letter of the stem.
In all the perfects it is וֹ and in the imperfects and imperatives
(before נָה) it is יְ_.

תִּצְלֶינָה, נְקַטּוֹתָ, סַבּוֹת

These vowels are always accented except before תֶּם and תֶּן.

6. An Aramaic form of the Qal imperfect, made by doubling
the first radical, is quite common, יִקֹּב he will curse, יִדֹּם he will
be silent.

VOCABULARY

גָּלַל	roll	פָּלַל	(Pi.) intervene, meditate (Hith.) pray
מָדַד	measure	אָרַר	curse
סָבַב	surround, turn	הָלַל	(Pi.) praise (Hith.) boast
קָלַל	be insignificant (Ni.) be light (Hi.) make light	חָנַן	be gracious (Pi.) make gracious (Hith.) make entreaty

EXERCISES

1. Write a synopsis of Qal, Niph'al, and Hiph'il using גָּלַל.

2. Translate and locate fully:

קַלּוּ, קִלֵּל, אָרוּר, אָרוֹר, גַּל, גֻּלַּל, יְקַלֵּל, הָקַל, קִלְקַל,
לְהִתְגַּלֵּל, מִתְגּלֵּל, הָלֵּל, אֲהַלֵּל, חַנּוֹתִי, מִתְחַנֵּן, יִתְמֹדֵד,
הֵסֵב, הַלְלוּ, יָחֹן, מַדּוֹתִי, סַבּוֹתִי, נָסֵב, מֵסֵב, הַלֵּל, חֹנֵּן, יָמֹד,
סֹבִּי, סֹב, פִּלַּלְתָּ, מְהֻלָּל, חָנוּן, נְהַלֵּל, חָנוּן, יְמַד, סֹבֵב, יְפַלֵּל,
מִתְהַלְּלִים, יְחֻנַּן, יְמֹדֵד, נָסַבּוּ, הִתְפַּלֵּל, מִדֵּד, סַבֵּב:

LESSON XXXV

THE MIDDLE VOWEL VERBS

(Ayin Waw and Ayin Yodh)

See Paradigm I (page 212)

Types: קוּם *rise,* בּוֹשׁ *be ashamed,* בִּין *discern*

In certain verbs the middle radical was originally ו or י, but this letter has either dropped out altogether, or remains only as a vowel letter. As a result, in many forms only two of the radicals appear. This is usually true of the Qal perfect: e. g., בֵּן, בָּא, מֵת, קָם. Since there is in these forms no indication of the original middle radical, the *infinitive construct* form is usually cited as the root, for there the ו or י is preserved: e. g., קוּם, בִּין, בּוֹא, מוּת.

Not all verbs which have a ו or י as the middle radical exhibit this peculiarity. In some cases the letter is strong enough to be retained as a consonant: e. g., צָוָה *command,* גָּוַע *expire,* חָיָה *live,* הָיָה *be.* These verbs are not classed as Middle Vowel verbs, and the rules here given do not apply to them.

As in strong verbs there are three classes of Middle Vowel verbs: *a*, *e*, and *o*. (Cf. קָטֵל, כָּבֵד, קָטֹן.) קוּם has the Qal perfect in *a*: קָם; מוּת in *e*: מֵת; בּוֹשׁ in *o*. The *o* type verb often retains the middle vowel letter where other types reject it: בּוֹשׁ, בּוֹשָׁה, בּוֹשׁוּ. (Note, however, that בּוֹא, *go in*, takes Qal perfect בָּא. So also the Ayin Yodh verbs: בִּין, Qal perfect, בָּן).

The following general rules apply to Middle Vowel verbs:

1. Medial ו never appears as a consonant. It either falls out or unites with the form:

קַוַל becomes קָל

קֻוְל becomes קוּל

נָקְוַם becomes נָקוֹם

2. The vowel of the preformative, which, after the contraction, stands in an open syllable before the tone, is heightened ◌ַ to ◌ָ in Hiph'il perfect and participle, (וֹ in Hoph'al) and ◌ַ to ◌ָ elsewhere:

נָקוֹם, יָקוּם, הוּקַם, יָקִים, הֵקִים

3. Before vowel afformatives the stem vowel, instead of being volatilized, as in the strong verb, is retained and accented:

יָמוּלוּ, נָפֹצוּ, יָבֹאוּ

4. Before consonantal afformatives a separating vowel (וֹ in perfect and ◌ִי in imperfect and imperative) is found in Niph'al and Hiph'il perfects and Qal imperfect. The Qal perfect shortens ◌ָ to ◌ַ, קַמְתִּי instead of קָמוֹתִי.

Notes

1. In the Ayin Yodh verbs the Qal imperfect is identical in form with the Hiph'il imperfect: יָשִׂית ,יָשִׁיר ,יָבִין ,יָשִׂים.

2. The verb בּוֹא (*come in*) keeps וֹ in the Qal imperfect where the other verbs have וּ (יָבוֹא).

3. Instead of the regular intensive stems we usually find Polel, Pilpel, Polal, or Hithpolel forms: קוֹמֵם ,כִּלְכֵּל ,קוֹמַם, הִתְקוֹמֵם.

4. When the separating vowel (וֹ) of the Niph'al perfect is accented, the וֹ of the stem is changed to וּ (for the sake of euphony): נְקוּלוֹת.

5. When the preposition לְ is prefixed to the infinitive construct it is pointed לָ (לָשׁוּב).

Vocabulary

גּוּר	*sojourn*	שׁוּב	*turn, return*
טוֹב	*be good*	בּוֹשׁ	*be ashamed*
קוּם	*rise* (Hi.) *raise up*	בִּין	*discern* (Hi.) *explain*
רוּץ	*run*	מוּת	*die*
שִׂים	*put, place*	שִׁיר	*sing*

Exercises

1. Write synopses using בּוֹשׁ ,שִׂים ,גּוּר.

2. Translate and locate fully:

יָבִין, בִּין, הֵבִין, אֶתְבּוֹנֵן, בּוֹשָׁה, מֵבִין, מֵבִישׁ, בּוֹשִׁים, גָּר,

יָגוּר, גַּרְתִּי, גּוּרִי, טוֹב, גֵּרִים, מִתְגּוֹרֵר, טוֹבוּ, הֲטִיבוֹתָ, אָמוּת,

מֵת, קַמְתָּ, מוֹת, נָקוּם, מְמוֹתֵת, קוּם, הֵמִית, יָמִית, הֲקִים,

יָקִים, מֵמִית, יוּמַת, רָץ, מֵקִים, הָקֵם, יָרוּץ, תָּרִיץ, לָרוּץ,

שָׂם, שַׂמְתִּי, שׁוּב, יָשִׂים, שָׁב, מֵשִׂים, שַׁבְתָּ, יוּשַׂם, הֲשִׁיבוֹתִי,

מֵשִׁיב, הוּשַׁב, שָׁר, יָשִׁיר, יוּשַׁר, לָשִׁיר:

LESSON XXXVI

THE PE YODH AND PE WAW VERBS

(The First Radical Yodh or Waw)

See Paradigm K (page 214)

Types: יָטַב *be good*, יָדַע *know*, יָרֵשׁ *inherit*

Since Yodh and Waw are weak letters they become quiescent after certain vowel sounds. They lose their consonantal character after most preformatives.

1. Six verbs are properly **Pe Yodh,** יָטַב *be good*, יָנַק *suck*, יָמַן *go to right*, יָשַׁר *be straight*, יָקַץ *awake*, יָלַל *howl*.

They retain the Yodh, יָטֵב, יְטַב, יִיטַב, יְטוֹב, יִטַב, יֵטַב, יְטוּב.

In the Hiph'il the Yodh unites with the vowel of the preformative, giving מֵיטִיב, יֵיטִיב, הֵיטִיב, ־ֵ.

2. Others are properly **Pe Waw** verbs, and are divided into two classes:

(a) Some **reject** the Waw in the Qal impf., imper. and inf. construct, יָרַד *go down*, יָדַע *know*, יָצָא *go out*, יָקַע *be dislocated*, יָשַׁב *sit, dwell*, יָלַד *bear*, יָחַד *be united*, (הָלַךְ *walk*).

Qal pf.	impf.	imper.	inf. construct
יָשַׁב	יֵשֵׁב	שֵׁב	שֶׁבֶת
יָדַע	יֵדַע	דַּע	דַּעַת
יָצָא	יֵצֵא	צֵא	צֵאת
הָלַךְ	יֵלֵךְ	לֵךְ	לֶכֶת

(b) Others **retain** the Waw, allowing it to stand as a Yodh with the vowel of the preformative, יָרַשׁ *possess*, יָרֵא *fear*, יָעַץ *advise*, יָעֵף *be weary*, יָשֵׁן *sleep*.

Qal pf.	impf.	imper.	inf. construct
יָרַשׁ	יִירַשׁ	יְרַשׁ (רַשׁ)	יְרשׁ (רֶשֶׁת)
יָבֵשׁ	יִיבַשׁ	יְבַשׁ	יְבשׁ (יִבְשֶׁת)

3. In the Hiph'il of verbs properly Pe Waw the original הוֹשִׁיב (הוֹשַׁב) appears as הוֹשִׁיב. (Likewise, מוֹשִׁיב, יוֹשִׁיב).

4. In the Niph'al perfect the original נָוְשַׁב becomes נוֹשַׁב. This is true both of Pe Yodh and of Pe Waw types. The Niph'al imperfect, imperative and infinitives behave as the strong verb יִוָּלֵד, הִוָּתֵר, תִּוָּרֵשׁ.

5. In the Hoph'al the original הָוְשַׁב becomes הוּשַׁב. (Likewise, מוּשַׁב, יוּשַׁב).

NOTES

1. The verb, יָכֹל *be able*, is irregular. The only imperfect used is the form יוּכַל which is a true Hoph'al. The infinitive construct is יְכֹלֶת.

2. The verb, הָלַךְ *walk*, is treated as a Pe Waw verb except in the Qal perfect, participle and infinite absolute, and throughout the Hithpa‘el. The infinitive construct is לֶכֶת.

3. When the preposition לְ is written with the infinitive construct it takes the form לְ (לָשֶׁבֶת).

4. The Qal imperative sometimes takes the cohortative ending רְדָה, שְׁבָה, לְכָה, ־ָה.

VOCABULARY

יָבֵשׁ	*be dry, dry up*	יָטַב	*be good* (Hi.) *do good*
יָלַד	*bring forth* (Hi.) *beget*	יָרֵא	*fear*
יָעַץ	*give counsel*	יָשַׁר	*be straight* (Pi.) *make straight*
יָשַׁב	*sit, dwell*	הָלַךְ	*go, walk*
יָדַע	*know*		

EXERCISES

1. Write a full synopsis of this verb using יָלַד.

2. Translate and locate fully:

יָלַד, הוֹדַע, אוֹבִישׁ, נוֹדַע, יָבְשׁוּ, יֵטַב, יֻלַּד,

יָדַעְתִּי, תֵּיבַשׁ, יָבוֹשׁ, יָדַע, נוֹדַע, הֵיטִיב, מוֹלִיד, תֵּיבַשׁ, דַּע,

יְדַעְתָּ, מֵיטִיב, יוֹעֵץ, הוֹבִישׁ, יָדַע, יוֹדִיעַ, תֵּלֶךְ, יָעוֹץ, הוֹבַשְׁתָּ,

יָדוּעַ, מוֹדִיעִים, יֻלַּד, נוֹעַץ, נוֹלַד, יְשַׁבְתָּם, יַשֵּׁר, מִתְהַלֵּךְ,

אוֹלִיד מוֹלִיכִים, לֵךְ, הוֹלֵךְ, הָלַכְתִּי, נֵלֵךְ, מְהַלֵּךְ, יִישַׁר,

יִרְאָה, יִירָא, יְרֵא, תִּוָּרֵא, אֵשֵׁב, שֵׁב, שֶׁבֶת, שְׁבוּ, מוֹשִׁיב:

LESSON XXXVII

A Story Concerning the Crossing of the Jordan (Continued)

וַיְדַבֵּר יְהוֹשֻׁעַ אֶל־בְּנֵי יִשְׂרָאֵל עוֹד לֵאמֹר כַּאֲשֶׁר יִסַּע
הָאָרוֹן מִמְּקוֹמוֹ וְאַתֶּם תִּסְעוּ מִמְּקוֹמְכֶם: אַךְ כַּעֲמֹד הַכֹּהֲנִים
עַל גְּדוֹת הַנָּהָר תַּעַמְדוּ גַם אַתֶּם: אַגִּיד לָכֶם מָתַי לִנְסֹעַ עוֹד
לֵאמֹר זֹאת הָעֵת לָגֶשֶׁת קְחוּ אֶת־כָּל־אֲשֶׁר־לָכֶם וּשְׂאוּ אֶת־
מַשָּׂאֲכֶם: בָּעֵת הַהִיא נָתַן אָמֵץ אִישׁ לְרֵעֵהוּ: נִקְרָא אִישׁ
לְרֵעֵהוּ לֵאמֹר אַל נִפְחָד: כָּכָה נִפְלָא: יֹאמְרוּ לָנוּ יַלְדֵּינוּ
מָחָר קְרָאתֶם לָנוּ וַנַּעֲבֹר בְּלִי פַחַד: יֹאמַר בֵּן לְאָבִיו קָרָאתָ
לִי בַיּוֹם הַהוּא בַת לְאִמָּהּ קָרוֹא קָרָאת לִי: כָּכָה יַפְלִיא יהוה
אֶת־הַיּוֹם הַזֶּה:

וַיַּעֲשׂוּ בְּנֵי יִשְׂרָאֵל כִּדְבַר יהוה: אָמַר יְהוֹשֻׁעַ הִתְקַדְּשׁוּ כִּי
יַעֲשֶׂה יהוה נִפְלָאוֹת בְּקִרְבְּכֶם וְכֵן עָשׂוּ: וַיְצַוּוּ אֹתָם הַשֹּׁטְרִים
לַעֲשׂוֹת כַּאֲשֶׁר צִוָּה יהוה בַכֹּל וְכֵן עָשׂוּ: וּבַעֲלוֹת הָעָם אֶל
הֶחָרָבָה אָמְרוּ יהוה עָשָׂה כִדְבָרוֹ טוֹב לָנוּ לַעֲשׂוֹת אֶת־כָּל־
אֲשֶׁר מְצַוֶּה הוּא:

Notes

1. וְאַתֶּם literal rendering: "and ye." אַתֶּם used for emphasis: "then *ye*, on *your part*, shall journey."

2. כַּעֲמֹד infinitive construct with preposition כְּ. Literal
rendering: "at the standing of . . . . . ." כְּ with infinitive
construct denotes "at the point when, just as, as soon as;" בְּ
with infinitive denotes duration: "in, when." Cf. בַּעֲלוֹת.

3. אֶת־כָּל־אֲשֶׁר־לָכֶם literally: "all which to you." A Hebrew idiom for expressing possession. "All that you have" (free translation).

4. בָּעֵת הַהִיא emphatic by virtue of position.

5. Distributive use of אִישׁ: "each to his fellow (or friend)." More literal rendering: "a man to his fellow."

6. יַלְדֵינוּ construct plural of יֶלֶד with 1st c. pl. suffix.

7. בְּלִי "without."

8. לְאִמָּהּ the noun אֵם with preposition לְ and 3rd f. sg. suffix.

9. קָרוֹא intensive use of infinitive absolute.

10. וַיְצַוּוּ Pi‘el imperfect with וַ consecutive from צָוָה (used mainly in the Pi‘el stem). The first וּ is a doubled consonant; the second a vowel=wǎ-yᵉtsǎw-wû.

11. כֹּל, בְּכֹל and preposition בְּ (בָּ before tone).

12. וּבַעֲלוֹת infinitive construct from עָלָה with preposition בְּ and וּ conjunctive. Literal rendering: "In the going up of . . ."

13. מְצַוֶּה הוּא participle used as finite verb. Here the subject follows the participle, contrary to common usage. This places the emphasis on the participle.

LESSON XXXVIII

The Numerals

1. The cardinal numbers, from *one* to *ten* inclusive, have each an appropriate form for the masculine and feminine genders as well as for the absolute and construct states.

2. The number *one* אֶחָד is an adjective. It usually stands after and agrees with its noun, אִישׁ אֶחָד *one man;* אִשָּׁה אַחַת *one woman*.

3. The numeral *two* שְׁנַיִם (f. שְׁתַּיִם) is a noun. It usually stands before and agrees with its noun, שְׁנֵי אֲנָשִׁים *two men;* (or שְׁנַיִם אֲנָשִׁים); שְׁתֵּי נָשִׁים *two women* (or שְׁתַּיִם נָשִׁים).

4. The numbers from *three* to *ten* are nouns and disagree in gender. They may stand before the noun in construct or, either before or after it, in absolute state, חֲמִשָּׁה בָנִים *five sons* or בָּנִים חֲמִשָּׁה or חֲמֵשֶׁת בָּנִים. (Note the use of the feminine forms with masculine nouns and the masculine form with feminine nouns, שֵׁשׁ יְלָדוֹת *six girls*.)

5. The numbers *eleven* to *nineteen* are formed by two separate words: the unit and the ten. The unit is the possessive. The noun is usually in the plural, חֲמִשָּׁה עָשָׂר בָּנִים *fifteen sons*.

6. The numbers *thirty, forty, fifty, sixty, seventy, eighty* and *ninety* are formed from the corresponding units with plural terminations. *Twenty* is plural of *ten*, עָשָׂר, עֶשְׂרִים, שְׁלֹשִׁים, etc. The noun is in the singular when the numeral precedes, in the plural when it follows the noun, שְׁלֹשִׁים שָׁנָה, שְׁלֹשִׁים שָׁנִים.

CARDINAL NUMBERS

	WITH MASCULINE NOUNS			WITH FEMININE NOUNS	
	Absolute	Construct		Absolute	Construct
1.	אֶחָד	אַחַד	א	אַחַת	אַחַת
2.	שְׁנַיִם	שְׁנֵי	ב	שְׁתַּיִם	שְׁתֵּי
3.	שְׁלֹשָׁה	שְׁלֹשֶׁת	ג	שָׁלֹשׁ	שְׁלֹשׁ
4.	אַרְבָּעָה	אַרְבַּעַת	ד	אַרְבַּע	אַרְבַּע
5.	חֲמִשָּׁה	חֲמֵשֶׁת	ה	חָמֵשׁ	חֲמֵשׁ
6.	שִׁשָּׁה	שֵׁשֶׁת	ו	שֵׁשׁ	שֵׁשׁ
7.	שִׁבְעָה	שִׁבְעַת	ז	שֶׁבַע	(שְׁבַע)
8.	שְׁמֹנָה	שְׁמֹנַת	ח	שְׁמֹנֶה	שְׁמֹנֶה
9.	תִּשְׁעָה	תִּשְׁעַת	ט	תֵּשַׁע	(תְּשַׁע)
10.	עֲשָׂרָה	עֲשֶׂרֶת	י	עֶשֶׂר	עֶשֶׂר
11.	אַחַד עָשָׂר / עַשְׁתֵּי עָשָׂר		יא	אַחַת עֶשְׂרֵה / עַשְׁתֵּי עֶשְׂרֵה	
12.	שְׁנֵים עָשָׂר / שְׁנֵי עָשָׂר		יב	שְׁתֵּים עֶשְׂרֵה / שְׁתֵּי עֶשְׂרֵה	
13.	שְׁלֹשָׁה עָשָׂר		יג	שְׁלֹשׁ עֶשְׂרֵה	
14.	אַרְבָּעָה עָשָׂר		יד	אַרְבַּע עֶשְׂרֵה	
15.	חֲמִשָּׁה עָשָׂר		טו	חֲמֵשׁ עֶשְׂרֵה	
16.	שִׁשָּׁה עָשָׂר		טז	שֵׁשׁ עֶשְׂרֵה	

With Masculine Nouns			With Feminine Nouns
17.	שִׁבְעָה עָשָׂר	יז	שְׁבַע עֶשְׂרֵה
18.	שְׁמֹנָה עָשָׂר	יח	שְׁמֹנֶה עֶשְׂרֵה
19.	תִּשְׁעָה עָשָׂר	יט	תְּשַׁע עֶשְׂרֵה

20.	עֶשְׂרִים	600.	שֵׁשׁ מֵאוֹת
21.	אֶחָד וְעֶשְׂרִים	700.	שְׁבַע מֵאוֹת
30.	שְׁלֹשִׁים	800.	שְׁמֹנֶה מֵאוֹת
40.	אַרְבָּעִים	900.	תְּשַׁע מֵאוֹת
50.	חֲמִשִּׁים	1,000.	אֶלֶף אֶחָד
60.	שִׁשִּׁים	2,000.	שְׁנֵי אֲלָפִים
70.	שִׁבְעִים	3,000.	שְׁלֹשֶׁת אֲלָפִים
80.	שְׁמֹנִים	4,000.	אַרְבַּעַת אֲלָפִים
90.	תִּשְׁעִים	5,000.	חֲמֵשֶׁת אֲלָפִים
100.	מֵאָה אַחַת	6,000.	שֵׁשֶׁת אֲלָפִים
200.	שְׁתֵּי מֵאוֹת	7,000.	שִׁבְעַת אֲלָפִים
300.	שְׁלֹשׁ מֵאוֹת	8,000.	שְׁמֹנַת אֲלָפִים
400.	אַרְבַּע מֵאוֹת	9,000.	תִּשְׁעַת אֲלָפִים
500.	חֲמֵשׁ מֵאוֹת	10,000.	עֲשֶׂרֶת אֲלָפִים רְבָבָה

The Ordinals from *one* to *ten* are adjectives formed from the corresponding cardinal numerals by the addition of the termination י‎ָ‎. Another י‎ָ‎ is inserted (when possible) between the second and third radical. After *ten* the cardinals are used for ordinals.

First	רִאשׁוֹן	*Sixth*	שִׁשִּׁי
Second	שֵׁנִי	*Seventh*	שְׁבִיעִי
Third	שְׁלִישִׁי	*Eighth*	שְׁמִינִי
Fourth	רְבִיעִי	*Ninth*	תְּשִׁיעִי
Fifth	חֲמִישִׁי	*Tenth*	עֲשִׂירִי

EXERCISES

שִׁשָּׁה בָנִים, בָּנוֹת שֵׁשׁ, שֵׁשׁ שָׁנִים, שֵׁשֶׁת יָמִים. עֲשָׂרָה אֲנָשִׁים,
פָּרִים עֲשָׂרָה, עֶשֶׂר שָׁנִים, עֲשֶׂרֶת יָמִים, עֲשֶׂרֶת הַדְּבָרִים.
אַרְבָּעָה עָשָׂר כְּבָשִׂים, שְׁלֹשָׁה עָשָׂר פָּרִים, שְׁנֵים עָשָׂר שִׁבְטֵי
יִשְׂרָאֵל; שְׁתֵּים עֶשְׂרֵה אֲבָנִים, שְׁלֹשׁ עֶשְׂרֵה עָרִים; עָרִים תֵּשַׁע
עֶשְׂרֵה. חֲמִשָּׁה עָשָׂר שֶׁקֶל, שְׁמֹנָה עָשָׂר אֶלֶף, אַרְבָּעָה עָשָׂר
יוֹם, שְׁנַיִם עָשָׂר אִישׁ, שְׁנֵי עָשָׂר בָּקָר; שְׁמֹנֶה עֶשְׂרֵה אַמָּה, שֵׁשׁ
עֶשְׂרֵה נֶפֶשׁ, תֵּשַׁע עֶשְׂרֵה שָׁנָה.

חָמֵשׁ שָׁנִים וְשִׁשִּׁים שָׁנָה, אַרְבָּעִים וְחָמֵשׁ שָׁנָה, שִׁבְעִים שָׁנָה
וְחָמֵשׁ שָׁנִים.

מֵאָה אִישׁ, מָאתַיִם שָׁנָה, תְּשַׁע מֵאוֹת שָׁנָה, שְׁלֹשׁ מֵאוֹת.
אֶלֶף אִישׁ, אֶלֶף פְּעָמִים, שִׁבְעַת אֲלָפִים פָּרָשִׁים, עֲשֶׂרֶת
אֲלָפִים אִישׁ:

LESSON XXXIX

READING ASSIGNMENT

וַיֹּאמֶר שְׁמוּאֵל אֶל־כָּל־יִשְׂרָאֵל הִנֵּה שָׁמַעְתִּי בְקוֹלְכֶם לְכֹל

אֲשֶׁר־אֲמַרְתֶּם לִי וָאַמְלִיךְ עֲלֵיכֶם מֶלֶךְ: וְעַתָּה הִנֵּה הַמֶּלֶךְ

מִתְהַלֵּךְ לִפְנֵיכֶם וַאֲנִי זָקַנְתִּי וָשַׂבְתִּי וּבָנַי הִנָּם אִתְּכֶם וַאֲנִי

הִתְהַלַּכְתִּי לִפְנֵיכֶם מִנְּעֻרַי עַד־הַיּוֹם הַזֶּה: הִנְנִי עֲנוּ בִי נֶגֶד יהוה

וְנֶגֶד מְשִׁיחוֹ אֶת־שׁוֹר מִי לָקַחְתִּי וַחֲמוֹר מִי לָקַחְתִּי וְאֶת־מִי

עָשַׁקְתִּי אֶת־מִי רַצּוֹתִי וּמִיַּד־מִי לָקַחְתִּי כֹפֶר וְאָשִׁיב לָכֶם:

וַיֹּאמְרוּ לֹא עֲשַׁקְתָּנוּ וְלֹא רַצּוֹתָנוּ וְלֹא־לָקַחְתָּ מִיַּד־אִישׁ מְאוּמָה:

וַיֹּאמֶר אֲלֵיהֶם עֵד יהוה בָּכֶם וְעֵד מְשִׁיחוֹ הַיּוֹם הַזֶּה כִּי לֹא

מְצָאתֶם בְּיָדִי מְאוּמָה וַיֹּאמְרוּ עֵד: וַיֹּאמֶר שְׁמוּאֵל אֶל־הָעָם

יהוה אֲשֶׁר עָשָׂה אֶת־מֹשֶׁה וְאֶת־אַהֲרֹן וַאֲשֶׁר הֶעֱלָה אֶת־

אֲבוֹתֵיכֶם מֵאֶרֶץ מִצְרָיִם: וְעַתָּה הִתְיַצְּבוּ וְאִשָּׁפְטָה אִתְּכֶם

לִפְנֵי יהוה אֵת כָּל־צִדְקוֹת יהוה אֲשֶׁר־עָשָׂה אִתְּכֶם וְאֶת

אֲבוֹתֵיכֶם:

NOTES

1. שָׁמַע + בְ means *to hearken*.

2. עֲלֵיכֶם the preposition עַל + the 2nd m. plu. suffix.

3. מִתְהַלֵּךְ note the force of the participle – continuous action (at present).

4. לִפְנֵיכֶם the preposition לְ + the substantive פָּנִים in the construct + the 2nd m. plu. pronominal suffix.

5. וַאֲנִי note the force of the pronoun (emphasis).

6. וְשַׂבְתִּי from שִׂיב *to be hoary with age.*

7. הִנָּם the particle הִנֵּה (*behold*) + the 3rd m. plu. suffix.

8. אִתְּכֶם the preposition אֵת (*with*) + the 2nd plu. suffix.

9. מִנְעָרַי the preposition מִן + the substantive נַעַר (*youth*) + 1st c. sg. suffix.

10. הִנְנִי see הִנָּם (above).

11. עֲנוּ Qal imperative from עָנָה *to answer, respond.*

12. מְשִׁיחוֹ noun + 3rd m. sg. suffix from מָשַׁח *to anoint.*

13. אֶת־שׁוֹר־מִי a question. Note the accusative.

14. רַצּוֹתִי from רָצַץ *to crush.*

15. אֲלֵיהֶם preposition אֶל (*unto*) + 3rd m. plu. suffix.

16. אֲבוֹתֵיכֶם plural of אָב + 2nd m. plu. suffix.

17. מִצְרַיִם *Egypt, the Egyptians.*

18. הִתְיַצְּבוּ note the force of the Hithpaʻel imperative, *get yourselves set.*

19. וְאִשָּׁפְטָה in the Niphʻal this verb means *to enter into controversy.*

LESSON XL

READING ASSIGNMENT

וַיֹּאמֶר יהוה אֶל־שְׁמוּאֵל עַד־מָתַי אַתָּה מִתְאַבֵּל אֶל־שָׁאוּל
וַאֲנִי מְאַסְתִּיו מִמְּלֹךְ עַל־יִשְׂרָאֵל מַלֵּא קַרְנְךָ שֶׁמֶן וְלֵךְ אֶשְׁלָחֲךָ
אֶל־יִשַׁי בֵּית־הַלַּחְמִי כִּי־רָאִיתִי בְּבָנָיו לִי מֶלֶךְ: וַיֹּאמֶר שְׁמוּאֵל
אֵיךְ אֵלֵךְ וְשָׁמַע שָׁאוּל וַהֲרָגָנִי: וַיֹּאמֶר יהוה עֶגְלַת בָּקָר תִּקַּח
בְּיָדֶךָ וְאָמַרְתָּ לִזְבֹּחַ לַיהוה בָּאתִי: וְקָרָאתָ לְיִשַׁי בַּזָּבַח וְאָנֹכִי

אוֹדִיעֲךָ אֶת אֲשֶׁר־תַּעֲשֶׂה וּמֵשַׁחְתָּ לִי אֵת אֲשֶׁר־אֹמַר אֵלֶיךָ:

וַיַּעַשׂ שְׁמוּאֵל אֵת אֲשֶׁר דִּבֶּר יהוה וַיָּבֹא בֵּית לָחֶם וַיֶּחֶרְדוּ

זִקְנֵי הָעִיר לִקְרָאתוֹ: וַיֹּאמֶר שָׁלֹם לִזְבֹּחַ לַיהוה בָּאתִי

הִתְקַדְּשׁוּ וּבָאתֶם אִתִּי בַּזָּבַח וַיְקַדֵּשׁ אֶת־יִשַׁי וְאֶת־בָּנָיו וַיִּקְרָא

לָהֶם לַזָּבַח: וַיַּעֲבֵר יִשַׁי שִׁבְעַת בָּנָיו לִפְנֵי שְׁמוּאֵל וַיֹּאמֶר

שְׁמוּאֵל אֶל־יִשַׁי לֹא־בָחַר יהוה בָּאֵלֶּה:

וַיִּשְׁלַח וַיְבִיאֵהוּ:   וַיֹּאמֶר יהוה קוּם מְשָׁחֵהוּ כִּי־זֶה הוּא:

וַיִּקַּח שְׁמוּאֵל אֶת־קֶרֶן הַשֶּׁמֶן וַיִּמְשַׁח אֹתוֹ בְּקֶרֶב אֶחָיו וַתִּצְלַח

רוּחַ־יהוה אֶל־דָּוִד מֵהַיּוֹם הַהוּא:

NOTES

1. עַד־מָתַי the preposition עַד *up to* + interrogative adverb מָתַי *when*.

2. וַאֲנִי Note the emphatic use of this pronoun.

3. מְאַסְתִּיו Qal perfect + the 3rd m. sg. suffix, written defectively.

4. מִמְּלֹךְ the preposition מִן + the infinitive construct.

5. וְלֵךְ Qal imperative from הָלַךְ *to walk* + waw conj.

6. בֵּית־הַלַּחְמִי *the Beth-lehemite.*

7. בְּבָנָיו the prep. בְּ + the noun בָּנִים + the 3rd m. sg. suffix.

8. אֵלֵךְ from הָלַךְ *to walk.*

9. תִּקַּח from לָקַח *to take.*

10. בָּאתִי from בּוֹא *to go in* or *come in* + 2 m. sg. suffix.

11. אוֹדִיעֲךָ Hiph'il from יָדַע *to know.*

12. אֹמַר from אָמַר *to say.* Note the defective writing.

13. אֵלֶיךָ the preposition אֶל *unto* + the 2nd m. sg. suffix.

14. וַיַּעַשׂ a shortened form for וַיַּעֲשֶׂה.

15. וּבָאתֶם note the use of waw consecutive and the imperfect used as an imperative.

16. אִתִּי the preposition אֵת *with* + the 1st c. sg. suffix.

17. וַיְבִיאֵהוּ Hiph'il impf. of בּוֹא + waw cons. + 3rd m. sg. suffix.

LESSON XLI

Reading Assignment

בְּרֵאשִׁית בָּרָא אֱלֹהִים אֵת הַשָּׁמַיִם וְאֵת הָאָרֶץ: וְהָאָרֶץ
הָיְתָה תֹהוּ וָבֹהוּ וְחֹשֶׁךְ עַל־פְּנֵי תְהוֹם וְרוּחַ אֱלֹהִים מְרַחֶפֶת
עַל־פְּנֵי הַמָּיִם: וַיֹּאמֶר אֱלֹהִים יְהִי אוֹר וַיְהִי־אוֹר: וַיַּרְא אֱלֹהִים
אֶת־הָאוֹר כִּי־טוֹב וַיַּבְדֵּל אֱלֹהִים בֵּין הָאוֹר וּבֵין הַחֹשֶׁךְ:
וַיִּקְרָא אֱלֹהִים לָאוֹר יוֹם וְלַחֹשֶׁךְ קָרָא לָיְלָה וַיְהִי־עֶרֶב וַיְהִי־
בֹקֶר יוֹם אֶחָד: נָתַן אֱלֹהִים מְאֹרוֹת לְהַבְדִּיל בֵּין הַיּוֹם וּבֵין
הַלָּיְלָה: וַיֹּאמֶר אֱלֹהִים נַעֲשֶׂה אָדָם בְּצַלְמֵנוּ כִּדְמוּתֵנוּ וְיִרְדּוּ:
וַיִּבְרָא אֱלֹהִים אֶת־הָאָדָם בְּצַלְמוֹ בְּצֶלֶם אֱלֹהִים בָּרָא אֹתוֹ
זָכָר וּנְקֵבָה בָּרָא אֹתָם: וַיַּרְא אֱלֹהִים אֶת־כָּל־אֲשֶׁר עָשָׂה
וְהִנֵּה־טוֹב מְאֹד וַיְהִי־עֶרֶב וַיְהִי בֹקֶר יוֹם הַשִּׁשִּׁי:

Notes

1. מְרַחֶפֶת a feminine participle from רָחַף, to agree with רוּחַ.

2. הַמָּיִם pausal form for הַמַּיִם.

3. יְהִי a jussive form from הָיָה, translated *let be*.

4. וַיִּרְא a shortened form instead of וַיִּרְאֶה.

5. נַעֲשֶׂה *let us make* (cohortative).

6. וְיִרְדּוּ a Qal imperfect of רָדָה *to have dominion*.

LESSON XLII

READING ASSIGNMENT

בְּרֵאשִׁית הָיָה הַדָּבָר וְהַדָּבָר הָיָה אֵת הָאֱלֹהִים וֵאלֹהִים
הָיָה הַדָּבָר: הוּא הָיָה בְרֵאשִׁית אֵת הָאֱלֹהִים: הַכֹּל נִהְיָה
עַל־יָדוֹ וּמִבַּלְעָדָיו לֹא נִהְיָה כָּל־אֲשֶׁר נִהְיָה: בּוֹ הָיוּ חַיִּים
וְהַחַיִּים הָיוּ אוֹר לִפְנֵי הָאָדָם: וְהָאוֹר הֵאִיר בַּחֹשֶׁךְ לֹא הִשִּׂיגוֹ:
וַיְהִי אִישׁ שָׁלוּחַ מֵאֵת הָאֱלֹהִים וּשְׁמוֹ יוֹחָנָן: הוּא בָא לְעֵדוּת
לְהָעִיד עַד־הָאוֹר לְמַעַן יַאֲמִינוּ כֻלָּם עַל־יָדוֹ: הוּא לֹא־הָיָה
הָאוֹר כִּי אִם־לְהָעִיד עַל־הָאוֹר: בֵּעוֹלָם הָיָה וְעַל־יָדוֹ נִהְיָה
הָעוֹלָם וְהָעוֹלָם לֹא יְדָעוֹ: הוּא בָא בְשֶׁלּוֹ וַאֲשֶׁר־הֵמָּה לוֹ לֹא
קִבְּלֻהוּ: וְהַמְקַבְּלִים אֹתוֹ הַמַּאֲמִינִים בִּשְׁמוֹ נָתַן עֹז לָמוֹ לִהְיוֹת
בָּנִים לֵאלֹהִים:

NOTES

1. This translation into Hebrew was made by Professor Delitzsch.

2. נִהְיָה Niph'al perfect from הָיָה.

3. בִּלְעָדָי וּמִבַּלְעָדָיו the conj. וְ + the prep. מִן + the form *without, apart from*.

4. הֵאִיר the causative idea from אוֹר *to be light*.

5. הִשִּׂיגוּ from נָשַׂג (Hi.) *to reach, overtake.*

6. עוֹלָם *world, age, antiquity, eternity.*

7. בְּשֶׁלּוֹ *through that which belongs to him* (שֶׁ + שֶׁל + בְּ).

8. קִבְּלֻהוּ defective writing for קִבְּלוּהוּ.

9. הַמְקַבְּלִים
   הַמַּאֲמִינִים } *participles (plural) + the article.*

10. לָמוֹ poetic for לוֹ.

LESSON XLIII

READING ASSIGNMENT (PSALM XXIII)

מִזְמוֹר לְדָוִד ⁽¹⁾יְהֹוָה רֹעִי לֹא אֶחְסָר: ⁽²⁾בִּנְאוֹת דֶּשֶׁא
יַרְבִּיצֵנִי עַל־מֵי מְנוּחוֹת יְנַהֲלֵנִי: ⁽³⁾נַפְשִׁי יְשׁוֹבֵב יַנְחֵנִי בְמַעְגְּלֵי־
צֶדֶק לְמַעַן שְׁמוֹ: ⁽⁴⁾גַּם כִּי־אֵלֵךְ בְּגֵיא צַלְמָוֶת לֹא־אִירָא רָע
כִּי־אַתָּה עִמָּדִי שִׁבְטְךָ וּמִשְׁעַנְתֶּךָ הֵמָּה יְנַחֲמֻנִי: ⁽⁵⁾תַּעֲרֹךְ לְפָנַי
שֻׁלְחָן נֶגֶד צֹרְרָי דִּשַּׁנְתָּ בַשֶּׁמֶן רֹאשִׁי כּוֹסִי רְוָיָה: ⁽⁶⁾אַךְ טוֹב
וָחֶסֶד יִרְדְּפוּנִי כָּל־יְמֵי חַיָּי וְשַׁבְתִּי בְּבֵית־יְהֹוָה לְאֹרֶךְ יָמִים:

NOTES

1. מִזְמוֹר לְדָוִד — These two words form a title to the psalm,
but in the Hebrew text are written as though a part of the poem.
The prep. לְ here probably expresses genitive relationship. It
is necessary to use this construction to express the idea of possession of an indefinite substantive. The construct relationship,
מִזְמוֹר דָּוִד, would mean, "*the* psalm of David." Many of the
psalms have this heading. It sometimes occurs in the form
לְדָוִד מִזְמוֹר, and sometimes simply לְדָוִד.

יְהֹוָה — This is not to be read Y*howah*. The personal name of God (probably Yahweh) was considered too sacred to be pronounced. Accordingly, the Hebrew always substituted another word, usually אֲדֹנָי, *my lord*, sometimes אֱלֹהִים, *God*. To indicate this reading, the Massoretes inserted the vowels of the substitute, though no change could be made in the inviolable consonants of the sacred text. The reader was expected to supply the proper consonants.

רֹעִי — properly Qal act. part. of verb רָעָה, used as a substantive. When suffix is added, final ה is dropped.

אֶחְסָר — final vowel lengthened from ◌ַ because of the poetical accent *silluk;* the syllable is said to be "in pause."

2. מֵי — construct of מַיִם, which occurs only in plural.

מְנֻחוֹת — plural of מְנֻחָה, *a quiet place.*

3. נַפְשִׁי — נֶפֶשׁ + 1st c. sg. suffix.

יְשׁוֹבֵב — Polel impf. of שׁוּב.

יַנְחֵנִי — Hiph. impf. of נָחָה, + 1st c. sg. suffix.

בְּמַעְגְּלֵי — construct plural of מַעְגָּל, *track, way, wagon trail.*

4. כִּי — This relative conjunction is used with various shades of meaning: indirect discourse ("that"); causal ("because"); result ("so that"); adversative ("but"); time ("when"); condition ("although", "even if"); etc. Here it expresses the conditional idea, reinforced by גַּם.

אֵלֵךְ — from הָלַךְ (וְלֵךְ).

צַלְמָוֶת — a poetical word, compounded of צֵל, *shadow, darkness*, and מָוֶת, *death;* lit., "thickest darkness;" fig., "great calamity or distress."

אִירָא — from יָרָא.

עִמָּדִי — The prep. עִם sometimes takes this form when 1st c. sg. suffix is added (also עִמִּי). It probably goes back to an old form of the prep., עִמָּד.

יְנַחֲמֻנִי — from נָחַם. יְנַחֲמוּ + 1st c. sg. suffix, with consequent shortening of וּ to ֻ.

5. תַּעֲרֹךְ — from עָרַךְ.

צֹרְרָי — Qal act. part. of צָרַר, *to press, be hostile;* as a substantive, *an enemy, adversary;* here m. pl. with 1 c. sg. suffix.

דִּשַּׁנְתָּ — The verb דָּשֵׁן in Qal means *to be fat;* in Pi'el, *to make fat,* or *cover with fat, oil;* hence, *anoint.* The more common word for anoint is מָשַׁח.

רְוָיָה — a rare noun meaning *an abundant drink, satisfying abundance,* derived from רָוָה, *io drink to the full.* Here used with כּוֹסִי as a nominal sentence: *my cup* (is, or contains) *an overflowing abundance.*

6. יִרְדְּפוּנִי — verb רָדַף, with 1st c. sg. suffix.

וְשַׁבְתִּי — This form as it stands is Qal perf., 1 c. sg. with waw consec. from שׁוּב, *return: and I shall return.* The general critical opinion, however, is that we should read וְשִׁבְתִּי, which is Qal inf. const. of יָשַׁב, *dwell,* + 1 c. sg. suffix: "my dwelling." The Massoretes give no indication that the vowel should be changed, but וְשַׁבְתִּי is difficult to construe, so we may assume the emendation: *and my dwelling* (shall be) *in the house of Yahweh.*

LESSON XLIV

Reading Assignment (Isaiah 5:1–7)

⁽¹⁾אָשִׁירָה נָּא לִידִידִי שִׁירַת דּוֹדִי לְכַרְמוֹ כֶּרֶם הָיָה לִידִידִי
בְּקֶרֶן בֶּן־שָׁמֶן: ⁽²⁾וַיְעַזְּקֵהוּ וַיְסַקְּלֵהוּ וַיִּטָּעֵהוּ שֹׂרֵק וַיִּבֶן מִגְדָּל
בְּתוֹכוֹ וְגַם־יֶקֶב חָצֵב בּוֹ וַיְקַו לַעֲשׂוֹת עֲנָבִים וַיַּעַשׂ בְּאֻשִׁים:
⁽³⁾וְעַתָּה יוֹשֵׁב יְרוּשָׁלַיִם וְאִישׁ יְהוּדָה שִׁפְטוּ־נָא בֵּינִי וּבֵין כַּרְמִי:
⁽⁴⁾מַה־לַּעֲשׂוֹת עוֹד לְכַרְמִי וְלֹא עָשִׂיתִי בּוֹ מַדּוּעַ קִוֵּיתִי לַעֲשׂוֹת
עֲנָבִים וַיַּעַשׂ בְּאֻשִׁים: ⁽⁵⁾וְעַתָּה אוֹדִיעָה־נָּא אֶתְכֶם אֵת אֲשֶׁר־
אֲנִי עֹשֶׂה לְכַרְמִי הָסֵר מְשׂוּכָּתוֹ וְהָיָה לְבָעֵר פָּרֹץ גְּדֵרוֹ וְהָיָה
לְמִרְמָס: ⁽⁶⁾וַאֲשִׁיתֵהוּ בָתָה לֹא יִזָּמֵר וְלֹא יֵעָדֵר וְעָלָה שָׁמִיר
וָשָׁיִת וְעַל הֶעָבִים אֲצַוֶּה מֵהַמְטִיר עָלָיו מָטָר: ⁽⁷⁾כִּי כֶרֶם
יהוה צְבָאוֹת בֵּית יִשְׂרָאֵל וְאִישׁ יְהוּדָה נְטַע שַׁעֲשׁוּעָיו וַיְקַו
לְמִשְׁפָּט וְהִנֵּה מִשְׂפָּח לִצְדָקָה וְהִנֵּה צְעָקָה:

Notes

1. אָשִׁירָה Qal impf. with cohortative ending. Cohortative
of entreaty or strong self-will. נָא is an enclitic particle: *I (we)
pray, now*. Hence, *let me sing, I pray*, or *I will sing now*.

יָדִיד adj. (poet.) *beloved*, const. יָדִיד, לִידִיד=לְיָדִיד.

שִׁירַת const. of שִׁירָה n. f. *song, ode*. Cognate accusative.

דּוֹד *beloved, friend, love;* from root דּוּד *rock, swing, fondle, love*.

שָׁמֶן pausal form for שֶׁמֶן (due to presence of silluḳ). Literal
rendering of the phrase: *on a horn, a son of fatness*. A Hebrew
idiom. A common construction for expressing a characteristic

or quality. Freely: *on a fatly nourished mountain horn* (i. e., Canaan).

2. יְעַזְּקֵהוּ Pi. impf. of עָזַק *dig: he digged it up thoroughly.*

סָקַל *stone, put to death by stoning;* Pi., *free from stones.*

יִטָּעֵהוּ Qal impf. of נָטַע. Verbs of planting, sowing, etc., take a double accusative.

שֹׂרֵק finest kind of eastern vine.

יִבֶן apocopated (shortened) form of imperfect. Full form: יִבְנֶה.

מִגְדָּל for adornment and protection.

וְגַם gives emphasis to what follows: *and also.* A wine-vat was hewn out of rock. This was a hard task. The performance of it indicated confident expectation.

וַיְקַו apocopated form: יְקַוֶּה (with ו consec.). From קָוָה *wait for* (orig. root prob. *twist, stretch;* idea of tension carried over to *wait for, endure*); intensive: *he waited diligently, expectantly.*

וַיַּעַשׂ apocopated form: יַעֲשֶׂה (with ו consec.). From עָשָׂה *do, make, produce, yield* (of grain, grapes, etc.).

בְּאֻשִׁים n. m. plu. *stinking, wild,* or *worthless grapes.* From בָּאַשׁ *have a bad smell, stink.*

The meaning of the song, which ends with verse 2, becomes evident: the vineyard, located in Canaan (the fatly nourished mountain horn), belonged to God; He digged it up, "stoned" it,

i. e., prepared it carefully, removing all obstructions, He then planted in it His choice group, the Hebrew people; He built a tower, hewed out a wine-vat, and waited expectantly for His people to bring forth fruit worthy of Him. Some have suggested that the tower represents Jerusalem, and the wine-vat, the Temple.

3. The prophet is here speaking. So closely is he identified with God that he speaks for God.

וְעַתָּה *and now.* Emphatic.

יוֹשֵׁב and אִישׁ are used in a collective sense.

4. *What more could I have done to my vineyard that I . . . . . .?*

לַעֲשׂוֹת the inf. const. with the prep. לְ is sometimes used to express possibility and is best translated by *can* or *could.*

מַדּוּעַ seeks for actual cause: *why, wherefore?*

5. The Lord of the vineyard speaks. *And now!* A tense moment.

אוֹדִיעָה Hi. cohortative of יָדַע.

עָשָׂה use of participle for vividness. Subject precedes.

הָסֵר probably Hi. inf. abs. from סוּר. הָסֵר and פָּרֹץ carry the bare ideas of the verbs. They are to be translated as imperfects or imperatives. (Harper's Syntax, p. 88.)

גָּדֵר a low, stone wall. *For trampling,* i. e., an open way for man and beast.

6. אֲשִׁיתֵהוּ Qal or Hi. impf. of שִׁית, *put, set, make.*

בָּתָה or בַּתָּה n. f. *Something cut off, ruin, desolation.*

מֵהַמְטִיר Hi. inf. const. with prep. מִן, from מטר.

7. The husk of the parable falls off. The heart of it is laid bare.

the planting of His delight—Judah was the seat of the Davidic dynasty.

Observe the play of words: צְדָקָה and צְעָקָה; מִשְׁפָּט and מִשְׂפָּח. מִשְׂפָּח derived (according to B.D.B.) from סָפַח, *pour out;* hence *bloodshed* (opposite of מִשְׁפָּט).

THE SYNTAX OF THE VERB

(These lessons on Syntax may be used as the teacher chooses.
The author has found it best to give them during
the second year of study).

SYNTAX OF HEBREW VERBS

Syntax (Lat. *syntaxis*, Grk. σύνταξις, from συντάσσειν, *to put together in order*) is "connected system or order." In reference to language, it means the due arrangement of words in sentences and their agreement.

The syntax of Hebrew verbs appears to depend upon three things: 1. the state of the verb; 2. the time indicated by the context; 3. the mood indicated by the verb and the context.

Clear interpretation of these points of syntax is essential to clear, distinctive translation. First of all, therefore, the broad fundamental facts concerning these points will be treated with a view to showing the way to distinctive translations. Afterwards the more varied developments will be treated.

I. STATE

State, as used in this discussion of distinctive translations, means condition of action, mind, body, or event. Let this use of the word "state" be carefully observed. Later it will be necessary to distinguish certain actions and states, setting them in contrast with each other, as in the comparison of stative and active verbs. Here the word "state" is much broader. It applies to the kind of condition indicated by any verb, active or stative, and describes it as complete, incomplete, continuous or imperative. In this connection, complete means finished or established; incomplete means not finished and so in beginning,

121

or not established and so subject to interruptions and repetitions; continuous means without interruption; imperative means commanded.

Obviously the state of a verb may be learned from its grammatical form. Perfects indicate completed states; imperfects, incomplete states; imperatives, imperative states; and participles, continuous states.

It needs to be remembered that those participial forms referred to here are the ones which serve as verbs. Many participial forms become nouns. They are to be treated as nouns.

Infinitives are not mentioned because they are never really verbs. They develop as verb forms and partake of certain verbal characteristics, but their true nature is nominal or adverbial. They will be treated later as nouns and adverbs.

II. TIME

Time, as used here, is that which distinguishes the state of the verb as before, now, or after.

The time of a Hebrew verb must be judged in the light of its context. There are no obvious markers in grammatical formation or syntactical arrangement. The reader must view the context as a whole, no matter whether it be a sentence, a paragraph, a passage, a book, or a sphere of knowledge, and discern the time that fits.

A time which is not related to another time, i. e. not indicated as coming before or after another time, will be designated by a single or simple name as a past, a present, or a future.

In beginning God created (a past) *the heavens and the earth,* Gen. 1:1.

The voice of thy brother's blood is crying (a present) *unto me,* Gen. 4:10.

And from thy face I shall be hid (a future) . . ., Gen. 4:14.

A time which is related to another time will be designated by a compound name, as previous-present or subsequent-past. Note that both parts of these names indicate time. Names like present perfect and future perfect are not used in the designation of time, because they mix the idea of state with that of time. It is desired that each point of syntax be judged separately.

A *previous past* is a time which was previous to another past time.

And he rested (a past) *on the seventh day from all his work which he had made* (a previous-past), Gen. 2:2.

A *previous present* is a present time which is previous to another present time.

Ah, sinful nation . . . children that deal corruptly! (a present) *They have forsaken* (a previous-present) *Yahweh,* Isa. 1:4.

A *previous future* is a future time which is thought of as previous to another future time.

Go (a future), *for Yahweh will have sent* (a previous-future) *thee,* I Samuel 20:22.

A *subsequent past* is a past time which was subsequent to another past time.

Then a breach was made (a past time) *in the city, and all the men of war proceeded to flee* (a subsequent-past) . . ., Jer. 52:7.

A *subsequent present* is a present time which is subsequent to another present time.

Lo, you see (a present) *the man is mad; wherefore then do you proceed to bring* (a subsequent present) *him to me,* I Sam. 21:15.

A *subsequent future* is a future time which will be subsequent to another future time.

And what will ye do (a future) *for the day of visitation* . . . . *Without me they shall bow down* (a future) *under the prisoners, and under the slain they shall proceed to fall* (a subsequent-future), Isa. 10:3,4.

III. MOOD

Mood originally meant mind, feeling, or heart. It is used now to describe one's spirit, attitude, or temper. In grammar it describes the subject's manner of feeling or thinking concerning the state of the verb.

The mood is indicative when the state is thought of as a fact, subjunctive when it is considered conditional or dependent, cohortative or jussive when one desires to urge the doing or the acceptance of it, imperative when one intends to command the doing or acceptance of it.

The **indicative** mood is indicated merely by the fact that the context calls for an affirmation. There is no special form of the verb to indicate it. However, it is helpful to note that the absence of those circumstances which mark the other moods is evidence that a verb is in the indicative.

The **subjunctive** mood is called for by the presence of a conditional idea. Subjunctive means sub-joined, dependent, conditional. When the context does not deal with a matter as an established fact but merely as possible, or desirable, or obligatory, we have a subjunctive mood.

The condition upon which the possibility, desirability or responsibility depends may be stated or merely understood. One may say, "I should go, because I am expected;" or, merely, "I should go," taking for granted that the reason for this responsibility is understood in view of the situation. The reader is expected to observe the occasion for a subjunctive idea in the context, no matter whether the condition be stated or not. It is not indicated by the verb form but by the context. It is helpful to note that almost all subjunctives are imperfects and apply to future time.

The **cohortative** and the **jussive** belong to the same mood. Both express desire, urgency, a sort of optative mood. Both appear with forms of the imperfect, the cohortative regularly with forms in the first person, and the jussive regularly with forms in the second or third person.

The cohortative is indicated by the addition of הֽ‎־ to the verb form.

Let me go, I pray thee, and return אֵלְכָה־נָּא וְאָשׁוּבָה, Ex. 4:18.

The jussive is indicated sometimes by the use of the negative particle אַל, sometimes by a vowel change, and sometimes by the context alone.

When the jussive idea is negative, אַל is used instead of the emphatic לֹא. Thus אַל with an imperfect practically always indicates a jussive.

. . . *Do not draw near* אַל־תִּקְרְבוּ *unto it* . . ., Josh. 3:4.

The vowel changes which occur in the jussive appear to be due to an added stress in pronunciation which the urgency of the mood produces. Such changes help to call attention to a jussive. However, the context must be considered. Similar changes occur under other conditions, and the context must also be considered in order to determine whether or not a plea is expressed.

And all the people said, Let live יְחִי *King Solomon*, I Kings 1:39. יְחִי appears here in place of יִחְיָה.

And whatsoever of thine is with thy brother let thy hand release תַּשְׁמֵט (it), Deut. 15:3. תַּשְׁמֵט appears here in place of תַּשְׁמִיט.

Whenever a jussive occurs with the context only to indicate that it is a jussive, the context shows with reasonable clearness that a plea is called for rather than a statement or a command.

And now, O God of Israel, let be confirmed יֵאָמֶן *I pray, thy words* . . . I Kings 8:26.

יֵאָמֶן in certain contexts should be translated "Will be confirmed." Here it is part of a prayer. The attitude of prayer calls for the jussive force.

The imperative is sometimes indicated by its own special form, sometimes by the use of an imperfect in the second person with לֹא, and sometimes by the context alone.

The special form of the imperative is used to express positive commands only.

Honor כַּבֵּד *thy father and thy mother*, Ex. 20: 12.

The imperfect in the second person with לֹא is used to express prohibitions.

Thou shalt not do לֹא־תַעֲשֶׂה *any work*, Ex. 20:10.

The imperfect in the second person may also be used to express a positive command. In such a case the context alone is relied upon to indicate the imperative idea.

Six days shalt thou labor תַּעֲבֹד, Ex. 20:9.

This word comes in the midst of the commandments, and a reader senses the fact immediately that God is commanding His people as to what to do in order to get ready for the Sabbath, not merely urging them to do it or making a statement as to what they will do.

IV. TYPES OF TRANSLATION

When the three foregoing points of syntax have been determined, their combination furnishes a guide to the translation. In existing translations there is a lack of uniformity in the handling of these points that causes a serious loss of clarity and vividness. Many have concluded that uniformity in the determination and translation of these points is impossible. Nevertheless, the present suggestions concerning them grow out of a belief that the Hebrew authors did work upon uniform principles in their use of them and that an attempt to regain the force of the original is worth the best of our efforts.

The table that follows suggests a distinctive translation for each. Only active verbs are used. However, the parallels for stative verbs may be worked out easily. These distinctive translations seek to express the essential idea in each combination in such a way that it may be clearly distinguished from all others. The manner of the distinctive translations cannot be rigidly emulated in every translation, but the essential idea can be maintained.

The examples given in the detailed treatments that follow are intended to demonstrate the possibility of maintaining the essential idea amid all the variations of translation. The wording of existing translations, preferably the American Revised, is used wherever it appears to be true to the essential idea, but a new wording is offered where existing translations seem to fail in making that idea clear. With each group of illustrations the combination of syntactical points is indicated so that comparison with the table of distinctive translations may be made.

A Table of Distinctive Translations for Hebrew Verbs

	State	Time	Mood	Translation
1.	Complete	Past	Indic.	*Killed.*
2.	Complete	Present	Indic.	*Kills.*
3.	Complete	Future	Indic.	*Shall kill.*
4.	Complete	Previous Past	Indic.	*Had killed.*
5.	Complete	Previous Pres.	Indic.	*Has killed.*
6.	Complete	Previous Fut.	Indic.	*Will have killed.* *Shall have killed.*
7.	Incomplete	Past	Indic.	*Repeatedly killed.*
8.	Incomplete	Present	Indic.	*Repeatedly kills.*
9.	Incomplete	Future	Indic.	*Will repeatedly kill.*
10.	Incomplete	Subseq't Past	Indic.	*Began to kill.* *Proceeded to kill.*
11.	Incomplete	Subseq't Pres.	Indic.	*Begins to kill.* *Proceeds to kill.*
12.	Incomplete	Subseq't Fut.	Indic.	*Will begin to kill.* *Will proceed to kill.*
13.	Continuous	Past	Indic.	*Was killing.*
14.	Continuous	Present	Indic.	*Is killing.*
15.	Continuous	Future	Indic.	*Will be killing.*
16.	Incomplete	Future	Subj.	*Could kill.* *Would kill.* *Should kill.*
17.	Complete	Previous Fut.	Subj.	*Could have killed.* *Would have killed.* *Should have killed.*
18.	Incomplete	Future	Cohor.	*Will kill.* *Let kill.*
19.	Incomplete	Future	Juss.	*Let kill.* *Do kill.*
20.	Incomplete	Future	Imper.	*Shalt kill.*
21.	Imperative	Future	Imper.	*Kill.*

THE INDICATIVE PERFECTS

A perfect designates an action or state as **completed** either in reality or in the thought of the speaker. It may represent its condition in the past, present or future. In any case the condition must be conceived of as **finished** or **completed**. The perfect always looks back upon a condition as belonging to the past just as the imperfect looks forward to it.

I. **A Simple Action** (.) (Greek Aorist). The perfect of narration denotes an action or state completed at a specific moment or period as indicated by the context.

There is no reference to any other event.

1. Past time (narration) (combination 1).

   God created בָּרָא *the heavens.* Gen. 1:1.

   To the woman he said אָמַר. Gen. 3:16.

   God proved נִסָּה *Abram.* Gen. 22:1.

   He sent שָׁלַח *letters.* Isa. 39:1

2. Present time (perfect of the immediate past) (English present) (combination 2).

   And him I appoint צִוִּיתִי *to be a prince.* I Kgs. 1:35.

   And now I send שָׁלַחְתִּי *a wise man.* II Chr. 2:12.

   I lift up הֲרִמֹתִי *my hand to Yahweh.* Gen. 14:22.

   (Deut. 26:3; Isa. 8:11; "*Thus says Yahweh.*")

3. Future time (considered completed because already determined or prophesied) (combination 3).

   Note, therefore, that the auxiliary verb used in each translation, the *will* or the *shall*, is the reverse of the one ordinarily used. Inasmuch as *will*, with the second and third persons, expresses mere futurity, the use of *shall* indicates the determination or prophecy. As *shall* with the first person indicates mere futurity, the use of *will* indicates the determination or prophecy.

a. **Perfect of Certainty** — The speaker is certain of the outcome or he has fully determined to make certain actions occur. This use is common in promises, decrees, threats, where the fulfilment is so certain that it is conceived as a completed act.

> *To thy seed I will give* נָתַתִּי *this land*. Gen. 15:18.
> *I know that Yahweh will save* הוֹשִׁיעַ. Ps. 20:7.
> *The field I will give to thee* נָתַתִּי. Gen. 23:11.
> (Ruth 4:3; Gen. 30:13; Num. 17:27; I Kgs. 3:13.)

b. The **prophetic perfect** portrays vividly and boldly a confidence that the speaker has in the certain fulfilment of a prediction. This use is found in the highest type of prophetic diction. It often is thrown into the midst of imperfects to indicate absolute confidence.

> *A child shall be born* יֻלַּד *to us*. Isa. 9:5.
> *A star shall proceed* דָּרַךְ *from Jacob*. Num. 24:17.
> *The people . . . shall see* רָאוּ *a great light*. Isa. 9:1.
> *It shall overflow* שָׁטַף. Isa. 8:8.
> (Isa. 5:13; 10:28; 11:8, 9; 28:2; Hos. 4:6; Amos 5:2.)

II. **A Simple Act completed** at a time previous to another act or state, thus resulting in a state of completion (cf. Greek Perfect) (•——).

1. Past time (**Pluperfect**)—The action is conceived of as finished prior to a point of time referred to in the past. (combination 4).

   And he put there the man whom he had formed יָצָר. Gen. 2:8.

   For he had not eaten אָכַל *bread.* I Sam. 28:20.

   And he rested . . . from all the work he had done. עָשָׂה. Gen. 2:2.

   (Gen. 2:5; 2:22; 18:8; 28:11; Isa. 6:6; I Kgs. 5:15.)

2. Present time (**Greek Perfect**)—The action is pictured as completed at some specific moment in the past but continues in its effects into the present (combination 5).

   They have forsaken עָזְבוּ *Yahweh.* Isa. 1:4.

   Who have set themselves שָׁתוּ *against me.* Ps. 3:7.

   He has hidden הִסְתִּיר *his face.* Ps. 10:11.

   (Gen. 32:11; Ps. 48:4; I Sam. 12:3; 14:29.)

3. Future time (**Future Perfect**)—Here we find finished action viewed in relation to another action still in the future (combination 6).

   Yahweh will have gone forth יָצָא. II Sam. 5:24.

   Yahweh will have given them נְתָנָם *into our hand.* I Sam. 14:10.

   Yahweh will have sent thee away שְׁלָחֲךָ. I Sam. 20:22.

   (Gen. 48:6; Mic. 5:2; Ruth 2:21; Isa. 4:4; 6:11.)

III. An action extended into a **state** (•–•–•–•–•).

1. State of **Specific Activity** (combination 1).

   He reigned מָלַךְ *three years.* I Kgs. 15:2.

They were fruitful פָּרוּ *and multiplied.* Ex. 1:7.

Twelve years they served עָבְדוּ. Gen. 14:4.

(Gen. 13:12; Ps. 45:10.)

2. **Perfect of experience (Gnomic Aorist).** The statement is
considered true because things of the same kind have
already happened. The author is certain that such prop-
ositions of a general character will hold good generally
(combination 2).

The cloud dissolves and goes כָּלָה וַיֵּלַךְ. Job 7:9.

An ox knows יָדַע *his master.* Isa. 1:3.

Grass withers יָבֵשׁ *flower fades* נָבֵל. Isa. **40:7.**

(Jer. 8:7; Ps. 7:16.)

IV. **A State** (——) (no real action).

1. **A mental or emotional state.** Stative verbs express a
physical or mental state or condition; see verbs to *know,
trust, rejoice, refuse, hate, love,* etc. (combination 2).

We remember זָכַרְנוּ *the fish.* Num. 11:5.

I love אָהַבְתִּי. Gen. 27:4.

I know יָדַעְתִּי *not the day of my death.* Gen. 27:2.

(Gen. 32:11; Jud. 14:16; Ex. 10:3.)

2. **A pure state of being;** see verbs meaning to *be righteous,
high, beautiful, old, weary, full, great, honorable,* etc.

I am old זָקַנְתִּי. Gen. 27:2.

I am little קָטֹנְתִּי. Gen. 32:11.

(Gen. 18:13; Isa. 1:11; 52:7; 55:9; Ps. 6:7.)

THE INDICATIVE IMPERFECTS

Action represented by the imperfect is unfinished whether in the past, present or future. The action is presented in movement rather than "in a condition of rest." It may be (1) repeated (**frequentative**), (2) just beginning (**incipient**), or (3) in a state of continuation (**progressive** or **adjectival**). It does not imply mere continuance. The participle is used to picture the uninterrupted action while the imperfect points to an action as beginning or recurring repeatedly.

> *A river was proceeding* יֹצֵא *out of the garden.* Gen. 2:10. (Participle)
>
> *A mist used to go up* יַעֲלֶה, Gen 2:6. (Imperfect)

I.   An action repeated (• • • •). The **frequentative** imperfect is used to describe reiterated actions, habits, customs or universal truths.

1. Past time (combination 7).

> *And a mist used to go up* יַעֲלֶה. Gen. 2:6.
> *Thus did Job continually* יַעֲשֶׂה. Job 1:5.
> *And so he did* יַעֲשֶׂה *year by year.* I Sam. 1:7.
> (Jud. 14:10; 21:25; II Sam. 1:22.)

2. Present time (combination 8).

   a. Facts that are accustomed to occur often in certain limits. (**Definite frequentative**)

> *Those who fear Yahweh he honors* יְכַבֵּד. Ps. 15:4.

   b. Truths universally admitted and facts that may occur at any time. (**Indefinite frequentative**)

Man looks upon . . . but Yahweh looks יִרְאָה *on the heart.* I Sam. 16:7.

3. Future time (combination 9).
He will be יְהִיָה *to thee for a mouth.* Ex. 4:16.
I shall draw water אֶשְׁאָב *for thy camel.* Gen. 24:19.
The children that will be born יִוָּלֵדוּ. Ps. 78:6.

II. An action begun at a time subsequent to that of another act or state, the **incipient** imperfect.

1. Past time (**Historical present**). The action is pictured as beginning or in movement. Used for vividness and color in poetry and prose (combination 10).
Then Moses proceeded to sing יָשִׁיר. Ex. 15:1.
Perish the day on which I was born אִוָּלֵד. Job 3:3.
I proceeded to bring you up אַעֲלֶה *out of Egypt.* Jud. 2:1.

2. Present time. For force and vividness the action is pictured as taking place while words are spoken (combination 11).
Kings of the earth begin to set themselves יִתְיַצְבוּ. Ps. 2:2.
The day has turned (pf.) *and the shadows of evening begin to lengthen* יִנָּטוּ. Jer. 6:4.
(Jud. 17:9; Num. 24:17; Hab. 3:9.)

3. Future time (combination 12).
I know (pf.) *that thou wilt surely proceed to be king* תִּמְלֹךְ. I Sam. 24:20.
Ye will henceforth be swept away תִּסָּפוּ. I Sam. 12:25.

Because the Egyptians will proceed to see יְרְאוּ *thee.*
Gen. 12:12.
(Gen. 16:12; 49:1; Ex. 6:1; 9:5.)

III. An action extended into a **state** (•–•–•–•), the **progressive** imperfect.

1. Past time (combination 7).
   And just as they continued to afflict them so they continued to multiply יִרְבֶּה. Ex. 1:12.

2. Present time (combination 8).
   As a lamp that burneth יִבְעָר. Isa. 62:1 (יִבְעָר).
   Afraid of a man that dies יָמוּת. Isa. 51:12.

3. Future time (combination 9).
   I will maintain אוֹכִיחַ *my ways.* Job 13:15.

IV. A **state** (——), the **adjectival** imperfect expressing a physical or mental state or a pure state of being. (No real action). See verbs to *know, trust, rejoice, refuse, hate, love, be high, be righteous, be full, be small, be old, be beautiful,* etc. (combinations 7, 8, 9).
   Benjamin is a wolf which ravens יִטְרָף. Gen. 49:27 (יִטְרֹף).

NOTE THE FOLLOWING: When the reference to time is single, only one action or state being involved, all perfects represent simple conditions, all imperfects repeated ones; when the reference to time is double, two actions or states being involved, all perfects represent previous conditions, all imperfects subsequent ones.

THE PARTICIPLES

Where stress is to be laid on the continuance of the action described the participle is always used. Its descriptive power is great. As a noun it does not involve any idea of time. As a verb its time is to be discerned from the context as that of any other verb. נָפַל may mean *falling* (Num. 24:4), *fallen* (Jud. 4:22) or *about to fall* (Jer. 37:14). The subject is presented in the continuous exercise of the action denoted by the verb. In the case of the passive participle the subject is presented as having the action continuously exercised upon him. The imperfect represented by a series of dots (. . . . . . .), multiplies an action, while the participle, represented by a line, (———), prolongs the action. One is **continual**, the other **continuous**.

Seraphim were standing עֹמְדִים *. . . with two he covered* יְכַסֶּה *his face.* Isa. 6:2.

I.   The **verbal** participles are all indicatives.

1. In its verbal use it may serve (a) to describe actions or (b) to emphasize the duration of a given state in the past. In reality it takes us back to the event and seeks to help us see the figures moving in the background. (combination 13).
   We were binding sheaves אֲנַחְנוּ מְאַלְּמִים. Gen. 37:7.
   They were going up הֵם עֹלִים.
   The sea was going הוֹלֵךְ *and storming* וְסֹעֵר. Jon. 1:11.

2. It may pull aside a screen and let us see what is going on at the present moment.   (combination 14).

Thy brother's blood is crying out צֹעֲקִים *unto me.* Gen. 4:10

From Sarai . . . I am fleeing בֹּרַחַת. Gen. 16:8.
Strangers are devouring אֹכְלִים *your land.* Isa. 1:7.
I am teaching you מְלַמֵּד. Deut. 4:1.

3. It may picture for us that which is about to happen. The action is represented as already under way. (combination 15).

Sarah will be bearing יֹלֶדֶת *a son.* Gen. 17:19.
We are about to destroy מַשְׁחִתִים *this place.* Gen. 19:13.
Behold I am bringing הִנְנִי מֵבִיא. Gen. 6:17.

NOTES

1. The subject usually precedes the participle.

2. When the subject is a pronoun it must be expressed.
Tomorrow thou shalt be slain אַתָּה מוּמָת. I Sam. 19:11.

3. The Niph'al participle has the sense of the Latin gerundive. נוֹרָא *to be feared,* נֶחְמָד *desirable,* נִכְבָּד *honorable.*

4. Some forms of the verb הָיָה are used with the active participle to form progressive tenses. The idea of duration is thus brought into fuller prominence.
Moses was keeping הָיָה רֹעֶה *the flock.* Ex. 3:1.
And let it be (permanently) *dividing* מַבְדִּיל. Gen. 1:6.

5. The negative used with the participle is usually אֵין. (It may be לֹא when attributive).

6. It may express the jussive sense.

Cursed be thou אָרוּר אַתָּה. Gen. 3:14.

II. The participle is construed as *a noun* in many cases and may be either the subject, predicate or object of the sentence.

Saviour מוֹשִׁיעַ, *friend (one loving)* אֹהֵב, *enemy* אֹיֵב, *seer (one seeing)* חֹזֶה, *shepherd (one feeding)* רֹעֶה.

In apposition with a noun it may be used as an adjective. *A devouring fire* אֵשׁ אֹכֶלֶת. Ex. 24:17 (Cf. Isa. 29:6).

When the participle has the article it takes on a new emphasis and must be rendered as a relative clause.

Yahweh who had appeared (or, *the one appearing*) הַנִּרְאָה *unto him.* Gen. 12:7.

His hand, the one stretched out הַנְּטוּיָה. Isa. 14:27.

THE SUBJUNCTIVE IMPERFECTS

The conditional ideas of the subjunctive mood are naturally expressed by imperfects. Except in rare instances, and then only in conditional sentences, imperfects are always used. Moreover, all subjunctives are in future time. The variations of translations, therefore, are indicated entirely by the nature of the contingency revealed in the context, i. e., whether it is a possibility, a desirability or a responsibility. (Combination 16).

1. **Possibility** is frequently expressed by the **auxiliary** *could. Can, may* and *might* are also used often.

If a man could be able יוּכַל *to number the dust of the*

earth, also thy seed could be numbered יִמָּנֶה. Gen. 13:16.

That it may be well יִיטַב with thee. Gen. 12:13.

Though your sins be as scarlet they may be white יַלְבִּינוּ as snow. Isa. 1:18.

Who may ascend יַעֲלֶה into thy holy hill. Ps. 24:3.

2. **Desirability** is frequently expressed by *would*. Each of these suggested auxiliaries, however, is subject to variations.

   If thou wouldst give me תִּתֶּן *half thy house, I would not go in* אָבֹא *with thee.* I Kgs. 13:8.

3. **Responsibility** is frequently expressed by *should*. This idea, however, has such variations as obligation and necessity; so *ought*, *must* and similar expressions are used.

   Who am I that I should go אֵלֵךְ *unto Pharaoh.* Ex. 3:11.
   But thou shouldst rule תִּמְשָׁל *over him.* Gen. 4:7.
   To know what Israel ought to do יַעֲשֶׂה. I Ch. 12:32.

THE SUBJUNCTIVE PERFECTS

In conditional sentences, the protasis sometimes states a condition which creates a responsibility, obligation or necessity so fixed that it is looked upon as inescapable. Then the apodosis uses a perfect to express the inescapable nature of that responsibility, obligation or necessity, though its mood be subjunctive and its time future. (Combination 17).

If you had kept them alive I should not kill הָרַגְתִּי *you.* Jud. 8:19.
Except Jehovah of hosts had left us a very small remnant, as Sodom we should become הָיִינוּ. Isa. 1:9.

THE COHORTATIVE, JUSSIVE, AND IMPERATIVE

In Hebrew just as in Arabic, there are two modified forms of the imperfect to give expression to desire on the part of the speaker. (Cf. Arabic, *Energic* and *Jussive*). The cohortative used in the **first** person, expresses the intention, will or desire of the author when he is the subject of the action, while the jussive, used in the **second** and **third** persons, expresses the desire, will or command of the author when some other person is the subject of the action.

I.   The **cohortative** expresses the will of the speaker in reference to his own actions. (Cf. Isa. 15:19; Deut. 33:16 and Ps. 20:4 for instances of its use in third person). When the speaker is free it expresses his **desire** or **determination.** When he is dependent upon others it expresses a **wish** or **request.** The form may be made more emphatic by the addition of the particle נָא.

The cohortative may express: (combination 18).

1. A strong **determination**—"*I will.*"
   I will eat אֹכְלָה *flesh.* Deut. 12:20.
   I will set אָשִׂימָה *a king over me.* Deut. 17:14.

2. An **exhortation** (in plural).
   Let us return נָשׁוּבָה *to Egypt.* Num. 14:4.

3. **A self-excitement.**

   Let us break asunder נְנַתְּקָה. Ps. 2:3.

4. **A request** or **entreaty.**

   Let me go up, I pray אֶעֱלֶה־נָּא. Gen. 50:5.

   Let me pass through אֶעְבְּרָה *thy land*. Num. 21:22.

5. **A simple consent** (yielding to constraint).

   Now let me die אָמוּתָה. Gen 46:30.

6. **A conditional** or final sentence.

   Ask of me and I will give וְאֶתְּנָה. Ps 2:8. (cf. use of co-hortative in imperative.)

II. The **jussive** is used in the second and third persons to express: (combination 19).

1. **A command** or **injunction** or **prohibition.**

   Let there be יְהִי *light*. Gen. 1:3.

   Let multiply יִרֶב (יִרְבֶּה). Gen. 1:22.

   Do not listen אַל־תִּשְׁמַע.

2. **A wish.**

   Let Yahweh establish יָקֶם *his word*. I Sam. 1:23.

3. **Permission.**

   Let him go up יַעַל *and build* וְיִבֶן. Ezra 1:3.

4. **Advice** or **suggestion.**

   Let Pharoah look out יֵרֶא *a man*. Gen. 41:33.

5. **A petition** or **entreaty** or **prayer.**

   Let thy servant remain, I pray יֵשֶׁב־נָא. Gen. 44:33.

   Let Yahweh watch יִצֶף *between me and thee*. Gen. 31:49.

6. **Conditional clauses** in the apodosis and the protasis. (cf. Arabic usage.)

III. The **imperfect** may also be used as an **imperative,** either in positive commands or prohibitions. (combination 20).

Six days thou shalt serve תַּעֲבֹד. Ex. 20:9.

Thou shalt not murder לֹא תִּרְצָח. Ex. 20:13.

Upon thy belly thou shalt go תֵלֵךְ. Gen. 3:14.

The following distinctions between prohibitions expressed by the imperfect and prohibitions expressed by the jussive are very helpful. "In prohibition, (1) in the second person, the ordinary imperfect takes לֹא and means *thou shalt not*, the jussive takes אַל and means *do not;* (2) in the third person, the ordinary imperfect takes לֹא and means *he shall not*, the jussive takes אַל and means *let him not.*"

IV. **Positive commands** are also expressed by the special imperative form but it never takes a negative. The force of this imperative appears to be practically the same as that of the imperative imperfect. The imperative imperfect may be more polite in certain situations, but the two are often interchanged for no apparent reason other than variety. This one is always used with the second person, and may express: (combination 21).

1. A **command.**

Speak דַּבֵּר *unto the children of Israel.* Lev. 1:2.

Fill מַלֵּא *the men's sacks.* Gen. 44:1.

Arise קוּם *go* לֵךְ *unto Nineveh.* Jonah 1:2.

2. An **exhortation.**

Break up נִירוּ your fallow ground for it is time to seek Yahweh. Hos. 10:12.

3. An **entreaty.**

Deliver me הַצִּילֵנִי. Ps. 31:3.

Arise קוּמָה and save us. Ps. 44:27.

4. **Permission.**

Where it is good in thine eyes, dwell שֵׁב. Gen. 20:15.

And he said unto him, run רוּץ. II Sam. 18:23.

5. **Strong assurances** (either promises or threats).

Thou shalt see רְאֵה the prosperity of Jerusalem. Ps. 128:5.

Cry aloud צַהֲלִי with thy voice. Isa. 10:30.

Occasionally a cohortative ה is added to an imperative. *Restore* הָשִׁיבָה *unto me the joy of thy salvation.* Ps. 51:14. The addition of the cohortative idea emphasizes the earnestness of the command, indicating that the author not merely calls for the fulfilment but also earnestly desires it. We might translate here after this fashion: *Restore — please! — unto me the joy of thy salvation.*

THE INFINITIVES

I.   The **Infinitive absolute,** an abstract verbal noun, is used to express the bare idea of the verbal action, or along with the inflected form to give emphasis to the expression of the action, or it may stand alone, almost with the force of an exclamation.

1. It may stand **instead of the finite verb** to express vividly and emphatically the essential idea of the verb.

   Behold! slaying הָרֹג *oxen! and killing* וְשָׁחֹט *sheep! eating* אָכֹל *flesh! and drinking* וְשָׁתוֹת *wine!* Isa. 22:13. *Remembering* זָכוֹר *the Sabbath day, six days thou shalt work.* Ex. 20:8, 9.

   Disguising הִתְחַפֵּשׂ *and coming* וָבֹא *into battle (will it be for me).* I Kgs. 22:30.

   Thus said Yahweh, eating אָכוֹל *and leaving over* וְהוֹתֵר *(shall it be).* II Kgs. 4:43.

   He did so walking הָלֹךְ *naked and barefoot.* Isa. 20:2.

2. It may stand **with the finite verb** to add emphasis or to describe the action of the preceding verb. Standing before the verb it adds an expression of intensity.

   He urgently besought me נִשְׁאֹל נִשְׁאַל. I Sam. 20:6.
   Thou shalt surely die מוֹת תָּמוּת. Gen. 2:17.
   The ox will certainly be stoned סָקוֹל יִסָּקֵל. Ex. 21:28.
   Wilt thou indeed rule over us? הֲמָלֹךְ תִּמְלֹךְ. Gen. 37:8.

3. **Constant progress** or complete existence of the action may be expressed by the use of the infinitive absolute following the main verb.

   He is gone (quite gone) (וַיֵּלֶךְ) הָלַךְ הָלוֹךְ. II Sam. 3:24.
   He went repeatedly out and in וַיֵּצֵא יָצוֹא וָשׁוֹב. Gen. 8:7.
   He went on, weeping וַיֵּלֶךְ הָלוֹךְ וּבָכֹה. II Sam. 3:16.
   And he gradually became greater and greater וַיֵּלֶךְ הָלוֹךְ וְגָדוֹל. I Chr. 11:9.

4. Some absolute infinitives (chiefly Hiph'il) have come to be construed as **adverbs**.

To walk humbly הַצְנֵעַ לֶכֶת. Mic. 6:8.

More הוֹתֵר. *Quickly* מַהֵר.

Diligently הַשְׁכֵּם (*to rise early*).

Much הַרְבֵּה. *Far* הַרְחֵק.

II. The **infinitive construct** as a verbal substantive is used like a gerund, taking suffixes and prepositions, and also has the government of its verb. It does not take the article.

1. **Standing alone** it may be:

(1) The **subject** of a nominal sentence.

Man's being alone is not good הֱיוֹת. Gen. 2:18.

Is wearying men too little for you? הַלְאוֹת. Isa. 7:13.

(2) In the **genitive**.

In the day of Yahweh's making עֲשׂוֹת. Gen. 2:4.

(3) In the **accusative** as object of the verb.

I know not to go out or come in צֵאת וָבֹא. I Kgs. 3:7.

2. With the preposition לְ the infinitive may express.

(1) **Design** or **purpose**.

He went up to worship לְהִשְׁתַּחֲוֹת *and to sacrifice* וְלִזְבֹּחַ. I Sam. 1:3.

(2) The **result**.

Thou shalt keep the charge of Yahweh so as to walk לָלֶכֶת *in his ways, to keep* לִשְׁמֹר *his statutes*. I Kgs. 2:3f.

(3) The **time of an action.**

   At Joab's sending לִשְׁלֹחַ *(when Joab sent).* II Sam. 18:29.

(4) A **periphrastic future.**

   The sun was about to set לָבוֹא. Gen. 15:12.

   Yahweh is (ready) to save me לְהוֹשִׁיעֵנִי. Isa. 38:20.

(5) A **gerundive** *(must, ought, is to be).*

   What is to be done לַעֲשׂוֹת *for thee?* II Kgs. 4:13.

The **negative infinitive** is formed by the use of the particle בִּלְתִּי with לְ.

I command thee not to eat לְבִלְתִּי אֲכָל־ *from it.* Gen. 3:11.

With the periphrastic or gerundive we usually find לֹא לְ or אֵין לְ.

The name of Yahweh must not be mentioned לֹא לְהַזְכִּיר. Amos 6:10.

WAW CONSECUTIVE WITH THE IMPERFECT

The primary forms, perfect and imperfect, are supplemented in Hebrew by two secondary forms made by prefixing the conjunction *waw* to the verb. When prefixed to a perfect it is to be translated as an imperfect. Joined to an imperfect it is to be translated as a perfect. A sentence begins with an ordinary perfect and is followed by one or more verbs in the imperfect with *waw* consecutive. This is the historical or narrative tense.

He found מָצָא *the place and lay down* וַיִּשְׁכַּב.

A sentence begins with the imperfect and is followed by one or more perfects with *waw* consecutive.

He will find יִמְצָא *the place and will lie down* וְשָׁכַב.

These verbs with *waw* consecutive are used in narration or prediction to carry forward the same idea as the first verb indicates.

The imperfect with *waw* continues the narrative in a connective way.

The serpent deceived me הִשִּׁיאַנִי *and I ate* וָאֹכֵל. Gen. 3:13.

He had not respect לֹא שָׁעָה *and Cain was angry* וַיִּחַר. Gen. 4:5.

Thou hast hearkened שָׁמַעְתָּ *to the voice and hast eaten* וַתֹּאכַל. Gen. 3:17.

He heard that he had been sick חָלָה *and was better* וַיֶּחֱזָק. Isa. 39:1.

It may continue a perfect of experience, a prophetic perfect, a participle, an infinitive or another imperfect with *waw*.

He blows נָשַׁף *upon them and they wither* וַיִּבָשׁוּ. Isa. 40:24.

A son shall be given נִתַּן *to us and shall be* וַתְּהִי . . . *and he shall call* וַיִּקְרָא. Isa. 9:5. (Prophetic perfect followed by imperfects with same meaning).

When I lifted up כַּהֲרִימִי *my voice and cried* וָאֶקְרָא. Gen. 39:18.

And Balaam arose וַיָּקָם *and saddled* וַיַּחֲבֹשׁ *and went* וַיֵּלֶךְ *and the anger of God was kindled* וַיִּחַר. Num. 22:21f.

NOTES

1. The *waw* is prefixed with ־ַ and daghesh-forte. Before א it takes ־ָ without the daghesh-forte.

וָאֶקְרָא, וַיִּקְרָא (cf. pointing of the article).

2. The tone is usually retracted from the last syllable to the penult, when the syllable is open.

וַתֵּלֶךְ, וַיֹּאמֶר.

3. Whenever possible the form is shortened.

וַיֵּד, וַיַּרְא, וַיִּבֶן, וַיִּקְטֵל.

4. *Waw* consecutive practically disappears from later Hebrew. Aramaic and post-biblical Hebrew authors do not use it at all.

5. When the verb is separated from its *waw* it lapses into the perfect.

And he called וַיִּקְרָא *to the light day, and to the darkness he called* קָרָא *night.* Gen. 1:5.

WAW CONSECUTIVE WITH THE PERFECT

In the statement of successive events or acts in the future *waw* with the perfect is used after the main verb in the imperfect or imperative. That verb fixes the starting point as the speaker passes successively forward in thought viewing each as completed in its turn.

If Israel shall err יִשְׁגּוּ *and it be hid* וְנֶעְלַם *and they do* וְעָשׂוּ *and shall be guilty* וְאָשֵׁמוּ *and it shall become known* וְנוֹדְעָה *then they shall offer* וְהִקְרִיבוּ *and shall bring* וְהֵבִיאוּ *and shall lay* וְסָמְכוּ. Lev. 4:13ff.

These verbs have the same variety of usages as the imperfects for which they are substituted. The waw continues the imperfect in the sense of a future.

God will be יִהְיֶה *with me and keep me* וּשְׁמָרַנִי.

It is used in a conditional or a subjunctive sense, to express command, or volition and following telic particles.

Every man should come יָבֹא *to me and I would do him justice* וְהִצְדַּקְתִּיו. II Sam. 15:4.

Lest he come יָבוֹא *and smite me* וְהִכַּנִי. Gen. 32:12.

That they may go יֵלְכוּ *and stumble* וְכָשְׁלוּ *and be broken* וְנִשְׁבָּרוּ. Isa. 28:13.

Thou mayest give it תִּתְּנֶנָּה *and he may eat it* וַאֲכָלָהּ. Deut. 14:21.

It is used with the imperfect to express what is general or customary in the present or the past.

On which one leans יִסָּמֵךְ *and it goes* וּבָא *into his hand.* Isa. 36:6.

A man flees יָנוּס *from a lion and a bear meets him* וּפְגָעוֹ. Amos 5:19.

A mist used to go up יַעֲלֶה *and water* וְהִשְׁקָה. Gen. 2:6. (See Gen. 29:2f; Ex. 33:7–11; Jud. 2:18f; 6:2–6; I Sam. 1:4–7 and I Kgs. 5:6–8 for examples of the use of *waw* consecutive with perfects to express graphic descriptions of past events more or less customary).

VOCABULARIES

According to כְּ

Against עַל (אֶל), בְּ

All כֹּל (כָּל-)

Among בְּתוֹךְ, בְּ

And וְ (וּ, וָ)

Anoint מָשַׁח

Be able יָכֹל

Bring forth יָלַד

Before נֶגֶד, טֶרֶם

Begin חָלַל

Be great גָּדַל

Be heavy כָּבֵד

Be righteous צָדַק

Between בֵּין

Bless בֵּרךְ (Pi.)

Blood דָּם

Book סֵפֶר

Bread לֶחֶם

Brother אָח

Bury קָבַר

By אֶל, בְּ

Call קָרָא

Capture לָכַד

Child יֶלֶד

Choose בָּחַר

City עִיר (f.)

Cleave, cling דָּבַק

Clothe לָבַשׁ

Command צוה (Pi.)

Come near קָרַב

Conceal סתר, כָּסָה (Ni.)

Consecrate קָדַשׁ (Pi.)

Consume אָכַל, בָּעַר

Covenant בְּרִית (f.)

Cover כָּפַר

Create בָּרָא

Cry out צָעַק

Curse קָלַל, אָרַר

Cut כָּרַת

Darkness חֹשֶׁךְ

Daughter בַּת (f.)

Day יוֹם

Deliver נצל (Hi.)

Destroy שָׁמַד

Divide בדל (Hi.)

Do עָשָׂה

Door דֶּלֶת (f.), פֶּתַח

Dove יוֹנָה (f.)

Draw near קָרַב

Dwell שָׁכַן, יָשַׁב

Earth אֶרֶץ

Eat אָכַל

Egypt מִצְרַיִם

Escape מלט (Ni.)

Evil רָעָה

Faces פָּנִים

Father אָב

Fight לָחַם (Ni.)

Fill מָלֵא

Find מָצָא

Fire אֵשׁ (f.)

Flesh בָּשָׂר

Foot רֶגֶל (f.)

For לְ (Prep.), כִּי (Conj.)

Friend רֵעַ, אֹהֵב

From מִן

Garden גַּן

Give נָתַן

Glory כָּבוֹד

Go הָלַךְ

God אֵל, אֱלֹהִים

Go down יָרַד

Gold זָהָב

Good טוֹב

Go out יָצָא

Great גָּדוֹל

Ground אֲדָמָה

Hand יָד (f.)

Hate שָׂנֵא

Have mercy רָחַם

He הוּא

Head רֹאשׁ

Heal רָפָא

Hear שָׁמַע

Heart לֵבָב, לֵב	Light אוֹר
Heavens שָׁמַיִם	Lord אָדוֹן
Heavy כָּבֵד	Love אָהַב
Hero גִּבּוֹר	Luminary מָאוֹר
Hide חָבָא, סָתַר	Man אָדָם, אִישׁ
Holy קָדוֹשׁ	Make king מָלַךְ (Hi.)
Honor כבד (Pi.)	Make known יָדַע (Hi.)
Horse סוּס	נָגַד (Hi.)
House בַּיִת	Minister שָׁרֵת (Pi.)
I אָנֹכִי, אֲנִי	Morning בֹּקֶר
I pray thee נָא	Moses מֹשֶׁה
In בְּ	Mother אֵם (f.)
Jehovah (יְהֹוָה) יהוה	Mountain הַר
Judge שָׁפַט	Name שֵׁם
Keep שָׁמַר	Night לַיִל, לַיְלָה
King, be מָלַךְ	Not אַל, לֹא
King מֶלֶךְ	Number סָפַר
Lad נַעַר	On בְּ, עַל
Land אֲדָמָה, אֶרֶץ (f.)	Over עַל
Large גָּדוֹל	Peace שָׁלוֹם
Law תּוֹרָה (f.)	People עַם
Learn לָמַד	Perfect תָּמִים

Perish אָבַד

Place מָקוֹם

Plant זָרַע, נָטַע

Pray פלל (Hith.)

Prince שַׂר

Princess שָׂרָה (f.)

Prophet נָבִיא

Pursue רָדַף

Refuse מָאַס

Reign מָלַךְ

Remember זָכַר

Rest שָׁבַת

Reveal גָּלָה

Righteousness צֶדֶק

Rise early שכם (Hi.)

River נָהָר

Roll גָּלַל

Rule מָשַׁל

Sabbath שַׁבָּת

Samuel שְׁמוּאֵל

Sanctify קדש (Pi.)

Say אָמַר

Sea יָם

See רָאָה

Seek בקש (Pi.)

Sell מָכַר

Send שָׁלַח

Separate בדל (Hi.)

Serve שֵׁרַת, עָבַד

She הִיא

Sin (noun) חַטָּאת, חַטָאָה (f.)

Sin (verb) חָטָא

Sit יָשַׁב

Slaughter הָרַג, שָׁחַט

Son בֵּן

Song שִׁיר

Speak דִּבֶּר (Pi.)

Star כּוֹכָב

Stone אֶבֶן

Stumble כָּשַׁל

Surround סָבַב

Swear שָׁבַע

Sword חֶרֶב (f.)

Take לָקַח

Teach לִמֵּד (Pi.)	Walk הָלַךְ
Tell אָמַר	Was (to be) הָיָה
That (dem.) הוּא, הִיא (f.)	Wash כָּבַס
That (rel.) אֲשֶׁר	Water מַיִם
The (הַ, הֶ, הָ) הַ·	Way דֶּרֶךְ
There שָׁם	We אֲנַחְנוּ, נַחְנוּ
They הֵם (m.), הֵן (f.)	What (int.) מָה
These אֵלֶּה	What (rel.) אֲשֶׁר
This זֶה (m.), זֹאת (f.)	When כִּי, אִם
Those הֵם (m.), הֵן (f.)	Which (rel.) אֲשֶׁר
Thou אַתָּה (m.), אַתְּ (f.)	Who (int.) מִי
Time פַּעַם (f.), עֵת (f.)	Who (rel.) אֲשֶׁר
To אֶל, לְ	Why מַדּוּעַ, לָמָּה
Tongue לָשׁוֹן	Wicked (adj.) רַע
Toward אֶל, לְ	With עִם, אֶת
Tree עֵץ	Witness עֵד
Trust בָּטַח	Woman אִשָּׁה (f.)
Unto אֶל, לְ	Word דָּבָר
Upon עַל, לְ	Write כָּתַב
Vessel כְּלִי	You אַתֶּם (m.), אַתֵּנָה (f.)
Visit פָּקַד	Year שָׁנָה (f.)
Voice קוֹל	Youth נַעַר, עֶלֶם

א

אָב father

אָבַד to perish, (Hi.) to destroy

אָבָה to be willing

אֶבְיוֹן needy, wretched

אָבַל mourn

אֶבֶן (f.) stone

אַבְרָם Abram

אָדוֹן lord, commander, master

אָדָם man

אֲדָמָה (f.) ground, earth

אֲדֹנָי Lord

אָהַב to love

אֹהֶל tent, hut, habitation

אָוֶן iniquity, vainness, emptiness

אוֹצָר treasury

אוֹר to be light, shine

אוֹר light

אוֹת sign

אָז then

אֹזֶן (f.) ear

אָזַן (Hi.) to listen, hear

אָח brother

אֶחָד (m.) one, (f.) אַחַת

אָחוֹת (f.) sister

אָחַז to seize, (Pi.) to enclose

אֲחֻזָּה (f.) possession

אַחַר after, behind

אַחֵר another, other

אַחֲרוֹן last

אַחֲרִית (f.) latter end

אִי where?

אֹיֵב enemy

אֵיךְ how? how!

אַיִל ram, stag

אַיִן nothing, there is **not**

אִישׁ man, husband

אַךְ yea, surely, only

אָכַל eat, devour, (Pu.) to be consumed, (Hi.) to feed

אֹכֶל food, (f.)

אַל- no, not, let not

אֵל God

אֶל unto

אֵלֶּה these

אֱלֹהִים God

אֱלִיל worthless; (pl.) idols

אַלְמָנָה (f.) widow

אֶלֶף ox, thousand

אֵם (f.) mother

אִם if, whether

אָמָה (f.) handmaid

אֱמוּנָה (f.) faithfulness, fidelity

אָמַן to be firm, (Ni.) to be faithful, (Hi.) to believe, trust

אָמֵץ to be alert, to be strong, (Pi.) to make firm

אָמַר to say, (Hi.) to avow

אֹמֶר saying, song

אֱמֶת (f.) truth, firmness

אֱנוֹשׁ man, mankind

אֲנַחְנוּ we

אָנֹכִי I, אֲנִי

אָסַף to gather, (Ni.) to assemble

אָסַר to bind, imprison

אַף nose, anger

אֵפוֹד ephod

אַרְבָּעָה four, אַרְבַּע

אַרְבָּעִים forty

אָרוֹן ark, chest

אֶרֶז cedar

אֹרַח way, path

אֲרִי lion

אֹרֶךְ length

אֶרֶץ (f.) earth

אָרַר to curse

אֵשׁ (f.) fire

אִשָּׁה (f.) woman, wife, female

אִשֶּׁה fire-offering

אָשֵׁם to be guilty, (Hi.) to punish

אָשַׁר to be straight, walk straight

אֲשֶׁר who, which (rel.)

אֵת (sign used before the definite accusative.)

אֵת with

אַתְּ (f.) thou

אַתָּה (m.) thou

אַתֶּם (m.) you

אַתֶּן (f.) you, אַתֵּנָה (f.)

ב

בְּ in, on, among

בְּאֵר (f.) well

בְּאֻשִׁים odious grapes

בָּגַד to deal treacherously

בֶּגֶד garment

בדל (Hi.) to separate, select

בֹּהוּ emptiness

בָּהַל to be afraid, (Pi.) to terrify

בְּהֵמָה (f.) beast, dumb brute

בּוֹא to go in

בּוֹר pit, grave

בּוֹשׁ to be ashamed

בָּזַז to plunder, spoil

בָּחַר to choose, prove

בָּטַח to trust

בֶּטֶן (f.) womb

בֵּין between, among

בִּין to perceive, (Hi.) to explain

בַּיִת house, tent

בָּכָה to weep

בְּכוֹר first-born, eldest

בְּלִי nothingness, not

בָּלַל to mingle, confuse

בָּלַע to swallow, (Pi.) to consume

בִּלְתִּי lest, that not

בָּמָה (f.) high place

בֵּן son

בָּנָה to build

בַּעַד behind, after

בַּעַל master, Baal

בָּעַר to consume, (Hi.) to kindle

בָּקַע to cleave, split

בָּקָר herd, cattle

בֹּקֶר morning

בקשׁ (Pi.) to seek, ask

בָּרָא to create, form

בַּרְזֶל iron

בָּרַח to flee, (Hi.) to drive away

בְּרִית (f.) covenant

בָּרַךְ to kneel down, bless

בֶּרֶךְ (f.) knee

בְּרָכָה (f.) blessing

בָּשָׂר flesh

בָּשַׁל to boil, ripen

בַּת (f.) daughter, girl, grand-
daughter

בָּתָה (f.) desolation

בְּתוֹךְ in the midst of

ג

גָּאוֹן pride, swelling

גָּאַל to redeem, deliver

גָּבַהּ to be high, to be proud

גִּבּוֹר hero

גְּבוּרָה (f.) might, strength

גָּבַר to be strong, (Hi.) to con-
firm, (Hith.) to behave
proudly

גֶּבֶר mighty one, man

גָּדָה (f.) bank

גָּדוֹל great, elder

גְּדִי kid, young goat

גָּדַל to be great, (Pi.) to cause
to grow, magnify

גּוֹי nation

גּוּר to sojourn, tarry

גּוֹרָל lot, voting-stone

גָּזַל to tear away, plunder

גַּיְא valley

גִּיל joy, exultation

גָּלָה to uncover, reveal, (Ni.)
to uncover oneself

גָּלַל to roll

גַּם also

גָּמַל to deal with, to do (good
or evil)

גָּמָל camel

גַּן garden

גָּנַב to steal

גֶּפֶן (f.) vine

גֵּר sojourner, stranger

גָּרַשׁ to drive out

ד

דֹּב bear

דָּבַק to cleave, cling

דָּבַר to speak (usually Pi.)

דָּבָר word, thing

דֶּבֶר plague, pestilence

דְּבַשׁ honey

דָּג fish, דָּגָה (f.)

דָּוִד David

דּוֹר generation, age

דִּין to rule, judge, (Ni.) to contend at law

דָּכָה (Pi.) to crush, trample

דֶּלֶת (f.) gate, door

דָּם blood

דָּמָה to be like, (Pi.) to compare

דְּמוּת (f.) likeness, image

דַּעַת (f.) knowledge

דַּרְדַּר thorny plant, thistles (col.)

דֶּרֶךְ way, journey

דָּרַשׁ to resort to, seek

דֶּשֶׁא grass

ה

ה the

הֲ (particle of interrogation)

הֶבֶל vapor, breath, Abel

הוּא (m.) he

הוּא (m.) that (dem.)

הוֹד glory, splendor

הִיא (f.) she

הִיא (f.) that (dem.)

הָיָה to be, to become

הֵיכָל temple

הָלַךְ to go, walk

הָלַל to be boastful, (Pi.) to praise

הֵם (m.) they, הֵמָּה

הָמוֹן multitude, tumult

הֵן (f.) they, הֵנָּה

הֵן behold!, הִנֵּה

הָפַךְ to turn, overthrow, (Ni.) to be changed

הַר mountain

הָרַג to kill

הָרָה to conceive

ו

ו and

ז

זֹאת (f.) this (dem.)

זָבַח to sacrifice

זֶבַח sacrifice

זֶה (m.) this (dem.)

זָהָב gold

זָהַר (Ni.) to be enlightened, (Hi.) to teach, warn

זוּר to be a stranger, (Ni.) to be estranged

זָכַר to remember

זָכָר male

זָמַר to prune, (Pi.) to sing

זָנָה to commit fornication

זָעַק to cry out

זָקֵן to be old

זָקֵן old man, elder

זְרֹעַ arm, strength

זָרַע to sow, (Hi.) to produce seed

זֶרַע seed

ח

חָבָא to hide, (Ni.) to hide oneself

חֶבֶל line, cord

חַג feast, festival

חָנַג to keep a feast

חָדַל to cease

חָדַשׁ (Pi.) to renew

חָדָשׁ fresh, new

חֹדֶשׁ new moon, month

חוּל to be in pain, writhe, bring forth

חוֹמָה (f.) wall

חוּץ outside, abroad

חָזָה to see, to gaze

חֹזֶה seer, prophet

חָזַק to be strong, (Hi.) to seize

חָטָא to miss, sin

חַטָּאת (f.) sin

חַי (adj.) living, fresh; (subst.) life חַיִּים (m. pl.)

חָיָה to live, (Pi.) to preserve alive

חַיָּה (f.) living creature, beast

חָכָם wise, skilful

חָכְמָה (f.) wisdom

חֵל bulwark, wall, rampart

חֵלֶב fat, marrow

חָלָה to be sick

חֲלוֹם dream

חָלַל to pollute, to pierce, (Hi.) to begin

חָלַם to dream

חָלַק to divide, plunder

חֵלֶק portion, share

חָמַד to take delight in, desire

חַמָּה (f.) heat, sun

חֲמוֹר (he)-ass

חָמָס violence, wickedness

חָמֵשׁ חֲמִשָּׁה five,

חֲמִשִּׁים fifty

חֵן favor, grace

חָנָה to encamp, bend down

חָנַן to be gracious, (Hith.) to entreat

חֶסֶד mercy, kindness

חָפֵץ to delight in

חֵץ arrow, handle

חָצַב to cut, hew out

חֲצִי half

חֹק statute, (f.)

חָרֵב to dry up, to be waste

חֶרֶב (f.) sword

חֹרֵב Horeb

חׇרְבָּה (f.) dry land

חָרַד to tremble, (Hi.) to terrify

חָרָה to be angry, burn

חֶרְפָּה (f.) reproach, shame

חָרַשׁ to plow, engrave, (Hi.) to be silent

חָשַׁב to think, impute

חֹשֶׁךְ darkness

חָתַת to be dismayed, (Hi.) to terrify

ט

טָהוֹר clean, pure

טָהֵר to be clean, (Pi.) to purify

טוֹב to be good

טוֹב good, kind

טַל dew

טָמֵא to be unclean, (Pi.) to defile

טֶרֶם before, not yet

י

יְאוֹר river, Nile

יָבֵשׁ to be dry

יַבָּשָׁה (f.) dry land

יָד (f.) hand

יָדָה to throw, cast, (Hi.) to praise, confess

יָדִיד one beloved

יָדַע to know, understand

יְהוּדָה Judah

יְהֹוָה Yahweh, יהוה

יְהוֹשֻׁעַ Joshua

יוֹחָנָן John

יוֹם day

יוֹמָם daily, by day

יוֹנָה (f.) dove

יַחַד (subst.) oneness, unity; (adv.) all alike, together

יָטַב to be good, (Hi.) to do well

יַיִן wine

יכח (Hi.) to decide, prove

יָכֹל to be able

יָלַד to bring forth, (Ni.) to be born, (Hi.) to beget

יֶלֶד child, youth

ילל (Hi.) to wail, lament

יָם sea

יָמִין (f.) right hand

ימן (Hi.) to turn to the right

יָנַק to suck

יָסַף to add, repeat

יָסַר to chastise, admonish

יָעַץ to advise, counsel, (Hith.) to conspire

יַעַר forest

יָצָא to go out, (Hi.) to bring out

יִצְחָק Isaac

יָצַק to pour out

יָצַר to form

יֵצֶר form, imagination

יֶקֶב wine-press

יָקַץ to awake

יָרֵא to fear, (Ni.) to be awe-inspiring

יָרַד to descend

יַרְדֵּן Jordan

יָרָה to throw, (Hi.) to teach

יְרוּשָׁלַיִם Jerusalem

יָרֵחַ moon

יָרַשׁ to possess, inherit

יִשְׂרָאֵל Israel

יֵשׁ there is

יָשַׁב to sit, dwell

יֹשֵׁב inhabitant

יְשׁוּעָה (f.) deliverance

יִשַׁי Jesse

ישׁע (Hi.) to deliver

יָשַׁר to be straight, upright, (Pi.) to make straight

יָשָׁר straight, upright

יתר (Ni.) to be left, (Hi.) to leave

יֶתֶר remnant

כ

כְּ as, like, according to

כָּבֵד to be heavy, to be honored

כָּבוֹד honor, glory

כָּבַס to wash, trample

כֶּבֶשׂ lamb

כֹּה thus, here

כֹּהֵן priest, minister

כּוֹכָב star

כּוּן (Hi.) to prepare, establish

כּוֹס (f.) cup

כֹּחַ strength

כִּי that, for, because

כָּכָה so, thus

כֹּל all

כֶּלֶב dog

כָּלָה to be complete, (Pi.) to finish

כְּלִי vessel, implement

כְּמוֹ as, like, as soon as

כֵּן thus, so

כָּנָף (f.) wing

כִּסֵּא throne, seat

כָּסָה to cover, conceal

כְּסִיל fool, dullard

כֶּסֶף silver, money

כָּעַס to be vexed, (Hi.) to provoke

כַּף (f.) palm of hand, sole

כפר (Pi.) to cover, (Pu.) to be atoned for

כֹּפֶר bribe, ransom

כְּרוּב cherub

כֶּרֶם vineyard

כָּרַת to cut off

כָּשַׁל to stumble

כָּתַב to write

כָּתֵף (f.) shoulder

ל

לְ to, for, at

לֹא not, no

לֵבָב heart, לֵב

לְבַד alone

לָבַשׁ to be clothed, put on

לוּן to lodge, pass the night

לחם to fight, do battle

לֶחֶם bread

לַיְלָה, לֵיל night

לָכַד to capture

לָכֵן therefore

לָמַד to learn, (Pi.) to teach

לָמָה why?

לְמַעַן in order that, to

לָקַח to take

לָשׁוֹן tongue

מ

מְאֹד very, exceedingly

מֵאָה (f.) hundred

מְאוּמָה anything

מָאוֹר luminary

מָאַן (Pi.) to refuse

מָאַס to reject

מִגְדָּל tower

מָגֵן shield

מִגְרָשׁ pasture

מִדְבָּר wilderness, desert, pasture

מָדַד to measure

מִדָּה (f.) measure

מַדּוּעַ why? wherefore?

מְדִינָה (f.) province

מָה what? how?

מִהַר (Pi.) to hasten

מוֹעֵד season, place

מוּת to die

מָוֶת death

מִזְבֵּחַ altar

מְזוּזָה (f.) doorpost

מִזְמוֹר psalm

מִזְרָח east, sunrise

מַחֲנֶה camp, army

מָחָר tomorrow

מַטֶּה rod, tribe

מָטַר (Hi.) to give rain, to rain

מָטָר rain

מִי who?

מַיִם (pl.) water, waters

מָכַר to sell

מָלֵא to be full

מַלְאָךְ angel, messenger

מְלָאכָה (f.) work, business

מָלוֹן lodging-place

מֶלַח salt

מִלְחָמָה (f.) war, fight, battle

מלט (Ni., Hith.) to escape, (Hi., Pi.) to deliver

מָלַךְ to be king, (Hi.) to make king

מֶלֶךְ king

מַלְכָּה (f.) queen

מַלְכוּת (f.) kingdom

מֶמְלָכָה (f.) kingdom

מִן out of, from, away from

מִנְחָה (f.) offering, present

מִסְפָּר number

מְעַט little, a few

מַעַל above

מַעֲשֶׂה work, doing, deed

מָצָא to find

מִצְוָה (f.) commandment

מִצְרַיִם Egypt, Egyptian

מִקְדָּשׁ sanctuary

מָקוֹם dwelling, place, abode

מִקְנֶה property, cattle

מַרְאֶה appearance, sight

מָרוֹם high place, height

מַשָּׂא burden, tribute

מְשׂוּכָה (f.) hedge

מִשְׁפָּח bloodshed

מֹשֶׁה Moses

מָשַׁח to anoint

מָשִׁיחַ anointed one

מִשְׁכָּן tabernacle, dwelling

מָשַׁל to rule

מָשָׁל proverb

מִשְׁעָן staff

מִשְׁפָּט judgment, sentence

מִשְׁקָל weight

מָתַי when

נ

נָא (enclitic particle of entreaty) "I pray"

נָוֶה (f.) pasture, habitation (pl. נָאוֹת)

נְאֻם oracle, utterance

נבא (Ni.) to prophesy

נבט (Hi.) to look

נָבִיא prophet

נֶגֶב south country

נָגַד (Hi.) to declare, tell

נֶגֶד before, in the presence of

נָגַע to touch, smite

נָגַשׁ to approach

נָד fugitive (ptc.)

נֵד heap, wall

נָדַח to banish, expel

נָדַר to vow

נֶדֶר vow

נהל (Pi.) to guide, lead

נָהָר river

נוּחַ to rest

נֹחַ Noah

נָחָה to guide, (Hi.) to lead

נָחַל to inherit, take

נַחַל valley, brook

נַחֲלָה (f.) possession, inheritance

נחם (Ni.) to repent, pity, (Pi.) to comfort

נַחְנוּ we

נָחָשׁ serpent

נְחֹשֶׁת (f.) bronze, copper

נָטָה to spread out, (Hi.) to incline, turn

נָטַע to plant

נֶטַע plant, plantation

נכה (Hi.) to smite

נכר (Hi.) to regard, know, (Ni.) to be unrecognized

נֶסֶךְ libation

נָסַע to remove, set out

נַעַר lad, servant

נַעֲרָה (f.) maiden, maid servant

נָפַל to fall

נֶפֶשׁ soul

נצב (Ni.) to stand, (Hi.) to set, place

נצח (Ni.) to endure, (Pi.) to excel, direct

נצל (Pi.) to plunder, (Hi.) to deliver

נצר to watch, guard

נְקֵבָה (f.) female

נָקָה (Pi.) to acquit, (Ni.) to be innocent

נָקִי innocent

נָקַם to avenge

נָשָׂא to lift, carry

נשׂג (Hi.) to reach, attain

נָשִׂיא chief, prince

נָשַׁק to kiss

נָתַן to give, establish

ס

סָבַב to turn, surround

סָבִיב circuit, around

סָגַר to shut, (Hi.) to deliver over

סוּס horse

סוּר to turn aside, (Hi.) to put away

סֶלַע rock, crag

סֹלֶת (f.) fine flour

סָמַךְ to lean, support

סָפַד to lament, mourn

סָפַר to count, (Pi.) to rehearse

סֵפֶר book

סָקַל to stone, (Pi.) to free from stones

סתר (Ni.) to conceal

ע

עָב dark, cloud

עָבַד to serve

עֶבֶד servant, laborer

עֲבוֹדָה (f.) slavery, servitude

עָבַר to pass over

עֵבֶר over, beyond

עֶגְלָה (f.) heifer

עַד (prep.) until; (subst.) eternity

עֵד witness

עֵדָה (f.) congregation, assembly

עֵדוּת (f.) testimony

עֵדֶן Eden

עָדַר to hoe

עוּד to bear witness, testify

עוֹד again

עוֹלָה (f.) burnt offering

עוֹלָם age, eternity, world

עָוֹן iniquity, guilt, punishment

עוֹף bird, fowl

עוּף to fly

עוּר to awake

עוֹר skin, leather

עֵז (f.) goat

עֹז strength

עָזַב to abandon, forsake

עזק (Pi.) to dig

עָזַר to help

עַיִן (f.) eye, fountain

עִיר (f.) city

עַל upon, over

עֵלִי Eli

עָלָה to go up

עֶלְיוֹן high, most high

עָלַם to hide, conceal

עַם people, nation

עִם along with, with

עָמַד to stand, (Hi.) to appoint

עִמָּד with

עָמָל labor, misery

עֵמֶק valley

עֵנָב grape

עָנָה to answer

עָנָה to suffer, (Pi.) to oppress

עֳנִי affliction

עָנָן cloud

עָפָר dust

עֵץ tree

עֵצָה (f.) counsel

עֶצֶם (f.) bone

עֵקֶב end, result; (prep. and conj.) because of

עֶרֶב evening

עֲרָבָה (f.) desert, plain

עֶרְוָה (f.) nakedness

עָרַךְ to arrange

עָשָׂה to do, make

עשׁק (Hith.) to strive, quarrel

עֲשָׂרָה ten, (f.) עֶשֶׂר

עֶשְׂרִים twenty

עָשָׁן smoke

עֵת (f.) time

עַתָּה now

פ

פֵּאָה (f.) side, corner

פָּדָה to ransom

פֶּה mouth

פֹּה here

פּוּץ to be scattered

פָּחַד to be afraid, tremble

פלא (Ni.) to be wonderful, to be extraordinary

פלל (Pi.) to intervene, pray

פְּלִשְׁתִּים Philistines

פֶּן lest (with imp.)

פָּנָה to turn

פָּנִים face (faces)

פָּעַל to do, make

פָּקַד to visit

פַּר bullock

פָּרַד to divide, separate

פְּרִי fruit

פָּרַץ to break through

פרר (Hi.) to break, frustrate

פָּרַשׂ to spread out

פָּשַׁע to rebel against

פֶּשַׁע rebellion, transgression

פָּתָה to be open, to be simple, (Pi.) to deceive, entice

פָּתַח to open

פֶּתַח door

צ

צֹאן (f.) flock

צָדַק to be right, (Pi., Hi.) to justify

צֶדֶק righteousness

צְדָקָה (f.) righteousness

צוה (Pi.) to command

צוּר rock

צָחַק to laugh

צֶלֶם image

צָמֵא to be thirsty

צֶמַח sprout, growth

צָעַק to cry out

צְעָקָה (f.) cry, outcry

צָפָה to keep watch

צַר adversary

צָרָה (f.) adversity

צָרַר to show hostility towards, vex

ק

קבל (Pi.) to receive, take

קָבַץ to collect, gather

קָבַר to bury

קָדוֹשׁ holy

קֶדֶם before, east

קָדַשׁ to be set apart, (Pi.) to consecrate, sanctify

קֹדֶשׁ holiness, sanctity, consecrated thing

קוֹל voice

קוּם to arise, stand

קָטַל to kill

קָטֹן small, younger

קָטֹן to be little

קְטֹרֶת (f.) incense

קַיִן_Cain

קִיר wall

קָלַל to be light, swift, (Pu.) to be cursed

קָנָה to acquire

קָנֶה stalk, reed

קֵץ end

קָצֶה end, extremity

קָצִיר harvest

קָרָא to call, to meet, to happen

קָרַב to come near

קָרְבָּן offering

קָרוֹב near

קֶרֶן (f.) horn

קָרַע to tear

קָשַׁר to bind, to conspire

קֶשֶׁת (f.) bow

ר

רָאָה to see

רֹאשׁ head

רִאשׁוֹן first, former

רֵאשִׁית (f.) beginning

רַב great, much, many

רֹב abundance

רָבַב to be many

רָבָה to be great, (Hi.) to multiply

רְבִיעִי fourth

רָבַץ to lie down

רָגַז to tremble, to be agitated

רֶגֶל (f.) foot

רָדָה to rule, have dominion

רָדַף to pursue

רוּחַ (f.) spirit, breath

רִיחַ (Hi.) to inhale, smell

רוּם to be exalted, to rise

רוּץ to run

רֹחַב breadth

רָחַם to love, (Pi.) to have compassion

רָחַף (Pi.) to hover, brood

רָחַץ to wash, bathe

רָחַק to be distant, (Hi.) to remove

רָחֹק distant

רִיב to strive, contend

רִיב strife

רֵיחַ savor, odor

רָכַב to ride

רֶכֶב chariot

רָם high (ptc.)

רָמַס to tread, trample

רָמַשׂ to creep

רָנַן to shout, give ringing cry

רַע evil

רֵעַ friend, neighbor

רָעָב famine

רָעָה to pasture, to tend

רֹעֶה shepherd

רָעַע to break, to be evil

רָפָא to heal

רָצָה to delight in, to be gracious to

רָצוֹן delight, favor

רָצַח to slay, murder

רָצַץ to break, crush, (Polel) to oppress

רַק only, thin

רָקִיעַ expanse

רָשָׁע evil, wicked

ש

שָׂבַע to be satisfied, sated

שָׂדֶה field, plain

שָׂחַק to laugh

שִׂיב to be gray, aged

שִׂים to put, place

שׂכל (Hi.) to be prudent, wise

שָׂמַח to rejoice, to be glad

שִׂמְחָה (f.) rejoicing, joy, festivity

שָׂנֵא to hate

שָׂעִיר hairy, goat

שָׂפָה (f.) lip, edge

שַׂר prince, head, chief

שָׂרָה (f.) Sarah

שָׂרַף to burn

שֹׂרֵק choicest vine

שׁ

שֶׁ (rel.) who, which, what

שָׁאוּל Saul

שְׁאוֹל (f.) Sheol, underworld

שָׁאַל to ask

שׁאר (Ni.) to be left, (Hi.) to leave

שְׁאֵרִית remnant

שֵׁבֶט rod, tribe, staff

שְׁבִיעִי seventh

שָׁבַע (Ni.) to swear, (Hi.) to
bind with an oath

שִׁבְעָה ,seven שֶׁבַע

שִׁבְעִים seventy

שָׁבַר to break in pieces

שָׁבַת to cease, rest, (Hi.) to
abolish

שַׁבָּת rest, Sabbath

שָׁדַד to ruin, devastate

שָׁוְא emptiness, iniquity

שׁוּב to turn back, return

שׁוֹפָר trumpet

שׁוֹר ox, bull

שָׁחָה to bow down

שָׁחַט to slaughter

שׁחת (Ni.) to be corrupted,
spoiled, (Hi.) to cor-
rupt, spoil

שָׁטַף to flow, to overwhelm

שִׁיר to sing

שִׁיר song

שִׁית to put, set

שַׁיִת thorns, briers

שָׁכַב to lie down

שָׁכַח to forget

שָׁכַל to be bereaved, (Pi.) to
make childless

שׁכם (Hi.) to rise early

שָׁכַן to dwell, (Hi.) to lay

שָׁכַר to be drunk, (Pi.) to
make drunk

שָׁלוֹם peace

שָׁלַח to send, (Pi.) to set free

שֻׁלְחָן table

שְׁלִישִׁי third

שלך (Hi.) to throw, cast

שָׁלֵם to be whole, to be complete, (Hi.) to make
peace

שֶׁלֶם peace offering

שְׁלֹשָׁה ,three שָׁלֹשׁ

שָׁם there

שֵׁם name

שמד (Ni. to be destroyed,
(Hi.) to destroy

שָׁמָּה thither

שְׁמוּאֵל Samuel

שָׁמַיִם heavens, sky

שָׁמִיר thorn, thorns

שָׁמֵם to be desolate

שְׁמָמָה (f.) desolation, waste

שֶׁמֶן oil, fatness, ointment

שְׁמֹנֶה eight, שְׁמֹנָה

שָׁמַע to hear

שָׁמַר to keep, watch

שֶׁמֶשׁ sun

שֵׁן (f.) tooth

שָׁנָה (f.) year

שֵׁנִי second

שְׁנַיִם (m.) two, שְׁתַּיִם (f.)

שַׁעַר (f.) gate, entrance

שַׁעֲשֻׁעִים (pl.) delight, pleasure

שִׁפְחָה (f.) maid-servant

שָׁפַט to judge

שָׁקָה (Hi.) to give to drink

שֶׁקֶל shekel

שֶׁקֶר falsehood, deception

שָׁרַץ to swarm

שֶׁרֶץ creeping things (coll.)

שרת (Pi.) to serve, minister

שִׁשָּׁה six, שֵׁשׁ

שִׁשִּׁי sixth

שִׁשִּׁים sixty

שָׁתָה to drink

ת

תֵּבָה (f.) ark

תֹּהוּ waste, formlessness

תְּהוֹם (f.) deep, abyss

תּוֹלְדוֹת (f.) generations, history

תּוֹעֵבָה (f.) abomination

תּוֹרָה (f.) law, instruction

תַּחַת under, beneath, instead of

תָּם whole, complete

תָּמִיד continuity

תָּמִים perfect

תָּמַם to finish, be complete

תִּפְאָרָה (f.) glory, splendor

תְּפִלָּה (f.) prayer

תָּפַשׂ to seize, catch

תָּקַע to thrust, strike

תְּרוּמָה (f.) heave-offering

תֵּשַׁע nine, תִּשְׁעָה

WORD LISTS

Some of the more common words are given in this table for review lessons. The teacher may assign them as early as he likes. The Hebrew word is given on page 179 and the English translation on page 183. The numbers correspond.

WORD LIST

(See page 20)

Some of the More Common Verbs

1	אָהַב	18	גָּנַב	35	חָטָא	52	לָחַם
2	אָכַל	19	גָּבַר	36	חָנַן	53	לָכַד
3	אָמַר	20	גָּדַל	37	חָשַׁב	54	לָמַד
4	אָסַף	21	גָּלָה	38	יָדָה	55	לָקַח
5	אָרַר	22	גָּלַל	39	יָדַע	56	מָאַס
6	בָּגַד	23	גָּרַשׁ	40	יָצָא	57	מָרַד
7	בָּחַר	24	דָּבַק	41	יָרֵא	58	מָהַר
8	בָּטַח	25	דָּבַר	42	יָרַד	59	מָטַר
9	בָּכָה	26	דָּרַשׁ	43	יָשַׁב	60	מָכַר
10	בָּנָה	27	הָלַל	44	כָּבַס	61	מָלֵא
11	בָּעַר	28	הָלַךְ	45	כָּלָה	62	מָלַט
12	בָּקַע	29	הָפַךְ	46	כָּסָה	63	מָלַךְ
13	בָּקַשׁ	30	הָרַג	47	כָּפַר	64	מָצָא
14	בָּרָא	31	זָבַח	48	כָּרַת	65	מָשַׁח
15	בָּרַךְ	32	זָכַר	49	כָּשַׁל	66	מָשַׁל
16	בָּשַׁל	33	זָקַן	50	כָּתַב	67	נָבַט
17	גָּאַל	34	חָדַל	51	לָבַשׁ	68	נָגַד

69	נֶגַע	85	עָבַד	101	קָטֹן	117	שָׁבַר
70	נָגַשׁ	86	עָבַר	102	קָלַל	118	שָׁבַת
71	נָחַל	87	עָזַב	103	קָרָא	119	שָׁחַט
72	נָטָה	88	עָזַר	104	קָרַב	120	שָׁטַף
73	נָטַע	89	עָמַד	105	רָאָה	121	שִׁיר
74	נָסַע	90	עָרַךְ	106	רָנַן	122	שָׁכַב
75	נָפַל	91	פָּדָה	107	רָדַף	123	שָׁכֵן
76	נָצַל	92	פָּלַל	108	רָחַם	124	שָׁכֶם
77	נָשָׂא	93	פָּקַד	109	רָנַן	125	שָׁלַח
78	נָתַן	94	פָּרַד	110	רָעָה	126	שָׁלַךְ
79	סָבַב	95	פָּשַׁע	111	רָפָא	127	שָׁמַע
80	סָגַר	96	צָדַק	112	שָׂכַל	128	שָׁמַר
81	סָמַךְ	97	צָוָה	113	שָׂנֵא	129	שָׁפַט
82	סָפַד	98	צָמֵא	114	שָׂרַף	130	תָּפַשׂ
83	סָפַר	99	קָבַר	115	שָׁאַל	131	תָּמַם
84	סָתַר	100	קָדַשׁ	116	שָׁבַע	132	תָּקַע

WORD LIST

(See page 34)

Some of the More Common Substantives

1	אָב	18	אַתָּה	35	דְּבַשׁ	52	חֵץ
2	אֶבֶן	19	בְּהֵמָה	36	דּוֹר	53	חֹק
3	אָדוֹן	20	בֵּין	37	דָּם	54	חֶרֶב
4	אֲדָמָה	21	בַּיִת	38	דֶּרֶךְ	55	חָרְפָּה
5	אוֹר	22	בֵּן	39	הֵיכָל	56	חָשֵׁךְ
6	אָח	23	בֹּקֶר	40	הִנֵּה	57	טוֹב
7	אֶחָד	24	בְּרִית	41	הַר	58	טָמֵא
8	אָדָם	25	בְּרָכָה	42	זָהָב	59	יָד
9	אִי	26	בַּת	43	חַג	60	יוֹם
10	אִישׁ	27	גִּבּוֹר	44	חוֹמָה	61	יַיִן
11	אֵל	28	גָּדוֹל	45	חוּץ	62	יֶלֶד
12	אֱלֹהִים	29	גּוֹי	46	חָכְמָה	63	יָם
13	אִם	30	גַּם	47	חֲלוֹם	64	יְשׁוּעָה
14	אַף	31	גָּמָל	48	חָמָס	65	כֹּהֵן
15	אֶרֶץ	32	גַּן	49	חָמֵשׁ	66	כּוֹכָב
16	אֵשׁ	33	גֵּר	50	חֵן	67	כֹּחַ
17	אִשָּׁה	34	דָּבָר	51	חֶסֶד	68	כִּי

181

131 רֵאשִׁית	111 עֵץ	90 מָקוֹם	69 כֹּל
132 רַב	112 עֵצָה	91 מָשִׁיחַ	70 כָּנָף
133 רֶגֶל	113 עֵת	92 מָשָׁל	71 כִּסֵּא
134 רוּחַ	114 עַתָּה	93 מִשְׁפָּט	72 כֶּרֶם
135 רֶכֶב	115 פֶּה	94 נָבִיא	73 לֵב
136 רַע	116 פֶּן	95 נָהָר	74 לֶחֶם
137 שָׂדֶה	117 פָּנִים	96 נַחֲלָה	75 לַיְלָה
138 שַׂר	118 פְּרִי	97 נַעַר	76 לָשׁוֹן
139 שַׁבָּת	119 צֹאן	98 סוּס	77 מְאֹד
140 שׁוֹפָר	120 צֶדֶק	99 סֵפֶר	78 מֵאָה
141 שׁוֹר	121 צְדָקָה	100 עֶבֶד	79 מָאוֹר
142 שִׁיר	122 קָדוֹשׁ	101 עָנָן	80 מִגְדָּל
143 שָׁלוֹם	123 קוֹל	102 עַד	81 מָגֵן
144 שֵׁם	124 קִיר	103 עֵדָה	82 מוֹעֵד
145 שְׁמֹנֶה	125 קָטוֹן	104 עוֹד	83 מִזְבֵּחַ
146 שָׁנָה	126 קֵץ	105 עַיִן	84 מִזְמוֹר
147 תֵּבָה	127 קָצִיר	106 עִיר	85 מַלְכָּה
148 תּוֹרָה	128 קָרוֹב	107 עַל	86 מֶלֶךְ
149 תָּמִים	129 קֶרֶן	108 עַם	87 מִנְחָה
150 תְּפִלָּה	130 רֹאשׁ	109 עָם	88 מַעֲשֶׂה
		110 עָפָר	89 מִצְוָה

WORD LIST (TRANSLATION)

(See page 179)

VERBS

1. Love
2. Eat
3. Say
4. Gather
5. Curse
6. Deal treacherously
7. Choose
8. Trust
9. Weep
10. Build
11. Consume
12. Cleave, split
13. Seek
14. Create
15. Bless
16. Boil
17. Redeem
18. Steal
19. Be strong, prevail
20. Be great
21. Reveal
22. Roll
23. Drive out
24. Cleave, cling
25. Speak
26. Tread, seek
27. Praise
28. Walk, go
29. Overturn
30. Kill
31. Sacrifice
32. Remember
33. Be old
34. Cease
35. Sin
36. Be gracious
37. Think, impute
38. Thank
39. Know
40. Go out
41. Be afraid
42. Go down
43. Sit, dwell
44. Wash
45. Complete
46. Conceal
47. Cover
48. Cut
49. Stumble
50. Write
51. Clothe, put on
52. Fight
53. Capture
54. Learn
55. Take
56. Refuse
57. Measure
58. Hasten
59. Rain
60. Sell

61. Be full	97. Command
62. Escape	98. Be thirsty
63. Reign	99. Bury
64. Find	100. Be holy
65. Anoint	101. Be small
66. Rule	102. Be light
67. Look	103. Call, meet
68. Make known	104. Draw near
69. Touch	105. See
70. Approach	106. Tremble
71. Inherit	107. Pursue
72. Stretch out	108. Have mercy
73. Plant	109. Sing, cry aloud
74. Depart	110. Feed, tend
75. Fall	111. Heal
76. Deliver, snatch	112. Be wise
77. Lift up	113. Hate
78. Give	114. Burn
79. Surround	115. Ask
80. Shut, close	116. Swear
81. Sustain	117. Break in pieces
82. Mourn	118. Rest, cease
83. Number	119. Slaughter
84. Conceal	120. Overflow
85. Serve	121. Sing
86. Pass over	122. Lie down
87. Abandon	123. Dwell
88. Assist	124. Rise early
89. Stand	125. Send
90. Arrange	126. Cast, throw
91. Redeem	127. Hear
92. Pray	128. Keep
93. Visit	129. Judge
94. Separate	130. Seize
95. Rebel	131. Be complete
96. Be righteous	132. Strike

WORD LIST (TRANSLATION)

(See page 181)

SUBSTANTIVES

1. Father
2. Stone
3. Master, Lord
4. Ground
5. Light
6. Brother
7. One
8. Man
9. Where
10. Man
11. God
12. God
13. Mother
14. Anger
15. Earth
16. Fire
17. Woman
18. Thou
19. Cattle, beast
20. Between
21. House
22. Son
23. Morning
24. Covenant
25. Blessing
26. Daughter
27. Hero
28. Great

29. Nation
30. Also
31. Camel
32. Garden
33. Sojourner
34. Word, thing
35. Honey
36. Generation
37. Blood
38. Way
39. Temple
40. Behold
41. Mountain
42. Gold
43. Feast, festival
44. Wall
45. Abroad
46. Wisdom
47. Dream
48. Violence
49. Five
50. Favor
51. Kindness
52. Arrow
53. Statute
54. Sword
55. Reproach
56. Darkness

57. Good
58. Unclean
59. Hand
60. Day
61. Wine
62. Child
63. Sea
64. Salvation
65. Priest
66. Star
67. Strength
68. For, because
69. All, every
70. Wing
71. Throne
72. Vineyard
73. Heart
74. Bread
75. Night
76. Tongue
77. Exceedingly
78. Hundred
79. Luminary
80. Tower
81. Shield
82. Season
83. Altar
84. Psalm
85. Queen
86. King
87. Offering
88. Deed, work
89. Command
90. Place
91. Anointed
92. Proverb

93. Judgment
94. Prophet
95. River
96. Inheritance
97. Boy, servant
98. Horse
99. Book
100. Servant
101. Cloud
102. Witness
103. Congregation
104. Again
105. Eye
106. City
107. Upon
108. People
109. With
110. Dust
111. Tree
112. Counsel
113. Time
114. Now
115. Mouth
116. Lest
117. Faces
118. Fruit
119. Flock
120. Righteousness
121. Righteousness
122. Holy
123. Voice
124. Wall
125. Small
126. End
127. Harvest
128. Near

129. Horn
130. Head
131. Beginning
132. Many, much
133. Foot
134. Spirit
135. Chariot
136. Bad, evil
137. Field
138. Prince
139. Sabbath

140. Trumpet
141. Ox
142. Song
143. Peace
144. Name
145. Eight
146. Year
147. Ark
148. Law, instruction
149. Perfect
150. Prayer

TRANSLATIONS

These three stories prepared and translated by
PROF. J. WASH WATTS, PH. D.

A Story Concerning the Covenant with Israel
See page 70 for the Hebrew

Yahweh taught Israel in the wilderness. And he spake to him according to these words, Just as I spake to Abraham thy father so I am speaking to thee. I am cutting a covenant with thee. Remember the commandments of Yahweh thy God to keep them and *I* will magnify thee. Sanctify thyself and honor thy God. Thou shalt learn these words and thou shalt bind them for a sign upon thy hands and thou shalt write them upon the door posts of thy house and upon thy gates. Also thou shalt indeed teach them to thy children. Thus thou shalt indeed make wise thy children.

Therefore the children of Israel said, It is good for us to be taught by Yahweh. "The judgments of Yahweh are truth . . . Also thy servant is warned by them: in the keeping of them is great reward." (Ps. 19:10b, 12). "Yahweh will reign forever and ever." (Ex. 15:18).

A Story Concerning the Crossing of the Jordan
See page 82 for the Hebrew

Joshua said unto the children of Israel, This day we shall pass over the Jordan. The priests will pass over before the people and they will stand in the midst of the Jordan until all the people have passed over. Yahweh is sending us in this way and we shall indeed hearken to his voice. I am confident that all of us are trusting in him. He is causing us to trust. We shall say, Yahweh is with us and we shall not perish.

And Joshua spake again, saying, Carry ye over with you twelve stones and set them up in your lodging place. Your children will ask in the future saying, What are these stones to you? and ye shall say to them, The waters of the Jordan were cut off before the ark of the covenant of Yahweh, the children of Israel did not refuse to pass over according to the word of Yahweh and they were not rejected as their fathers were rejected in the wilderness; therefore these stones are for a memorial to the children of Israel forever.

A Story Concerning the Crossing of the Jordan (Continued)
See page 90 for the Hebrew

Yahweh said unto Joshua, This day I shall begin the magnifying of thee in the eyes of all Israel that they may know that just as I was with Moses I will be with thee. Say thou to them, By this ye should know that there is a living god in your midst and he will certainly dispossess for your sake the nations which are dwelling in the land. When the soles of the feet of the priests rest in the waters of the Jordan, the waters going down from above will be cut off and they will stand as one heap and the waters going down upon The Sea of The Salt will be exhausted until all the people will have finished passing over. This Yahweh will do for the sake of the understanding of all the peoples of the earth the hand of Yahweh that mighty it is and for the sake of the putting of the fear of Yahweh in your hearts.

And in that day Yahweh indeed began to magnify Joshua. The priests were standing in the midst of the Jordan until the completion of all the word which Yahweh had commanded Joshua. And it came to pass just as the priests finished passing over, the waters began to return to their place. And the children of Israel said in their hearts, Lovingkindness will encompass all those trusting in Yahweh as it is encompassing Joshua to-day; hallelujah!; praise ye the name of Yahweh.

A Story Concerning the Crossing of the Jordan (Continued)
See page 100 for the Hebrew

And Joshua spake unto the children of Israel again, saying, Just as the ark shall journey from its place then ye shall journey from your place. However, when the priests stand upon the banks of the river, ye shall stand also ye. I shall make known to thee when to journey again, saying, This is the time to draw near, take all that is yours, and carry your baggage. In that time we shall give encouragement each to his fellow. We shall call each to his fellow, saying, Let us not be afraid. Thus we shall be distinguished. Our children will say to us in the future, Ye called to us and we passed over without fear. A son will say to his father, Thou didst call to me in that day; a daughter to her mother, Thou didst indeed call to me. Thus Yahweh will make wonderful this day.

And the children of Israel did according to the word of Yahweh. Joshua said, Sanctify yourselves for Yahweh will perform wonders in your midst; and so they did. And the officers commanded them to do just as Yahweh commanded in everything; and so they did. And when the people went up unto the dry ground, they said, Yahweh is doing according to his word. It is good for us to do all which he is commanding.

PARADIGMS

		Qal	Qal (Middle O)	Qal (Middle E)	Niph'al
Perfect	3 m. s.	קָטַל	קָטֹן	כָּבֵד	נִקְטַל
	3 f. s.	קָטְלָה	קָטְנָה	כָּבְדָה	נִקְטְלָה
	2 m. s.	קָטַלְתָּ	קָטֹנְתָּ	כָּבַדְתָּ	נִקְטַלְתָּ
	2 f. s.	קָטַלְתְּ	קָטֹנְתְּ	כָּבַדְתְּ	נִקְטַלְתְּ
	1 c. s.	קָטַלְתִּי	קָטֹנְתִּי	כָּבַדְתִּי	נִקְטַלְתִּי
	3 c. p.	קָטְלוּ	קָטְנוּ	כָּבְדוּ	נִקְטְלוּ
	2 m. p.	קְטַלְתֶּם	קְטָנְתֶּם	כְּבַדְתֶּם	נִקְטַלְתֶּם
	2 f. p.	קְטַלְתֶּן	קְטָנְתֶּן	כְּבַדְתֶּן	נִקְטַלְתֶּן
	1 c. p.	קָטַלְנוּ	קָטֹנּוּ	כָּבַדְנוּ	נִקְטַלְנוּ
Imperfect	3 m. s.	יִקְטֹל	יִקְטַן	יִכְבַּד	יִקָּטֵל
	3 f. s.	תִּקְטֹל	תִּקְטַן	תִּכְבַּד	תִּקָּטֵל
	2 m. s.	תִּקְטֹל	תִּקְטַן	תִּכְבַּד	תִּקָּטֵל
	2 f. s.	תִּקְטְלִי	תִּקְטְנִי	תִּכְבְּדִי	תִּקָּטְלִי
	1 c. s.	אֶקְטֹל	אֶקְטַן	אֶכְבַּד	אֶקָּטֵל
	3 m. p.	יִקְטְלוּ	יִקְטְנוּ	יִכְבְּדוּ	יִקָּטְלוּ
	3 f. p.	תִּקְטֹלְנָה	תִּקְטַנָּה	תִּכְבַּדְנָה	תִּקָּטַלְנָה
	2 m. p.	תִּקְטְלוּ	תִּקְטְנוּ	תִּכְבְּדוּ	תִּקָּטְלוּ
	2 f. p.	תִּקְטֹלְנָה	תִּקְטַנָּה	תִּכְבַּדְנָה	תִּקָּטַלְנָה
	1 c. p.	נִקְטֹל	נִקְטַן	נִכְבַּד	נִקָּטֵל
Impv.	2 m. s.	קְטֹל	קְטַן	כְּבַד	הִקָּטֵל
	2 f. s.	קִטְלִי	קִטְנִי	כִּבְדִי	הִקָּטְלִי
	2 m. p.	קִטְלוּ	קִטְנוּ	כִּבְדוּ	הִקָּטְלוּ
	2 f. p.	קְטֹלְנָה	קְטַנָּה	כְּבַדְנָה	הִקָּטַלְנָה
Inf.	Absol.	קָטוֹל	קָטוֹן	כָּבוֹד	הִקָּטֵל (נִקְטֹל)
	Const.	קְטֹל	קְטֹן	כְּבֹד, כְּבַד	הִקָּטֵל
Part.	Active	קֹטֵל		כָּבֵד	
	Passive	קָטוּל			נִקְטָל

(handwritten margin note beside Impv.: Follows Imperfect w/o preformative)

at kPau

Pi'el	Pu'al	Hithpa'el	Hiph'il	Hoph'al
קִטֵּל	קֻטַּל	הִתְקַטֵּל	הִקְטִיל	הָקְטַל
קִטְּלָה	קֻטְּלָה	הִתְקַטְּלָה	הִקְטִילָה	הָקְטְלָה
קִטַּלְתָּ	קֻטַּלְתָּ	הִתְקַטַּלְתָּ	הִקְטַלְתָּ	הָקְטַלְתָּ
קִטַּלְתְּ	קֻטַּלְתְּ	הִתְקַטַּלְתְּ	הִקְטַלְתְּ	הָקְטַלְתְּ
קִטַּלְתִּי	קֻטַּלְתִּי	הִתְקַטַּלְתִּי	הִקְטַלְתִּי	הָקְטַלְתִּי
קִטְּלוּ	קֻטְּלוּ	הִתְקַטְּלוּ	הִקְטִילוּ	הָקְטְלוּ
קִטַּלְתֶּם	קֻטַּלְתֶּם	הִתְקַטַּלְתֶּם	הִקְטַלְתֶּם	הָקְטַלְתֶּם
קִטַּלְתֶּן	קֻטַּלְתֶּן	הִתְקַטַּלְתֶּן	הִקְטַלְתֶּן	הָקְטַלְתֶּן
קִטַּלְנוּ	קֻטַּלְנוּ	הִתְקַטַּלְנוּ	הִקְטַלְנוּ	הָקְטַלְנוּ
יְקַטֵּל	יְקֻטַּל	יִתְקַטֵּל	יַקְטִיל	יָקְטַל
תְּקַטֵּל	תְּקֻטַּל	תִּתְקַטֵּל	תַּקְטִיל	תָּקְטַל
תְּקַטֵּל	תְּקֻטַּל	תִּתְקַטֵּל	תַּקְטִיל	תָּקְטַל
תְּקַטְּלִי	תְּקֻטְּלִי	תִּתְקַטְּלִי	תַּקְטִילִי	תָּקְטְלִי
אֲקַטֵּל	אֲקֻטַּל	אֶתְקַטֵּל	אַקְטִיל	אָקְטַל
יְקַטְּלוּ	יְקֻטְּלוּ	יִתְקַטְּלוּ	יַקְטִילוּ	יָקְטְלוּ
תְּקַטֵּלְנָה	תְּקֻטַּלְנָה	תִּתְקַטֵּלְנָה	תַּקְטֵלְנָה	תָּקְטַלְנָה
תְּקַטְּלוּ	תְּקֻטְּלוּ	תִּתְקַטְּלוּ	תַּקְטִילוּ	תָּקְטְלוּ
תְּקַטֵּלְנָה	תְּקֻטַּלְנָה	תִּתְקַטֵּלְנָה	תַּקְטֵלְנָה	תָּקְטַלְנָה
נְקַטֵּל	נְקֻטַּל	נִתְקַטֵּל	נַקְטִיל	נָקְטַל
קַטֵּל		הִתְקַטֵּל	הַקְטֵל	
קַטְּלִי		הִתְקַטְּלִי	הַקְטִילִי	
קַטְּלוּ	NONE	הִתְקַטְּלוּ	הַקְטִילוּ	NONE
קַטֵּלְנָה		הִתְקַטֵּלְנָה	הַקְטֵלְנָה	
קַטֹּל (קַטֵּל)	קֻטֹּל	(הִתְקַטֹּל)	הַקְטֵל	הָקְטֵל
קַטֵּל	(קֻטֵּל)	הִתְקַטֵּל	הַקְטִיל	הָקְטֵל
מְקַטֵּל		מִתְקַטֵּל	מַקְטִיל	מָקְטָל
	מְקֻטָּל			מָקְטָל

		Qal		Niph'al	Pi'el
Perfect	3 m. s.	עָטַל		נֶעְטַל	עִטֵּל
	3 f. s.	עָטְלָה		נֶעֶטְלָה	עִטְּלָה
	2 m. s.	עָטַלְתָּ		נֶעֶטַלְתָּ	עִטַּלְתָּ
	2 f. s.	עָטַלְתְּ		נֶעֶטַלְתְּ	עִטַּלְתְּ
	1 c. s.	עָטַלְתִּי		נֶעֶטַלְתִּי	עִטַּלְתִּי
	3 c. p.	עָטְלוּ		נֶעֶטְלוּ	עִטְּלוּ
	2 m. p.	עֲטַלְתֶּם		נֶעֶטַלְתֶּם	עִטַּלְתֶּם
	2 f. p.	עֲטַלְתֶּן		נֶעֶטַלְתֶּן	עִטַּלְתֶּן
	1 c. p.	עָטַלְנוּ		נֶעֶטַלְנוּ	עִטַּלְנוּ
Imperfect	3 m. s.	יֶעְטַל	יַעְטֹל	יֵעָטֵל	יְעַטֵּל
	3 f. s.	תֶּעְטַל	תַּעְטֹל	תֵּעָטֵל	תְּעַטֵּל
	2 m. s.	תֶּעְטַל	תַּעְטֹל	תֵּעָטֵל	תְּעַטֵּל
	2. f. s.	תֶּעְטְלִי	תַּעְטְלִי	תֵּעָטְלִי	תְּעַטְּלִי
	1 c. s.	אֶעְטַל	אֶעְטֹל	אֵעָטֵל	אֲעַטֵּל
	3 m. p.	יֶעְטְלוּ	יַעְטְלוּ	יֵעָטְלוּ	יְעַטְּלוּ
	3 f. p.	תֶּעֱטַלְנָה	תַּעֲטֹלְנָה	תֵּעָטַלְנָה	תְּעַטֵּלְנָה
	2 m. p.	תֶּעְטְלוּ	תַּעְטְלוּ	תֵּעָטְלוּ	תְּעַטְּלוּ
	2 f. p.	תֶּעֱטַלְנָה	תַּעֲטֹלְנָה	תֵּעָטַלְנָה	תְּעַטֵּלְנָה
	1 c. p.	נֶעְטַל	נַעְטֹל	נֵעָטֵל	נְעַטֵּל
Impv.	2 m. s.	עֲטַל	עֲטֹל	הֵעָטֵל	עַטֵּל
	2 f. s.	עִטְלִי	עִטְלִי	הֵעָטְלִי	עַטְּלִי
	2 m. p.	עִטְלוּ	עִטְלוּ	הֵעָטְלוּ	עַטְּלוּ
	2 f. p.	עֲטַלְנָה	עֲטֹלְנָה	הֵעָטַלְנָה	עַטֵּלְנָה
Inf.	Absol.	עָטוֹל		נַעְטוֹל	עַטֹּל
	Const.	עֲטֹל		הֵעָטֵל	עַטֵּל
Part.	Active	עֹטֵל			מְעַטֵּל
	Passive	עָטוּל		נֶעְטָל	

Pu'al	Hithpa'el	Hiph'il	Hoph'al
עֻטַּל	הִתְעַטֵּל	הֶעְטִיל	הָעֳטַל
עֻטְּלָה	הִתְעַטְּלָה	הֶעְטִילָה	הָעָטְלָה
עֻטַּלְתָּ	הִתְעַטַּלְתָּ	הֶעְטַלְתָּ	הָעֳטַלְתָּ
עֻטַּלְתְּ	הִתְעַטַּלְתְּ	הֶעְטַלְתְּ	הָעֳטַלְתְּ
עֻטַּלְתִּי	הִתְעַטַּלְתִּי	הֶעְטַלְתִּי	הָעֳטַלְתִּי
עֻטְּלוּ	הִתְעַטְּלוּ	הֶעְטִילוּ	הָעָטְלוּ
עֻטַּלְתֶּם	הִתְעַטַּלְתֶּם	הֶעְטַלְתֶּם	הָעֳטַלְתֶּם
עֻטַּלְתֶּן	הִתְעַטַּלְתֶּן	הֶעְטַלְתֶּן	הָעֳטַלְתֶּן
עֻטַּלְנוּ	הִתְעַטַּלְנוּ	הֶעְטַלְנוּ	הָעֳטַלְנוּ
יְעֻטַּל	יִתְעַטֵּל	יַעְטִיל	יָעֳטַל
תְּעֻטַּל	תִּתְעַטֵּל	תַּעְטִיל	תָּעֳטַל
תְּעֻטַּל	תִּתְעַטֵּל	תַּעְטִיל	תָּעֳטַל
תְּעֻטְּלִי	תִּתְעַטְּלִי	תַּעְטִילִי	תָּעֳטְלִי
אֲעֻטַּל	אֶתְעַטֵּל	אַעְטִיל	אָעֳטַל
יְעֻטְּלוּ	יִתְעַטְּלוּ	יַעְטִילוּ	יָעֳטְלוּ
תְּעֻטַּלְנָה	תִּתְעַטַּלְנָה	תַּעְטֵלְנָה	תָּעֳטַלְנָה
תְּעֻטְּלוּ	תִּתְעַטְּלוּ	תַּעְטִילוּ	תָּעֳטְלוּ
תְּעֻטַּלְנָה	תִּתְעַטַּלְנָה	תַּעְטֵלְנָה	תָּעֳטַלְנָה
נְעֻטַּל	נִתְעַטֵּל	נַעְטִיל	נָעֳטַל
	הִתְעַטֵּל	הַעְטֵל	
NONE	הִתְעַטְּלִי	הַעְטִילִי	NONE
	הִתְעַטְּלוּ	הַעְטִילוּ	
	הִתְעַטֵּלְנָה	הַעְטֵלְנָה	
עֻטֹּל	(הִתְעַטֹּל)	הַעְטֵל	הָעֳטֵל
(עֻטַּל)	הִתְעַטֵּל	הַעְטִיל	הָעֳטֵל
	מִתְעַטֵּל	מַעְטִיל	
מְעֻטָּל			מָעֳטָל

		Qal	Niph'al	Pi'el
Perfect	3 m. s.	קָאַל	נִקְאַל	קֵאַל
	3 f. s.	קָאֲלָה	נִקְאֲלָה	קֵאֲלָה
	2 m. s.	קָאַלְתָּ	נִקְאַלְתָּ	קֵאַלְתָּ
	2 f. s.	קָאַלְתְּ	נִקְאַלְתְּ	קֵאַלְתְּ
	1 c. s.	קָאַלְתִּי	נִקְאַלְתִּי	קֵאַלְתִּי
	3 c. p.	קָאֲלוּ	נִקְאֲלוּ	קֵאֲלוּ
	2 m. p.	קָאַלְתֶּם	נִקְאַלְתֶּם	קֵאַלְתֶּם
	2 f. p.	קָאַלְתֶּן	נִקְאַלְתֶּן	קֵאַלְתֶּן
	1 c. p.	קָאַלְנוּ	נִקְאַלְנוּ	קֵאַלְנוּ
Imperfect	3 m. s.	יִקְאַל	יִקָּאֵל	יְקָאֵל
	3 f. s.	תִּקְאַל	תִּקָּאֵל	תְּקָאֵל
	2 m. s.	תִּקְאַל	תִּקָּאֵל	תְּקָאֵל
	2 f. s.	תִּקְאֲלִי	תִּקָּאֲלִי	תְּקָאֲלִי
	1 c. s.	אֶקְאַל	אֶקָּאֵל	אֲקָאֵל
	3 m. p.	יִקְאֲלוּ	יִקָּאֲלוּ	יְקָאֲלוּ
	3 f. p.	תִּקְאַלְנָה	תִּקָּאַלְנָה	תְּקָאַלְנָה
	2 m. p.	תִּקְאֲלוּ	תִּקָּאֲלוּ	תְּקָאֲלוּ
	2 f. p.	תִּקְאַלְנָה	תִּקָּאַלְנָה	תְּקָאַלְנָה
	1 c. p.	נִקְאַל	נִקָּאֵל	נְקָאֵל
Impv.	2 m. s.	קְאַל	הִקָּאֵל	קָאֵל
	2 f. s.	קְאֲלִי	הִקָּאֲלִי	קָאֲלִי
	2 m. p.	קְאֲלוּ	הִקָּאֲלוּ	קָאֲלוּ
	2 f. p.	קְאַלְנָה	הִקָּאַלְנָה	קָאַלְנָה
Inf.	Absol.	קָאוֹל	נִקְאוֹל	קָאֹל
	Const.	קְאַל	הִקָּאֵל	קָאֵל
Part.	Active	קֹאֵל		מְקָאֵל
	Passive	קָאוּל	נִקְאָל	

Pu'al	Hithpa'el	Hiph'il	Hoph'al
קָאַל	הִתְקָאַל	הִקְאִיל	הָקְאַל
קָאֲלָה	הִתְקָאֲלָה	הִקְאִילָה	הָקְאֲלָה
קָאַלְתָּ	הִתְקָאַלְתָּ	הִקְאַלְתָּ	הָקְאַלְתָּ
קָאַלְתְּ	הִתְקָאַלְתְּ	הִקְאַלְתְּ	הָקְאַלְתְּ
קָאַלְתִּי	הִתְקָאַלְתִּי	הִקְאַלְתִּי	הָקְאַלְתִּי
קָאֲלוּ	הִתְקָאֲלוּ	הִקְאִילוּ	הָקְאֲלוּ
קָאַלְתֶּם	הִתְקָאַלְתֶּם	הִקְאַלְתֶּם	הָקְאַלְתֶּם
קָאַלְתֶּן	הִתְקָאַלְתֶּן	הִקְאַלְתֶּן	הָקְאַלְתֶּן
קָאַלְנוּ	הִתְקָאַלְנוּ	הִקְאַלְנוּ	הָקְאַלְנוּ
יְקָאַל	יִתְקָאַל	יַקְאִיל	יָקְאַל
תְּקָאַל	תִּתְקָאַל	תַּקְאִיל	תָּקְאַל
תְּקָאַל	תִּתְקָאַל	תַּקְאִיל	תָּקְאַל
תְּקָאֲלִי	תִּתְקָאֲלִי	תַּקְאִילִי	תָּקְאֲלִי
אֲקָאַל	אֶתְקָאַל	אַקְאִיל	אָקְאַל
יְקָאֲלוּ	יִתְקָאֲלוּ	יַקְאִילוּ	יָקְאֲלוּ
תְּקָאַלְנָה	תִּתְקָאַלְנָה	תַּקְאֵלְנָה	תָּקְאַלְנָה
תְּקָאֲלוּ	תִּתְקָאֲלוּ	תַּקְאִילוּ	תָּקְאֲלוּ
תְּקָאַלְנָה	תִּתְקָאַלְנָה	תַּקְאֵלְנָה	תָּקְאַלְנָה
נְקָאַל	נִתְקָאַל	נַקְאִיל	נָקְאַל
	הִתְקָאֵל	הַקְאֵל	
NONE	הִתְקָאֲלִי	הַקְאִילִי	NONE
	הִתְקָאֲלוּ	הַקְאִילוּ	
	הִתְקָאֵלְנָה	הַקְאֵלְנָה	
		הַקְאֵל	הָקְאַל
קָאֹל	הִתְקָאֵל	הַקְאִיל	הָקְאֵל
	מִתְקָאֵל	מַקְאִיל	
מְקָאָל			מָקְאָל

		Qal	Niph'al	P'iel
Perfect	3 m. s.	קָטַח	נִקְטַח	קִטַּח
	3 f. s.	קָטְחָה	נִקְטְחָה	קִטְּחָה
	2 m. s.	קָטַחְתָּ	נִקְטַחְתָּ	קִטַּחְתָּ
	2 f. s.	קָטַחַתְּ	נִקְטַחַתְּ	קִטַּחַתְּ
	1 c. s.	קָטַחְתִּי	נִקְטַחְתִּי	קִטַּחְתִּי
	3 c. p.	קָטְחוּ	נִקְטְחוּ	קִטְּחוּ
	2 m. p.	קְטַחְתֶּם	נִקְטַחְתֶּם	קִטַּחְתֶּם
	2 f. p.	קְטַחְתֶּן	נִקְטַחְתֶּן	קִטַּחְתֶּן
	1 c. p.	קָטַחְנוּ	נִקְטַחְנוּ	קִטַּחְנוּ
Imperfect	3 m. s.	יִקְטַח	יִקָּטַח	יְקַטַּח
	3 f. s.	תִּקְטַח	תִּקָּטַח	תְּקַטַּח
	2 m. s.	תִּקְטַח	תִּקָּטַח	תְּקַטַּח
	2 f. s.	תִּקְטְחִי	תִּקָּטְחִי	תְּקַטְּחִי
	1 c. s.	אֶקְטַח	אֶקָּטַח	אֲקַטַּח
	3 m. p.	יִקְטְחוּ	יִקָּטְחוּ	יְקַטְּחוּ
	3 f. p.	תִּקְטַחְנָה	תִּקָּטַחְנָה	תְּקַטַּחְנָה
	2 m. p.	תִּקְטְחוּ	תִּקָּטְחוּ	תְּקַטְּחוּ
	2 f. p.	תִּקְטַחְנָה	תִּקָּטַחְנָה	תְּקַטַּחְנָה
	1 c. p.	נִקְטַח	נִקָּטַח	נְקַטַּח
Impv.	2 m. s.	קְטַח	הִקָּטַח	קַטַּח
	2 f. s.	קִטְחִי	הִקָּטְחִי	קַטְּחִי
	2 m. p.	קִטְחוּ	הִקָּטְחוּ	קַטְּחוּ
	2 f. p.	קְטַחְנָה	הִקָּטַחְנָה	קַטַּחְנָה
Inf.	Absol.	קָטוֹחַ	נִקְטֹחַ	קַטֵּח
	Const.	קְטֹחַ	הִקָּטֵח	קַטֵּח
Part.	Active	קֹטֵח		מְקַטֵּח
	Passive	קָטוּחַ	נִקְטָח	

Pu'al	Hithpa'el	Hiph'il	Hoph'al
קֻטַּח	הִתְקַטַּח	הִקְטִיחַ	הָקְטַח
קֻטְּחָה	הִתְקַטְּחָה	הִקְטִיחָה	הָקְטְחָה
קֻטַּחְתָּ	הִתְקַטַּחְתָּ	הִקְטַחְתָּ	הָקְטַחְתָּ
קֻטַּחְתְּ	הִתְקַטַּחַתְּ	הִקְטַחַתְּ	הָקְטַחַתְּ
קֻטַּחְתִּי	הִתְקַטַּחְתִּי	הִקְטַחְתִּי	הָקְטַחְתִּי
קֻטְּחוּ	הִתְקַטְּחוּ	הִקְטִיחוּ	הָקְטְחוּ
קֻטַּחְתֶּם	הִתְקַטַּחְתֶּם	הִקְטַחְתֶּם	הָקְטַחְתֶּם
קֻטַּחְתֶּן	הִתְקַטַּחְתֶּן	הִקְטַחְתֶּן	הָקְטַחְתֶּן
קֻטְּחְנוּ	הִתְקַטְּחְנוּ	הִקְטַחְנוּ	הָקְטַחְנוּ
יְקֻטַּח	יִתְקַטַּח	יַקְטִיחַ	יָקְטַח
תְּקֻטַּח	תִּתְקַטַּח	תַּקְטִיחַ	תָּקְטַח
תְּקֻטַּח	תִּתְקַטַּח	תַּקְטִיחַ	תָּקְטַח
תְּקֻטְּחִי	תִּתְקַטְּחִי	תַּקְטִיחִי	תָּקְטְחִי
אֲקֻטַּח	אֶתְקַטַּח	אַקְטִיחַ	אָקְטַח
יְקֻטְּחוּ	יִתְקַטְּחוּ	יַקְטִיחוּ	יָקְטְחוּ
תְּקֻטַּחְנָה	תִּתְקַטַּחְנָה	תַּקְטַחְנָה	תָּקְטַחְנָה
תְּקֻטְּחוּ	תִּתְקַטְּחוּ	תַּקְטִיחוּ	תָּקְטְחוּ
תְּקֻטַּחְנָה	תִּתְקַטַּחְנָה	תַּקְטַחְנָה	תָּקְטַחְנָה
נְקֻטַּח	נִתְקַטַּח	נַקְטִיחַ	נָקְטַח
	הִתְקַטַּח	הַקְטַח	
NONE	הִתְקַטְּחִי	הַקְטִיחִי	NONE
	הִתְקַטְּחוּ	הַקְטִיחוּ	
	הִתְקַטַּחְנָה	הַקְטֵחְנָה	
קֻטַּח		הַקְטֵחַ	הָקְטֵחַ
קֻטֹּח	הִתְקַטַּח	הַקְטִיחַ	הָקְטַח
	מִתְקַטֵּח	מַקְטִיחַ	
מְקֻטָּח			מָקְטָח

		Qal		Niph'al	Pi'el
Perfect	3 m. s.		נָטַל	נִטַּל	נִטֵּל
	3 f. s.		נָטְלָה	נִטְּלָה	נִטְּלָה
	2 m. s.		נָטַלְתָּ	נִטַּלְתָּ	נִטַּלְתָּ
	2 f. s.		נָטַלְתְּ	נִטַּלְתְּ	נִטַּלְתְּ
	1 c. s.		נָטַלְתִּי	נִטַּלְתִּי	נִטַּלְתִּי
	3 c. p.		נָטְלוּ	נִטְּלוּ	נִטְּלוּ
	2 m. p.		נְטַלְתֶּם	נִטַּלְתֶּם	נִטַּלְתֶּם
	2 f. p.		נְטַלְתֶּן	נִטַּלְתֶּן	נִטַּלְתֶּן
	1 c. p.		נָטַלְנוּ	נִטַּלְנוּ	נִטַּלְנוּ
Imperfect	3 m. s.	יִטַּל	יִטֹּל	יִנָּטֵל	יְנַטֵּל
	3 f. s.	תִּטַּל	תִּטֹּל	תִּנָּטֵל	תְּנַטֵּל
	2 m. s.	תִּטַּל	תִּטֹּל	תִּנָּטֵל	תְּנַטֵּל
	2 f. s.	תִּטְּלִי	תִּטְּלִי	תִּנָּטְלִי	תְּנַטְּלִי
	1 c. s.	אֶטַּל	אֶטֹּל	אֶנָּטֵל	אֲנַטֵּל
	3 m. p.	יִטְּלוּ	יִטְּלוּ	יִנָּטְלוּ	יְנַטְּלוּ
	3 f. p.	תִּטַּלְנָה	תִּטֹּלְנָה	תִּנָּטַלְנָה	תְּנַטֵּלְנָה
	2 m. p.	תִּטְּלוּ	תִּטְּלוּ	תִּנָּטְלוּ	תְּנַטְּלוּ
	2 f. p.	תִּטַּלְנָה	תִּטֹּלְנָה	תִּנָּטַלְנָה	תְּנַטֵּלְנָה
	1 c. p.	נִטַּל	נִטֹּל	נִנָּטֵל	נְנַטֵּל
Impv.	2 m. s.	טַל	נְטֹל	הִנָּטֵל	נַטֵּל
	2 f. s.	טְלִי	נִטְלִי	הִנָּטְלִי	נַטְּלִי
	2 m. p.	טְלוּ	נִטְלוּ	הִנָּטְלוּ	נַטְּלוּ
	2 f. p.	טַלְנָה	נְטֹלְנָה	הִנָּטַלְנָה	נַטֵּלְנָה
Inf. Absol.		נָטוֹל	נָטוֹל	הִנָּטֵל	נַטֵּל
Const.		טֶלֶת	נְטֹל	הִנָּטֵל	נַטֵּל
Part. Active			נֹטֵל		מְנַטֵּל
Passive			נָטוּל	נִטָּל	

Pu'al	Hithpa'el	Hiph'il	Hoph'al
נֻטַּל	הִתְנַטֵּל	הִטִּיל	הֻטַּל
נֻטְּלָה	הִתְנַטְּלָה	הִטִּילָה	הֻטְּלָה
נֻטַּלְתָּ	הִתְנַטַּלְתָּ	הִטַּלְתָּ	הֻטַּלְתָּ
נֻטַּלְתְּ	הִתְנַטַּלְתְּ	הִטַּלְתְּ	הֻטַּלְתְּ
נֻטַּלְתִּי	הִתְנַטַּלְתִּי	הִטַּלְתִּי	הֻטַּלְתִּי
נֻטְּלוּ	הִתְנַטְּלוּ	הִטִּילוּ	הֻטְּלוּ
נֻטַּלְתֶּם	הִתְנַטַּלְתֶּם	הִטַּלְתֶּם	הֻטַּלְתֶּם
נֻטַּלְתֶּן	הִתְנַטַּלְתֶּן	הִטַּלְתֶּן	הֻטַּלְתֶּן
נֻטַּלְנוּ	הִתְנַטַּלְנוּ	הִטַּלְנוּ	הֻטַּלְנוּ
יְנֻטַּל	יִתְנַטֵּל	יַטִּיל	יֻטַּל
תְּנֻטַּל	תִּתְנַטֵּל	תַּטִּיל	תֻּטַּל
תְּנֻטַּל	תִּתְנַטֵּל	תַּטִּיל	תֻּטַּל
תְּנֻטְּלִי	תִּתְנַטְּלִי	תַּטִּילִי	תֻּטְּלִי
אֲנֻטַּל	אֶתְנַטֵּל	אַטִּיל	אֻטַּל
יְנֻטְּלוּ	יִתְנַטְּלוּ	יַטִּילוּ	יֻטְּלוּ
תְּנֻטַּלְנָה	תִּתְנַטַּלְנָה	תַּטֵּלְנָה	תֻּטַּלְנָה
תְּנֻטְּלוּ	תִּתְנַטְּלוּ	תַּטִּילוּ	תֻּטְּלוּ
תְּנֻטַּלְנָה	תִּתְנַטַּלְנָה	תַּטֵּלְנָה	תֻּטַּלְנָה
נְנֻטַּל	נִתְנַטֵּל	נַטִּיל	נֻטַּל
	הִתְנַטֵּל	הַטֵּל	
	הִתְנַטְּלִי	הַטִּילִי	
NONE	הִתְנַטְּלוּ	הַטִּילוּ	**NONE**
	הִתְנַטֵּלְנָה	הַטֵּלְנָה	
נֻטַּל	(הִתְנַטֵּל)	הַטֵּל	הֻטַּל
(נֻטַּל)	הִתְנַטֵּל	הַטִּיל	
	מִתְנַטֵּל	מַטִּיל	
מְנֻטָּל			מֻטָּל

		Qal	Niph'al	Pi'el
Perfect	3 m. s.	קָטָא	נִקְטָא	קִטֵּא
	3 f. s.	קָטְאָה	נִקְטְאָה	קִטְּאָה
	2 m. s.	קָטֵאתָ	נִקְטֵאתָ	קִטֵּאתָ
	2 f. s.	קָטֵאת	נִקְטֵאת	קִטֵּאת
	1 c. s.	קָטֵאתִי	נִקְטֵאתִי	קִטֵּאתִי
	3 c. p.	קָטְאוּ	נִקְטְאוּ	קִטְּאוּ
	2 m. p.	קְטָאתֶם	נִקְטֵאתֶם	קִטֵּאתֶם
	2 f. p.	קְטָאתֶן	נִקְטֵאתֶן	קִטֵּאתֶן
	1 c. p.	קָטֵאנוּ	נִקְטֵאנוּ	קִטֵּאנוּ
Imperfect	3 m. s.	יִקְטָא	יִקָּטֵא	יְקַטֵּא
	3 f. s.	תִּקְטָא	תִּקָּטֵא	תְּקַטֵּא
	2 m. s.	תִּקְטָא	תִּקָּטֵא	תְּקַטֵּא
	2 f. s.	תִּקְטְאִי	תִּקָּטְאִי	תְּקַטְּאִי
	1 c. s.	אֶקְטָא	אֶקָּטֵא	אֲקַטֵּא
	3 m. p.	יִקְטְאוּ	יִקָּטְאוּ	יְקַטְּאוּ
	3 f. p.	תִּקְטֶאנָה	תִּקָּטֶאנָה	תְּקַטֶּאנָה
	2 m. p.	תִּקְטְאוּ	תִּקָּטְאוּ	תְּקַטְּאוּ
	2 f. p.	תִּקְטֶאנָה	תִּקָּטֶאנָה	תְּקַטֶּאנָה
	1 c. p.	נִקְטָא	נִקָּטֵא	נְקַטֵּא
Impv.	2 m. s.	קְטָא	הִקָּטֵא	קַטֵּא
	2 f. s.	קְטְאִי	הִקָּטְאִי	קַטְּאִי
	2 m. p.	קְטְאוּ	הִקָּטְאוּ	קַטְּאוּ
	2 f. p.	קְטֶאנָה	הִקָּטֶאנָה	קַטֶּאנָה
Inf.	Absol.	קָטוֹא	נִקְטֹא	קַטֹּא
	Const.	קְטֹא	הִקָּטֵא	קַטֵּא
Part.	Active	קֹטֵא		מְקַטֵּא
	Passive	קָטוּא	נִקְטָא	

Pu'al	Hithpa'el	Hiph'il	Hoph'al
קֻטָּא	הִתְקַטֵּא	הִקְטִיא	הָקְטָא
קֻטְּאָה	הִתְקַטְּאָה	הִקְטִיאָה	הָקְטְאָה
קֻטֵּאתָ	הִתְקַטֵּאתָ	הִקְטֵאתָ	הָקְטֵאתָ
קֻטֵּאת	הִתְקַטֵּאת	הִקְטֵאת	הָקְטֵאת
קֻטֵּאתִי	הִתְקַטֵּאתִי	הִקְטֵאתִי	הָקְטֵאתִי
קֻטְּאוּ	הִתְקַטְּאוּ	הִקְטִיאוּ	הָקְטְאוּ
קֻטֵּאתֶם	הִתְקַטֵּאתֶם	הִקְטֵאתֶם	הָקְטֵאתֶם
קֻטֵּאתֶן	הִתְקַטֵּאתֶן	הִקְטֵאתֶן	הָקְטֵאתֶן
קֻטֵּאנוּ	הִתְקַטֵּאנוּ	הִקְטֵאנוּ	הָקְטֵאנוּ
יְקֻטָּא	יִתְקַטֵּא	יַקְטִיא	יָקְטָא
תְּקֻטָּא	תִּתְקַטֵּא	תַּקְטִיא	תָּקְטָא
תְּקֻטָּא	תִּתְקַטֵּא	תַּקְטִיא	תָּקְטָא
תְּקֻטְּאִי	תִּתְקַטְּאִי	תַּקְטִיאִי	תָּקְטְאִי
אֲקֻטָּא	אֶתְקַטֵּא	אַקְטִיא	אָקְטָא
יְקֻטְּאוּ	יִתְקַטְּאוּ	יַקְטִיאוּ	יָקְטְאוּ
תְּקֻטֶּאנָה	תִּתְקַטֶּאנָה	תַּקְטֶאנָה	תָּקְטֶאנָה
תְּקֻטְּאוּ	תִּתְקַטְּאוּ	תַּקְטִיאוּ	תָּקְטְאוּ
תְּקֻטֶּאנָה	תִּתְקַטֶּאנָה	תַּקְטֶאנָה	תָּקְטֶאנָה
נְקֻטָּא	נִתְקַטֵּא	נַקְטִיא	נָקְטָא
	הִתְקַטֵּא	הַקְטֵא	
NONE	הִתְקַטְּאִי	הַקְטִיאִי	NONE
	הִתְקַטְּאוּ	הַקְטִיאוּ	
	הִתְקַטֶּאנָה	הַקְטֶאנָה	
—		הַקְטֵא	—
	הִתְקַטֵּא	הַקְטִיא	
	מִתְקַטֵּא	מַקְטִיא	
מְקֻטָּא			מָקְטָא

		Qal	Niph'al	Pi'el
Perfect	3 m. s.	קָטָה	נִקְטָה	קִטָּה
	3 f. s.	קָטְתָה	נִקְטְתָה	קִטְּתָה
	2 m. s.	קָטִיתָ	נִקְטֵיתָ	קִטֵּיתָ
	2 f. s.	קָטִית	נִקְטֵית	קִטֵּית
	1 c. s.	קָטִיתִי	נִקְטֵיתִי	קִטֵּיתִי
	3 c. p.	קָטוּ	נִקְטוּ	קִטּוּ
	2 m. p.	קְטִיתָם	נִקְטֵיתָם	קִטֵּיתָם
	2 f. p.	קְטִיתָן	נִקְטֵיתָן	קִטֵּיתָן
	1 c. p.	קָטִינוּ	נִקְטֵינוּ	קִטֵּינוּ
Imperfect	3 m. s.	יִקְטֶה	יִקָּטֶה	יְקַטֶּה
	3 f. s.	תִּקְטֶה	תִּקָּטֶה	תְּקַטֶּה
	2 m. s.	תִּקְטֶה	תִּקָּטֶה	תְּקַטֶּה
	2 f. s.	תִּקְטִי	תִּקָּטִי	תְּקַטִּי
	1 c. s.	אֶקְטֶה	אֶקָּטֶה	אֲקַטֶּה
	3 m. p.	יִקְטוּ	יִקָּטוּ	יְקַטּוּ
	3 f. p.	תִּקְטֶינָה	תִּקָּטֶינָה	תְּקַטֶּינָה
	2 m. p.	תִּקְטוּ	תִּקָּטוּ	תְּקַטּוּ
	2 f. p.	תִּקְטֶינָה	תִּקָּטֶינָה	תְּקַטֶּינָה
	1 c. p.	נִקְטֶה	נִקָּטֶה	נְקַטֶּה
Impv.	2 m. s.	קְטֵה	הִקָּטֵה	קַטֵּה
	2 f. s.	קְטִי	הִקָּטִי	קַטִּי
	2 m. p.	קְטוּ	הִקָּטוּ	קַטּוּ
	2 f. p.	קְטֶינָה	הִקָּטֶינָה	קַטֶּינָה
Inf.	Absol.	קָטֹה	נִקְטֹה	קַטֹּה (קַטֵּה)
	Const.	קְטוֹת	הִקָּטוֹת	קַטּוֹת
Part.	Active	קֹטֶה		מְקַטֶּה
	Passive	קָטוּי	נִקְטֶה	

Pu'al	Hithpa'el	Hiph'il	Hoph'al
קֻטָּה	הִתְקַטָּה	הִקְטָה	הָקְטָה
קֻטְּתָה	הִתְקַטְּתָה	הִקְטָתָה	הָקְטָתָה
קֻטֵּיתָ	הִתְקַטֵּיתָ	הִקְטֵיתָ	הָקְטֵיתָ
קֻטֵּית	הִתְקַטֵּית	הִקְטֵית	הָקְטֵית
קֻטֵּיתִי	הִתְקַטֵּיתִי	הִקְטֵיתִי	הָקְטֵיתִי
קֻטּוּ	הִתְקַטּוּ	הִקְטוּ	הָקְטוּ
קֻטֵּיתֶם	הִתְקַטִּיתֶם	הִקְטִיתֶם	הָקְטֵיתֶם
קֻטֵּיתֶן	הִתְקַטִּיתֶן	הִקְטִיתֶן	הָקְטֵיתֶן
קֻטֵּינוּ	הִתְקַטֵּינוּ	הִקְטֵינוּ	הָקְטֵינוּ
יְקֻטֶּה	יִתְקַטֶּה	יַקְטֶה	יָקְטֶה
תְּקֻטֶּה	תִּתְקַטֶּה	תַּקְטֶה	תָּקְטֶה
תְּקֻטֶּה	תִּתְקַטֶּה	תַּקְטֶה	תָּקְטֶה
תְּקֻטִּי	תִּתְקַטִּי	תַּקְטִי	תָּקְטִי
אֲקֻטֶּה	אֶתְקַטֶּה	אַקְטֶה	אָקְטֶה
יְקֻטּוּ	יִתְקַטּוּ	יַקְטוּ	יָקְטוּ
תְּקֻטֶּינָה	תִּתְקַטֶּינָה	תַּקְטֶינָה	תָּקְטֶינָה
תְּקֻטּוּ	תִּתְקַטּוּ	תַּקְטוּ	תָּקְטוּ
תְּקֻטֶּינָה	תִּתְקַטֶּינָה	תַּקְטֶינָה	תָּקְטֶינָה
נְקֻטֶּה	נִתְקַטֶּה	נַקְטֶה	נָקְטֶה
NONE	הִתְקַטֵּה	הַקְטֵה	**NONE**
	הִתְקַטִּי	הַקְטִי	
	הִתְקַטּוּ	הַקְטוּ	
	הִתְקַטֶּינָה	הַקְטֶינָה	
קֻטֹּה		הַקְטֵה	הָקְטֵה
קֻטּוֹת	הִתְקַטּוֹת	הַקְטוֹת	הָקְטוֹת
	מִתְקַטֶּה	מַקְטֶה	
מְקֻטֶּה			מָקְטֶה

		Qal	Niph'al	Po'el
Perfect	3 m. s.	קָט	נָקַט	קוֹטֵט
	3 f. s.	קָטָה	נָקְטָה	קוֹטְטָה
	2 m. s.	קַטּוֹתָ	נְקַטּוֹתָ	קוֹטַטְתָּ
	2 f. s.	קַטּוֹת	נְקַטּוֹת	קוֹטַטְתְּ
	1 c. s.	קַטּוֹתִי	נְקַטּוֹתִי	קוֹטַטְתִּי
	3 c. p.	קָטּוּ	נָקְטוּ	קוֹטְטוּ
	2 m. p.	קַטּוֹתֶם	נְקַטּוֹתֶם	קוֹטַטְתֶּם
	2 f. p.	קַטּוֹתֶן	נְקַטּוֹתֶן	קוֹטַטְתֶּן
	1 c. p.	קַטּוֹנוּ	נְקַטּוֹנוּ	קוֹטַטְנוּ
Imperfect	3 m. s.	יָקֹט / יִקַּט	יִקַּט	יְקוֹטֵט
	3 f. s.	תָּקֹט / תִּקַּט	תִּקַּט	תְּקוֹטֵט
	2 m. s.	תָּקֹט / תִּקַּט	תִּקַּט	תְּקוֹטֵט
	2 f. s.	תָּקֹטִי / תִּקְּטִי	תִּקְּטִי	תְּקוֹטְטִי
	1 c. s.	אָקֹט / אֶקַּט	אֶקַּט	אֲקוֹטֵט
	3 m. p.	יָקֹטּוּ / יִקְּטוּ	יִקְּטוּ	יְקוֹטְטוּ
	3 f. p.	תְּקֹטֶינָה / תִּקַּטְנָה	תִּקַּטְנָה	תְּקוֹטֵטְנָה
	2 m. p.	תָּקֹטּוּ / תִּקְּטוּ	תִּקְּטוּ	תְּקוֹטְטוּ
	2 f. p.	תְּקֹטֶינָה / תִּקַּטְנָה	תִּקַּטְנָה	תְּקוֹטֵטְנָה
	1 c. p.	נָקֹט / נִקַּט	נִקַּט	נְקוֹטֵט
Impv.	2 m. s.	קֹט	הִקַּט	קוֹטֵט
	2 f. s.	קֹטִי	הִקַּטִי	קוֹטְטִי
	2 m. p.	קֹטּוּ	הִקַּטּוּ	קוֹטְטוּ
	2 f. p.	קְטֶינָה	הִקַּטֶינָה	קוֹטֵטְנָה
Inf.	Absol.	קָטוֹט	הִקּוֹט	קוֹטֵט
	Const.	קֹט	הִקַּט	קוֹטֵט
Part.	Active	קֹטֵט		מְקוֹטֵט
	Passive	קָטוֹט	נָקֹט	

same as Hoph'al of (ע"ו)

Po'al	Hithpo'el	Hiph'il	Hoph'al
קוֹטֵט	הִתְקוֹטֵט	הֵקֵט	הוּקַט
קוֹטְטָה	הִתְקוֹטְטָה	הֵקֵטָּה	הוּגַקְטָּה
קוֹטַטְתָּ	הִתְקוֹטַטְתָּ	הֲקֵטּוֹתָ	הוּקַטּוֹתָ
קוֹטַטְתְּ	הִתְקוֹטַטְתְּ	הֲקֵטּוֹת	הוּקַטּוֹת
קוֹטַטְתִּי	הִתְקוֹטַטְתִּי	הֲקֵטּוֹתִי	הוּקַטּוֹתִי
קוֹטְטוּ	הִתְקוֹטְטוּ	הֵקֵטּוּ	הוּגַקְטוּ
קוֹטַטְתֶּם	הִתְקוֹטַטְתֶּם	הֲקֵטּוֹתֶם	הוּקַטּוֹתֶם
קוֹטַטְתֶּן	הִתְקוֹטַטְתֶּן	הֲקֵטּוֹתֶן	הוּקַטּוֹתֶן
קוֹטַטְנוּ	הִתְקוֹטַטְנוּ	הֲקֵטּוֹנוּ	הוּקַטּוֹנוּ
יְקוֹטֵט	יִתְקוֹטֵט	יָקֵט	יוּקַט (יָקַט)
תְּקוֹטֵט	תִּתְקוֹטֵט	תָּקֵט	תּוּקַט
תְּקוֹטֵט	תִּתְקוֹטֵט	תָּקֵט	תּוּקַט
תְּקוֹטְטִי	תִּתְקוֹטְטִי	תָּקֵטִּי	תּוּגַקְטִי
אֲקוֹטֵט	אֶתְקוֹטֵט	אָקֵט	אוּקַט
יְקוֹטְטוּ	יִתְקוֹטְטוּ	יָקֵטּוּ	יוּגַקְטוּ
תְּקוֹטֵטְנָה	תִּתְקוֹטֵטְנָה	תָּקֵטֶּינָה	תּוּקַטֶּינָה
תְּקוֹטְטוּ	תִּתְקוֹטְטוּ	תָּקֵטּוּ	תּוּגַקְטוּ
תְּקוֹטֵטְנָה	תִּתְקוֹטֵטְנָה	תָּקֵטֶּינָה	תּוּקַטֶּינָה
נְקוֹטֵט	נִתְקוֹטֵט	נָקֵט	נוּקַט
NONE	הִתְקוֹטֵט	הָקֵט	NONE
	הִתְקוֹטְטִי	הָקֵטִּי	
	הִתְקוֹטְטוּ	הָקֵטּוּ	
	הִתְקוֹטֵטְנָה	הַקְטֵּינָה	
	הִתְקוֹטֵט	הָקֵט	
קוֹטֵט		הָקֵט	הוּקַט
	מִתְקוֹטֵט	מֵקֵט	
מְקוֹטָט			מוּקָט

		Qal (ע"ו) A	Qal (ע"ו) E	Qal (ע"ו) O	Qal (ע"י)
Perfect	3 m. s.	קָל	מֵת	בּוֹשׁ	קָל
	3 f. s.	קָלָה	מֵתָה	בּוֹשָׁה	קָלָה
	2 m. s.	קַלְתָּ	מַתָּה	בֹּשְׁתָּ	קַלְתָּ
	2 f. s.	קַלְתְּ	מַתְּ	בֹּשְׁתְּ	קַלְתְּ
	1 c. s.	קַלְתִּי	מַתִּי	בֹּשְׁתִּי	קַלְתִּי
	3 c. p.	קָלוּ	מֵתוּ	בּוֹשׁוּ	קָלוּ
	2 m. p.	קַלְתֶּם	מַתֶּם	בָּשְׁתֶּם	קַלְתֶּם
	2 f. p.	קַלְתֶּן	מַתֶּן	בָּשְׁתֶּן	קַלְתֶּן
	1 c. p.	קַלְנוּ	מַתְנוּ	בֹּשְׁנוּ	קַלְנוּ
Imperfect	3 m. s.	יָקוּל	יָמוּת	יֵבוֹשׁ	יָקִיל
	3 f. s.	תָּקוּל	תָּמוּת	תֵּבוֹשׁ	תָּקִיל
	2 m. s.	תָּקוּל	תָּמוּת	תֵּבוֹשׁ	תָּקִיל
	2 f. s.	תָּקוּלִי	תָּמוּתִי	תֵּבוֹשִׁי	תָּקִילִי
	1 c. s.	אָקוּל	אָמוּת	אֵבוֹשׁ	אָקִיל
	3 m. p.	יָקוּלוּ	יָמוּתוּ	יֵבוֹשׁוּ	יָקִילוּ
	3 f. p.	תְּקוּלֶינָה	תְּמוּתֶינָה	תֵּבוֹשְׁנָה	תְּקִילֶינָה
	2 m. p.	תָּקוּלוּ	תָּמוּתוּ	תֵּבוֹשׁוּ	תָּקִילוּ
	2 f. p.	תְּקוּלֶינָה	תְּמוּתֶינָה	תֵּבוֹשְׁנָה	תְּקִילֶינָה
	1 c. p.	נָקוּל	נָמוּת	נֵבוֹשׁ	נָקִיל
Impv.	2 m. s.	קוּל	מוּת	בּוֹשׁ	קִיל
	2 f. s.	קוּלִי	מוּתִי	בּוֹשִׁי	קִילִי
	2 m. p.	קוּלוּ	מוּתוּ	בּוֹשׁוּ	קִילוּ
	2 f. p.	קֹלְנָה	מֹתְנָה	בֹּשְׁנָה	———
Inf.	Absol.	קוֹל	מוֹת	בּוֹשׁ	קוֹל
	Const.	קוּל	מוּת	בּוֹשׁ	קִיל
Part.	Active	קָל	מֵת	בּוֹשׁ	קָל
	Passive	קוּל			קוּל קִיל

(handwritten: = same as ע״ו)   *Hithpolel*

Niph'al	Polel	Polal	Hiph'il	Hoph'al
נָקוֹל	קוֹלֵל	קוֹלַל	הֵקִיל	הוּקַל
נָקוֹלָה	קוֹלְלָה	קוֹלְלָה	הֵקִילָה	הוּקְלָה
נְקוֹלֹוֹתָ	קוֹלַלְתָּ	etc.	הֲקִילֹוֹתָ	הֻגַּלְתָּ
נְקוֹלוֹת	קוֹלַלְתְּ		הֲקִילוֹת	הוּקַלְתְּ
נְקוֹלֹוֹתִי	קוֹלַלְתִּי		הֲקִילֹוֹתִי	הֻגַּלְתִּי
נָקוֹלוּ	קוֹלְלוּ		הֵקִילוּ	הוּקְלוּ
נְקוֹלוֹתֶם	קוֹלַלְתֶּם		הֲקִילוֹתֶם	הֻקַלְתֶּם
נְקוֹלוֹתֶן	קוֹלַלְתֶּן		הֲקִילוֹתֶן	הֻקַלְתֶּן
נְקוֹלוֹנוּ	קוֹלַלְנוּ		הֲקִילוֹנוּ	הֻגַּלְנוּ
יֵקוֹל	יְקוֹלֵל	יְקוֹלַל	יָקִיל	יוּקַל
תֵּקוֹל	תְּקוֹלֵל	תְּקוֹלַל	תָּקִיל	תּוּקַל
תֵּקוֹל	תְּקוֹלֵל	etc.	תָּקִיל	תּוּקַל
תֵּקוֹלִי	תְּקוֹלְלִי		תָּקִילִי	תּוּקְלִי
אֵקוֹל	אֲקוֹלֵל		אָקִיל	אוּקַל
יֵקוֹלוּ	יְקוֹלְלוּ		יָקִילוּ	יוּקְלוּ
תֵּקוֹלֶנָה	תְּקוֹלֵלְנָה		תְּקֵלְנָה	תּוּקַלְנָה
תֵּקוֹלוּ	תְּקוֹלְלוּ		תָּקִילוּ	תּוּקְלוּ
תֵּקוֹלֶנָה	תְּקוֹלֵלְנָה		תְּקֵלְנָה	תּוּקַלְנָה
נִקוֹל	נְקוֹלֵל		נָקִיל	נוּקַל
הֵקוֹל	קוֹלֵל		הָקֵל	
הֵקוֹלִי	קוֹלְלִי	NONE	הֲקִילִי	NONE
הֵקוֹלוּ	קוֹלְלוּ		הֲקִילוּ	
הֵקוֹלֶנָה	קוֹלֵלְנָה		הֲקֵלְנָה	
הֵקוֹל	קוֹלֵל		הָקֵל	—
הֵקוֹל		—	הָקִיל	—
—	מְקוֹלֵל	—	מֵקִיל	—
נָקוֹל	—	מְקוֹלָל	—	מוּקָל

		Qal	Niph'al	Qal (prop. פ"י)	Hiph'il (prop. פ"י)
Perfect	3 m. s.	אָטַל	נֶאֱטַל	יָטַל	הֵיטִיל
	3 f. s.	etc.	etc.	etc.	הֵיטִילָה
	2 m. s.	same as	same as	Regular	הֵיטַלְתָּ
	2 f. s.	Pe Guttural	Pe Guttural		הֵיטַלְתְּ
	1 c. s.				הֵיטַלְתִּי
	3 c. p.				הֵיטִילוּ
	2 m. p.				הֵיטַלְתֶּם
	2 f. p.				הֵיטַלְתֶּן
	1 c. p.				הֵיטַלְנוּ
Imperfect	3 m. s.	יֹאטַל (יֵאָטֵל)	same as	יִיטַל	יֵיטִיל
	3 f. s.	תֹּאטַל	Pe Guttural	תִּיטַל	תֵּיטִיל
	2 m. s.	תֹּאטַל		תִּיטַל	תֵּיטִיל
	2 f. s.	תֹּאטְלִי		תִּיטְלִי	תֵּיטִילִי
	1 c. s.	אֹטַל		אִיטַל	אֵיטִיל
	3 m. p.	יֹאטְלוּ		יִיטְלוּ	יֵיטִילוּ
	3 f. p.	תֹּאטַלְנָה		תִּיטַלְנָה	תֵּיטֵלְנָה
	2 m. p.	תֹּאטְלוּ		תִּיטְלוּ	תֵּיטִילוּ
	2 f. p.	תֹּאטַלְנָה		תִּיטַלְנָה	תֵּיטֵלְנָה
	1 c. p.	נֹאטַל		נִיטַל	נֵיטִיל
Impv.	2 m. s.	אֱטַל	same as	יְטַל	הֵיטֵל
	2 f. s.	אִטְלִי	Pe Guttural	יִטְלִי	הֵיטִילִי
	2 m. p.	אִטְלוּ		יִטְלוּ	הֵיטִילוּ
	2 f. p.	אֱטַלְנָה		יְטַלְנָה	הֵיטֵלְנָה
Inf.	Absol.	אָטוֹל	same as	יָטוֹל	הֵיטֵל
	Const.	אֱטֹל	Pe Guttural	יְטֹל	הֵיטִיל
Part.	Active	אֹטֵל	same as	יֹטֵל	מֵיטִיל
	Passive	אָטוּל	Pe Guttural	יָטוּל	

Qal		Niph'al	Hiph'il	Hoph'al
	יֵטֵל	נוֹטֵל	הוֹטִיל	הוּטַל
	etc.	נוֹטְלָה	הוֹטִילָה	הוּטְלָה
	Regular	נוֹטַלְתָּ	הוֹטַלְתָּ	הוּטַלְתָּ
		נוֹטַלְתְּ	הוֹטַלְתְּ	הוּטַלְתְּ
		נוֹטַלְתִּי	הוֹטַלְתִּי	הוּטַלְתִּי
		נוֹטְלוּ	הוֹטִילוּ	הוּטְלוּ
		נוֹטַלְתֶּם	הוֹטַלְתֶּם	הוּטַלְתֶּם
		נוֹטַלְתֶּן	הוֹטַלְתֶּן	הוּטַלְתֶּן
		נוֹטַלְנוּ	הוֹטַלְנוּ	הוּטַלְנוּ
יֵטֵל	יִטַּל	יִנָּטֵל	יוֹטִיל	יוּטַל
תֵּטֵל	תִּטַּל	etc.	תּוֹטִיל	תּוּטַל
תֵּטֵל	תִּטַּל	Regular	תּוֹטִיל	תּוּטַל
תֵּטְלִי	תִּטְּלִי		תּוֹטִילִי	תּוּטְלִי
אֵטֵל	אִטַּל		אוֹטִיל	אוּטַל
יֵטְלוּ	יִטְּלוּ		יוֹטִילוּ	יוּטְלוּ
תֵּטַלְנָה	תִּטַּלְנָה		תּוֹטֵלְנָה	תּוּטַלְנָה
תֵּטְלוּ	תִּטְּלוּ		תּוֹטִילוּ	תּוּטְלוּ
תֵּטַלְנָה	תִּטַּלְנָה		תּוֹטֵלְנָה	תּוּטַלְנָה
נֵטֵל	נִטַּל		נוֹטִיל	נוּטַל
טֵל	יְטַל	הִוָּטֵל	הוֹטֵל	
טְלִי	יְטְלִי	הִוָּטְלִי	הוֹטִילִי	NONE
טְלוּ	יְטְלוּ	הִוָּטְלוּ	הוֹטִילוּ	
טֵלְנָה	יְטַלְנָה	הִוָּטֵלְנָה	הוֹטֵלְנָה	
יָטוֹל	יְטוֹל		הוֹטֵל	——
טֶלֶת	יְטַל	הִוָּטֵל	הוֹטִיל	——
	יֵטֵל		מוֹטִיל	
	יָטוּל	נוֹטָל	נוֹטָל	מוּטָל

		1 c. s.	2 m. s.	2 f. s.	3 m. s.	3 f. s.
Perfect	3 m. s.	קְטָלַנִי	קְטָלְךָ	קְטָלֵךְ (ֵךְ-)	קְטָלָהוּ קְטָלוֹ	קְטָלָהּ
	3 f. s.	קְטָלַתְנִי	קְטָלָתְךָ	קְטָלָתֶךְ	קְטָלָתְהוּ קְטָלָתּוּ	קְטָלָתָּה
	2 m. s.	קְטַלְתַּנִי קְטַלְתָּנִי	——	——	קְטַלְתָּהוּ קְטַלְתּוֹ	קְטַלְתָּהּ
	2 f. s.	קְטַלְתִּינִי	——	——	קְטַלְתִּיהוּ קְטַלְתִּיו	קְטַלְתִּיהָ
	1 c. s.	——	קְטַלְתִּיךָ	קְטַלְתִּיךְ	קְטַלְתִּיו	קְטַלְתִּיהָ
	3 c. p.	קְטָלוּנִי	קְטָלוּךָ	קְטָלוּךְ	קְטָלוּהוּ	קְטָלוּהָ
	2 m. p.	קְטַלְתּוּנִי	——	——	קְטַלְתּוּהוּ	(קְטַלְתּוּהָ)
	1 c. p.	——	קְטַלְנוּךָ	קְטַלְנוּךְ	קְטַלְנוּהוּ	קְטַלְנוּהָ
Perf.	Mid. E. 3 m. s.	קְטָלַנִי	קְטָלְךָ	קְטָלֵךְ	קְטָלוֹ	קְטָלָהּ
Imperfect	3 m. s.	יִקְטְלֵנִי	יִקְטָלְךָ	יִקְטָלֵךְ	יִקְטְלֵהוּ	יִקְטְלֶהָ יִקְטְלָהּ
	With Nun Ep.	יִקְטְלֵנִי	יִקְטָלְךָ	——	יִקְטְלֶנּוּ	יִקְטְלֶנָּה
	3 m. p.	יִקְטְלוּנִי	יִקְטְלוּךָ	יִקְטְלוּךְ	יִקְטְלוּהוּ	יִקְטְלוּהָ
	2 f. p.	תִּקְטְלוּנִי	——	——	תִּקְטְלוּהוּ	תִּקְטְלוּהָ
Impv.	2 m. s.	קָטְלֵנִי	——	——	קָטְלֵהוּ	קָטְלֶהָ קָטְלָהּ
Inf.	Const.	קָטְלִי קְטָלֵנִי	קָטְלְךָ קָטְלֶךָ	קָטְלֵךְ	קָטְלוֹ	קָטְלָהּ

1 c. p.	2 m. p.	2 f. p.	3 m. p.	3 f. p.
קְטָלָנוּ	קְטַלְכֶם	(יִקְטָלְכֶן)	קְטָלָם	קְטָלָן
קְטַלְתָּנוּ	—	—	קְטַלְתָּם	(יִקְטָלַתַּן)
קְטַלְתָּנוּ	—	—	קְטָלְתָּם	(יִקְטָלְתָּן)
קְטַלְתִּינוּ	—	—	קְטָלְתִּים	(יִקְטַלְתִּין)
—	קְטַלְתִּיכֶם	(יִקְטַלְתִּיכֶן)	קְטַלְתִּים	קְטַלְתִּין
קְטָלוּנוּ	—	—	קְטָלוּם	קְטָלוּן
קְטָלְתּוּנוּ	—	—	(קְטָלְתּוּם)	(יִקְטָלְתּוּן)
—	קְטָלְנוּכֶם	(קְטָלְנוּכֶן)	קְטָלְנוּם	(יִקְטָלְנוּן)
קְטֶלָנוּ	קְטֶלְכֶם	(יִקְטֶלְכֶן)	קְטֶלָם	קְטֶלָן
יִקְטְלֵנוּ	יִקְטָלְכֶם	(יִקְטָלְכֶן)	יִקְטְלֵם	(יִקְטְלֵן)
יִקְטְלֵנוּ				
יִקְטְלוּנוּ	יִקְטְלוּכֶם	(יִקְטְלוּכֶן)	יִקְטְלוּם	יִקְטְלוּן
תִּקְטְלוּנוּ	—	—	תִּקְטְלוּם	תִּקְטְלוּן
קָטְלֵנוּ	—	—	קָטְלֵם	—
קָטְלֵנוּ	קָטְלְכֶם / קָטְלְכֶם	קָטְלְכֶן / קָטְלְכֶן	קָטְלֵם	קָטְלֵן

		Strong Verb	Pe Guttural	Ayin Guttural	Lamedh Guttural	Pe Nun	Lamedh Aleph	Lamedh He	Doubled Ayin	Middle Vowel	Pe Waw — Pe Yodh
Qal	Perf.	קָטַל	עָמַד	בָּחַר	שָׁלַח	נָגַשׁ	מָצָא	גָּלָה	סָבַב	קָם, קוֹם	יָשַׁב, יָשֵׁב
	Impf.	יִקְטֹל	יַעֲמֹד	יִבְחַר	יִשְׁלַח	יִגַּשׁ, יִתֵּן	יִמְצָא	יִגְלֶה	יָסֹב, יִסֹּב	יָקוּם	יֵשֵׁב, יִיטַב
	Impv.	קְטֹל	עֲמֹד	בְּחַר	שְׁלַח	גַּשׁ, תֵּן	מְצָא	גְּלֵה	סֹב	קוּם	שֵׁב, יְרַשׁ
	Inf. A.	קָטוֹל	עָמוֹד	בָּחוֹר	שָׁלוֹחַ	נָגוֹשׁ	מָצוֹא	גָּלֹה	סָבוֹב	קוֹם	יָשׁוֹב
	Inf. C.	קְטֹל	עֲמֹד	בְּחֹר	שְׁלֹחַ	גֶּשֶׁת	מְצֹא	גְּלוֹת	סֹב	קוּם	שֶׁבֶת, רֶדֶת
	Ptc. A.	קֹטֵל	עֹמֵד	בֹּחֵר	שֹׁלֵחַ	נֹגֵשׁ	מֹצֵא	גֹּלֶה	סֹבֵב	קָם	יֹשֵׁב
	Ptc. P.	קָטוּל	עָמוּד	בָּחוּר	שָׁלוּחַ	נָגוּשׁ	מָצוּא	גָּלוּי	סָבוּב	קוּם	יָשׁוּב
Niph'al	Perf.	נִקְטַל	נֶעֱמַד	נִבְחַר	נִשְׁלַח	נִגַּשׁ	נִמְצָא	נִגְלָה	נָסַב	נָקוֹם	נוֹשַׁב
	Impf.	יִקָּטֵל	יֵעָמֵד	יִבָּחֵר	יִשָּׁלַח	יִנָּגֵשׁ	יִמָּצֵא	יִגָּלֶה	יִסַּב	יִקּוֹם	יִוָּשֵׁב
	Impv.	הִקָּטֵל	הֵעָמֵד	הִבָּחֵר	הִשָּׁלַח	הִנָּגֵשׁ	הִמָּצֵא	הִגָּלֵה	הִסַּב	הִקּוֹם	הִוָּשֵׁב
	Inf. A.	נִקְטוֹל	נַעֲמֹד	נִבְחוֹר	נִשְׁלוֹחַ	נִגּוֹשׁ	נִמְצוֹא	נִגְלֹה	הִסּוֹב	הִקּוֹם	הִוָּשֵׁב
	Inf. C.	הִקָּטֵל	הֵעָמֵד	הִבָּחֵר	הִשָּׁלַח	הִנָּגֵשׁ	הִמָּצֵא	הִגָּלוֹת	הִסַּב	הִקּוֹם	הִוָּשֵׁב
	Part.	נִקְטָל	נֶעֱמָד	נִבְחָר	נִשְׁלָח	נִגָּשׁ	נִמְצָא	נִגְלֶה	נָסָב	נָקוֹם	נוֹשָׁב
Pi'el	Perf.	קִטֵּל	עִמֵּד	בֵּרַךְ	שִׁלַּח	נִגֵּשׁ	מִצֵּא	גִּלָּה	סֹבֵב	קִיֵּם	יִשַּׁב
	Impf.	יְקַטֵּל	יְעַמֵּד	יְבָרֵךְ	יְשַׁלַּח	יְנַגֵּשׁ	יְמַצֵּא	יְגַלֶּה	יְסֹבֵב	יְקַיֵּם	יְיַשֵּׁב
	Impv.	קַטֵּל	עַמֵּד	בָּרֵךְ	שַׁלַּח	נַגֵּשׁ	מַצֵּא	גַּלֵּה	סֹבֵב	קַיֵּם	יַשֵּׁב
	Inf. A.	קַטֵּל	עַמֵּד	בָּרֵךְ	שַׁלֵּחַ	נַגֵּשׁ	מַצֵּא	גַּלֵּה	סֹבֵב	קַיֵּם	יַשֵּׁב

Paradigm of the Regular Verb — Pi‘el, Pu‘al, Hiph‘il, Hoph‘al (root קטל)

Hoph‘al Part.	Hoph‘al Inf. A. / Inf. C.	Hoph‘al — / Impf.	Hoph‘al Perf.	Hiph‘il Part.	Hiph‘il Inf. C.	Hiph‘il Inf. A.	Hiph‘il Impv.	Hiph‘il Impf.	Hiph‘il Perf.	Pu‘al Part.	Pu‘al — / Impf.	Pu‘al Perf.	Pi‘el Part.	Pi‘el Inf. C.
מָקְטָל	הָקְטֵל	יָקְטַל	הָקְטַל	מַקְטִיל	הַקְטִיל	הַקְטֵל	הַקְטֵל	יַקְטִיל	הִקְטִיל	מְקֻטָּל	יְקֻטַּל	קֻטַּל	מְקַטֵּל	קַטֵּל
מָקְטֶלֶת	הָקְטֶלֶת	יָקְטְלוּ	הָקְטְלָה	מַקְטֶלֶת	הַקְטִילִי		הַקְטִילִי	תַּקְטִיל	הִקְטִילָה	מְקֻטֶּלֶת	תְּקֻטַּל	קֻטְּלָה	מְקַטֶּלֶת	
מָקְטָלִים	הָקְטָלִים	תָּקְטַל	הָקְטַלְתָּ	מַקְטִילִים	הַקְטִילוּ		הַקְטִילוּ	תַּקְטִיל	הִקְטַלְתָּ	מְקֻטָּלִים	תְּקֻטַּל	קֻטַּלְתָּ	מְקַטְּלִים	
מָקְטָלוֹת		תָּקְטְלִי	הָקְטַלְתְּ	מַקְטִילוֹת			הַקְטֵלְנָה	תַּקְטִילִי	הִקְטַלְתְּ	מְקֻטָּלוֹת	תְּקֻטְּלִי	קֻטַּלְתְּ	מְקַטְּלוֹת	
		אָקְטַל	הָקְטַלְתִּי					אַקְטִיל	הִקְטַלְתִּי		אֲקֻטַּל	קֻטַּלְתִּי		
		יָקְטְלוּ	הָקְטְלוּ					יַקְטִילוּ	הִקְטִילוּ		יְקֻטְּלוּ	קֻטְּלוּ		
		תָּקְטַלְנָה	הָקְטַלְתֶּם					תַּקְטֵלְנָה	הִקְטַלְתֶּם		תְּקֻטַּלְנָה	קֻטַּלְתֶּם		
		תָּקְטְלוּ	הָקְטַלְתֶּן					תַּקְטִילוּ	הִקְטַלְתֶּן		תְּקֻטְּלוּ	קֻטַּלְתֶּן		
מוּקָם		יוּקַם	הוּקַם	מֵקִים	הָקִים		הָקֵם	יָקִים	הֵקִים	מְקוֹמָם	יְקוֹמַם	קוֹמַם	מְקוֹמֵם	קוֹמֵם
מָגְלֶה		יָגְלֶה	הָגְלָה	מַגְלֶה	הַגְלוֹת	הַגְלֵה	הַגְלֵה	יַגְלֶה	הִגְלָה	מְגֻלֶּה	יְגֻלֶּה	גֻּלָּה	מְגַלֶּה	גַּלּוֹת